European Integration and the Functioning of Product Markets

Edited by

Adriaan Dierx

Directorate General for Economic and Financial Affairs
European Commission

Fabienne Ilzkovitz

Directorate General for Economic and Financial Affairs
European Commission
Associate Professor of Economics
University of Brussels and ICHEC, Belgium

Khalid Sekkat

Professor of Economics
DULBEA
University of Brussels, Belgium

PUBLISHED ON BEHALF OF THE COMMISSION OF
EUROPEAN COMMUNITIES

Edward Elgar

Cheltenham, UK • Northampton, MA, USA

Published by
Edward Elgar Publishing Limited
Glensanda House
Montpellier Parade
Cheltenham
Glos GL50 1UA
UK

Edward Elgar Publishing, Inc.
136 West Street
Suite 202
Northampton
Massachusetts 01060
USA

A catalogue record for this book
is available from the British Library

ISBN   1 84376 393 1
EU ISBN 92–894–3470–8   Cat. number: CK-43-02-195-EN-C

Publications Office

Publications.eu.int

Printed and bound in Great Britain by MPG Books Ltd, Bodmin, Cornwall

Contents

Contributors

Russell Davidson, GREQAM, University of Aix-Marseilles II.
Steve Davies, University of East Anglia.
Adriaan Dierx, Directorate-General for Economic and Financial Affairs, European Commission.
Michel Fouquin, CEPII and University of Paris I.
Michael Gasiorek, University of Sussex and GREQAM, University of Aix-Marseilles II.
Fabienne Ilzkovitz, Directorate-General for Economic and Financial Affairs, European Commission, University of Brussels and ICHEC.
Bruce Lyons, University of East Anglia.
Karen-Helene Midelfart, NHH, Bergen and CEPR.
Henry G. Overman, London School of Economics and CEPR.
Karl Pichelmann, Directorate-General for Economic and Financial Affairs, European Commission and University of Brussels.
Stephen J. Redding, London School of Economics and CEPR.
Werner Röger, Directorate-General for Economic and Financial Affairs, European Commission.
Laura Rondi, CERIS-CNR, Torino.
Khalid Sekkat, DULBEA, University of Brussels.
Leo Sleuwaegen, VLGMS, KULeuven and Erasmus University, Rotterdam.
David Ulph, University College London and Analysis and Research Office, Inland Revenue, London.
Davide Vannoni, University of Turin and CERIS-CNR, Torino.
Richard Vaughan, University College London.
Anthony J. Venables, London School of Economics and CEPR.
Reinhilde Veugelers, KULeuven and CEPR.
Alan Winters, University of Sussex and CEPR.

Acknowledgements

We are very grateful to Klaus Regling, Director General, for his continuous support and for giving us the opportunity to communicate to the policy and research communities the results of the research programme of the Directorate-General for Economic and Financial Affairs on product market integration in the EU. We thank Jan Host Schmidt, Director, for his numerous comments and feedback, which have substantially enriched and improved the substance of this book. Without the secretarial assistance provided by Sarah Vitiello it would have been very difficult to complete this book. Karel Havik and Alberto Garralon were responsible for data processing and statistical analysis. We owe them many thanks. At the same time, we would like to thank the Commission staff for having helped us to investigate and report on Europe's achievements in economic integration. Nevertheless, the opinions expressed by authors are their own and do not necessarily reflect the policy line of the European Commission.

Foreword

The process of European economic integration has contributed to building an area of growth and prosperity. Over the past decade, a number of important steps have been taken aimed at creating better-integrated goods and services markets in Europe. The completion of the Single Market Programme (SMP) in 1992 established the principle of a free circulation of goods, services, capital and persons inside the European Union (EU). Economic and Monetary Union (EMU) was the logical subsequent major step in the continuing process of European economic integration. It complements the SMP by facilitating cross-border transactions and making markets more transparent.

Europe's achievements in terms of economic integration have attracted worldwide interest and are seen as an example for other regions to follow. A dozen years after the completion of the Single Market Programme and almost half a dozen years following EMU, it is time to look back and examine the extent to which the different measures taken to create integrated and better functioning product markets have been a factor in raising EU growth. In doing so, one needs to consider the growth effects of other developments such as globalisation and technological progress, which lie outside the immediate realm of the European integration process. Clearly, it is difficult to disentangle the effects of the SMP from those of EMU and other advances in economic integration.

The present assessment of the impact of European product market integration goes beyond that of earlier studies on the impact of the SMP, such as the Cecchini Report or the 1996 Internal Market Review. The Cecchini Report could only provide an ex-ante assessment of the SMP, while the 1996 Review was based on data for only a couple of years post-1992. In the meantime, significant new information has become available, which enables tracking the effects of the SMP on market conditions, firm behaviour and the structure of industry. This information is particularly valuable because it allows the creation of an empirical mirror image of the theoretical underpinnings of the EU's product market reform policies. The intention of the SMP and the EMU was to facilitate market entry and stimulate competition on EU product markets through the removal of non-tariff barriers and exchange rate movements respectively. Increased competition meant a decline in market power and increased economic efficiency, which in turn contributes to higher productivity and potential growth.

This volume provides an in-depth investigation of the different channels through which European economic integration has affected product market functioning and how such effects have fed into macroeconomic outcomes. While clearly indicating the benefits of economic integration, the book also highlights a number of weaknesses in the functioning of European product markets pointing to the need for an increased and coordinated economic reform effort.

The establishment of EMU has been a catalyst for increased product market surveillance, and Broad Economic Policy Guidelines, which are the main instrument for economic policy coordination in the European Union, now include recommendations for product market reforms at both the Community and the national level. The Lisbon strategy, launched by EU heads of state and government in March 2000, also aims to improve the product market performance by challenging the European Union to become the most competitive and dynamic knowledge-based economy in the world before the end of the decade. If successful, this reform effort should help improve the functioning of EMU by increasing the capacity of the European economy to adjust to changes in the international environment and to face the technological challenge. Moreover, it should help raise the level of potential growth by transforming the EU into a more competitive and dynamic economy. Finally, EU enlargement implies a further expansion of the Internal Market, which offers an opportunity for further gains in economic efficiency and growth.

The book builds on a number of studies carried out by acknowledged academic experts for the Directorate General for Economic and Financial Affairs of the European Commission. The aim of this study programme was to assess the functioning of European product markets ten years after the completion of the Single Market Programme. The different authors have made a substantial effort to extract the principal messages from their work and to include them in this volume's chapters. The work by academic experts has been complemented by analyses carried out by staff of the European Commission, which has helped to provide more of a policy perspective on the different issues raised.

Klaus Regling
Director General for Economic
and Financial Affairs
European Commission

1. Product market integration in the EU: an overview

Adriaan Dierx, Fabienne Ilzkovitz and Khalid Sekkat

The ten-year anniversary of the Single Market Programme (SMP) offers an excellent opportunity to look back and examine how economic integration has affected product market functioning in the European Union (EU). Although markets for goods and services have been influenced by other developments (for example, globalisation and Economic and Monetary Union (EMU)), the SMP remains an important driver of change in EU product markets. EMU, which should be seen as a subsequent stage in the continuing process of European integration, complements the SMP by facilitating cross-border transactions and making markets more transparent. The reduction in cross-border transaction costs and the elimination of exchange rate risk within the euro area are expected to stimulate trade and foreign investment. Moreover, the increased clarity of differences in price levels between Member States should encourage arbitrage and contribute to price convergence.

This volume provides an in-depth analysis of the consequences of the on-going process of European market integration. It covers microeconomic aspects such as the level of competition, the strategic behaviour of firms and the structure and location of European industry as well as macroeconomic ones such as the impact of product market integration on growth and employment and on the European Union's exposure to asymmetric shocks.

The volume contains eight chapters. This opening chapter presents the analytical framework, which links together the different chapters of this book and gives an overview of its contents. The four following chapters deal with microeconomic aspects of integration. Chapter 2 develops a theoretical framework and provides indicators to investigate the impact of the increase in price transparency associated with the arrival of the euro on European product markets. Chapters 3, 4 and 5 look at enterprises' reactions to the change in the economic environment brought about by the SMP and at the resulting impact on the structure of European industry. Chapter 3 focuses on the impact on the industrial and geographical diversification of leading firms in European manufacturing. In Chapter 4, the impact of market integration on industrial concentration and industry performance is examined. Chapter 5 provides a comprehensive analysis of changes that have occurred in country specialisation, geographic concentration and location of industry over the recent decades. The three remaining chapters deal with more macroeconomic aspects. Chapter 6 looks at the employment and growth impact of product market reforms carried out over the last decade. Chapter 7 focuses on the impact of euro/dollar fluctuations on European manufacturing by examining the differences in sector sensitivity to exchange rate fluctuations. Chapter 8 is more forward looking. It discusses how the changes in industry structure associated with the process of EU integration may affect the exposure of EU Member States to asymmetric shocks, such as those originating from euro/dollar fluctuations. Chapters 2 to 5 and Chapter 7 are based on external studies commissioned by the Directorate-General for Economic and Financial Affairs of the European Commission, while staff of this Directorate-General have prepared Chapters 1, 6 and 8.

ANALYTICAL FRAMEWORK

Table 1.1 describes the analytical framework used in this volume to examine the microeconomic impact of EU product market integration. The table makes a distinction between the effects of the reduction of barriers to cross-border activities inside the EU (as a result of both the SMP and EMU), and the increased price transparency associated mostly with EMU. The table also distinguishes between the expected effects on markets (viewed as short-term effects), on the behaviour of firms (in the medium term) and on the organisation of industry (in the long term). The table gives a simplified view. It is for example very difficult to fully separate the impact of the lowering of non-tariff trade barriers from that of greater price transparency. Similarly, it is not evident that changes in market conditions, firm conduct and industrial organisation necessarily occur in sequential order. Rather, these different elements are in a continuous and dynamic interaction.[1]

By eliminating non-tariff barriers to intra-EU trade and exchange rate fluctuations, the Single Market Programme and EMU facilitate market entry[2] by new firms and therefore the introduction of new brands into the different national markets. Therefore, inter-brand competition is expected to rise. A decline in profit margins, in particular for producers that fail to adapt, will result. A second effect of EMU is the increased transparency of price differences between the countries in the euro area, especially since 2002 when the euro notes and coins were put into circulation. This increased transparency makes it more difficult for multinational enterprises to segment national markets geographically and maintain profit margins, as higher price transparency reduces information costs and increases the ability of consumers or their surrogates to engage in cross-border arbitrage (see Chapter 2). Hence by reducing the ability of manufacturers to price discriminate between Member States, the common currency will increase intra-brand competition. Such transparency effects are likely to be reinforced by the increased importance of electronic commerce with its relatively low level of cross-border search costs (European Commission, 2001). By changing the conditions of competition, product market integration should thus lead to an increase in allocative efficiency, that is, prices should move closer to marginal costs.

Table 1.1   The effects of the SMP and EMU on EU product markets

	Reduction of barriers to cross-border activities inside the EU (due to the SMP and EMU)	Increased price transparency (due to EMU mostly)
Short-term effects Level of competition in product markets rises	Market entry↑ Inter-brand competition↑ Allocative efficiency↑ Profit margins↓	Intra-brand competition↑ Market segmentation↓ Allocative efficiency↑ Profit margins↓
Medium-term effects Firms change production strategy	Sectoral diversification↓ Multinationality↑ Productive efficiency↑ Profit margins↑	Product differentiation↑ Sectoral diversification↓ Market power↑ Profit margins↑ Vertical linkages↑
Long-term effects Changes in the structure of industry	Industrial concentration (at Member State level)↓ Spatial concentration↑↓ Inter-industry trade↓ Intra-industry trade↑	Intra-industry trade↑

Increased competition and the subsequent decline in profit margins may cause firms to make greater efforts to reduce production costs or implement strategies to increase their market power (see Chapters 2 and 3). In order to reduce production costs, one option is to concentrate production in sectors where the firm has a leading position in the market ('return to core business'), implying a decline in sectoral diversification. Another option is to exploit economies of scale by expanding into new geographical markets. This will inevitably imply a strengthening of the multinational character of the firm. Such changes should be reflected in average cost reductions, that is, gains in productive efficiency, and thus should contribute to the restoration of profit margins. In order to regain market power, one option, facilitated by the increased price transparency, is to come to a tacit agreement amongst producers and distributors to set high prices. However, the increased risk of collusion can be counteracted by an effective application of competition policy. Another option is to increase product differentiation. If a firm's product can be clearly distinguished from that of competitors or from its own product marketed in other countries, the firm's ability to set prices at the desired level can be increased. However, product differentiation requires investments in R&D and advertising. To avoid spreading their limited investment resources, firms may be forced to focus on their core business and to abandon non-essential activities. This is another explanation for the decline in sectoral diversification. Finally, intra-brand competition may give rise to a strengthening of vertical linkages. Sellers may attempt to establish contractual or ownership arrangements with distributors in order to protect profits currently achieved through price discrimination.

The implications of these changes in company behaviour for industrial concentration are not immediately evident, as there are offsetting developments. At the level of individual Member States, a decline in industrial concentration is likely to occur mainly because of market entry by foreign firms. This would probably be a more important factor than the failure or takeover of national firms. At the level of the EU as a whole, market integration may lead to an increase in industrial concentration because mutual entry does not imply an increase in the total number of firms. While failures or takeovers will increase industrial concentration at the European level, the smaller number of firms is expected to compete more intensely across borders. It is difficult to decide a priori what the net impact will be. However, the empirical analysis suggests that the strategic reactions of firms are unlikely to offset the positive effect of integration on the performance of the European economy (see Chapter 4).

With firms having expanded their markets beyond national borders, it is only natural for them to reconsider the location of production facilities, raising the questions of whether, and how, closer European integration affects the location of economic activity. Krugman (1991a and 1991b) argued that aggregate production would become more concentrated in the regions closest to the largest markets, as companies would increasingly exploit the agglomeration and other scale economies present in a more integrated Europe. This basic argument was further developed in the 1990s within the context of the so-called 'New Economic Geography'.[3] However, as the concentration of economic activity in the EU core increases, the price of immobile production factors may increase and congestion may appear (that is, negative agglomeration economies). If this is the case, a further reduction of intra-EU trade barriers may lead to a re-dispersion of economic activity over space. As firms concentrate and re-disperse, they may affect the specialisation of countries and regions in different activities.

The impact on industrial specialisation depends on two forces working in opposite directions. On the one hand, the removal of barriers to trade should lead to a reduction in transport and transaction costs and thus allow a better exploitation of scale economies in production. Such a development would be reflected in an increased specialisation of the EU Member States. On the other hand, European integration has contributed to a convergence of factor endowments (see Aiginger et al., 1999) and the removal of exchange rate variability, which would be expected to lead to an increase in intra-industry trade and a decline in industrial specialisation (see European Commission, 1996 and 1997; Frankel and Rose, 1997; and Fontagné and Freudenberg, 1999).[4] For Europe, there is empirical evidence for both lines of thought. While production specialisation seems to have been rising since the early 1980s, export specialisation has remained more or less unchanged and there has been a notable increase in the relative importance of intra-industry trade (see Chapter 5).

The analytical framework described above illustrates how the SMP and EMU may affect the conditions of competition and the organisation of industry in the EU, an issue that is further elucidated in Chapters 2 through 5. These microeconomic effects can in turn have an impact on the macroeconomic performance of the EU economy, which is examined in Chapters 6, 7 and 8.

MICROECONOMIC EFFECTS OF PRODUCT MARKET INTEGRATION

Chapter 2 by Gasiorek et al. discusses the issue of market integration, price transparency and price convergence. This chapter starts by analysing the impact of European integration on price levels and price dispersion. This analysis shows that following the completion of the SMP a significant price convergence was visible for the countries in the EU core, that is, countries with relatively stable exchange rates, while a significant divergence away from the EU average was detected for other countries – upwards in Scandinavia and downwards in the Iberian peninsula. These empirical results give some support to the theoretical argument according to which some reduction in price dispersion is expected to arise from the greater integration and exchange rate stability resulting from EMU.

This chapter also proposes a microeconomic model to analyse the impact of the greater transparency of prices associated with EMU. This microeconomic model distinguishes three channels through which price transparency may affect price–cost margins. First, an increase in price transparency reduces the search costs and facilitates price comparisons between products for consumers. Second, it improves the information available to producers and widens the possibilities of collusion between them. Third, it creates possibilities of arbitrage between countries for consumers, distributors and wholesalers, thereby increasing the price elasticity of demand. The first and the third mechanisms should reduce price–cost margins while the second one should increase them. On the whole, price transparency has opposite effects on price levels and price–cost margins depending on whether it makes it easier for consumers or producers to detect price changes. In that respect, the chapter argues that the costs to the large producers of collecting information on prices across markets are already relatively low and that therefore the single currency is likely to have a relatively limited impact on the information available to producers. The greater impact should come from the improved consumer price transparency and from the greater scope for arbitrage to frustrate marketing strategies based on price discrimination.

The effects of higher price transparency also depend on the characteristics of the industries. These effects should be smaller in industries with differentiated products because it is more difficult for consumers to compare prices, in industries selling intermediate products to other firms because producers already have good information on prices, in highly concentrated industries because the degree of collusion could be greater and in industries with strong vertical linkages which make it possible to preserve price discrimination.

Building on the above theoretical analysis, a computable general equilibrium model is developed comprising 15 countries and 50 manufacturing sectors. It investigates the potential impact of greater price transparency for producers and consumers on economic welfare. Simulation results show increased output as a result of increased price transparency in a large majority of manufacturing sectors and lower mark-ups in all but one of them. Therefore, if the single currency in Europe does have a greater positive impact on consumer transparency than on producer transparency, one can expect pro-competitive effects resulting in a decrease in price–cost margins and an increase in output.

Chapter 3 by Rondi, Sleuwaegen and Vannoni traces the changing industrial and geographical diversification strategy of leading firms over the decade 1987–1997. The chapter uses a market share matrix to analyse the distribution of production of leading firms in the European Union across sectors and Member States.

The results suggest a tendency for firms to refocus on their core businesses. It appears that the competitive rise of R&D and advertising expenditures in the larger and more integrated market has encouraged firms to divest secondary activities. There are, however, differences over time: it is only after 1993 that the movement of a return to the core became truly evident. Since the completion of the SMP was expected to lead firms to reorganise their corporate structures before the end of 1992, this somewhat surprising result suggests that the return to the core may still be in progress. There is also evidence of a convergence of corporate structures across EU Member States. Countries that in 1987 were hosting the most industrially diversified leaders have undergone a considerable reduction in diversified operations.

At the same time firms have increasingly expanded and/or re-balanced their geographical operations across Member States, thereby strongly increasing the multinational character of their production over time. Amongst the SMP sensitive industries, for example, leading firms in high-tech industries characterised by a high percentage of public procurement strongly reduced their industrial diversification, while at the same time increasing their geographical diversification. The simultaneous movements of a return to the core and increased multinationality seem to suggest that there is a trade-off between industrial and geographical diversification as possible routes to growth. However, this hypothesis could not be confirmed as surviving leaders appear to have pursued both diversification strategies at the same time.

The fourth chapter by Veugelers examines the impact of such strategic reactions on industrial concentration and industry performance, using the same market share matrix but over the period 1987–2000.

The results suggest that average production concentration did not change very much before 1997 but slightly increased afterwards. However, for some industries there have been dramatic changes over the 1990s, and especially in the post-1993 period. The highly concentrated sectors especially have witnessed a decline in concentration, but nevertheless remain at above average concentration levels. There has also been considerable turbulence in market leadership in EU manufacturing industries. By 2000, the top five companies from 1987 had lost more than half their production share and in most of the sectors with a dominant leader in 1987, a new leader had emerged in 2000, often with an even greater market share.

Chapter 4 concludes by attempting to make the link between industry concentration and industry performance. The results suggest that productivity growth is significantly higher in industries with declining concentration levels. In addition, productivity and profitability are higher in concentrated industries, while the speed of decline in price dispersion is slower.

Chapter 5 by Midelfart, Overman, Redding and Venables tracks the impact of market integration on country specialisation and the geographical concentration of manufacturing activity in the European Union. It also analyses the determinants of location of activities in the EU.

The data on product specialisation show that, since the early 1980s, there has been a gradual increase in production specialisation, which has been rather more abrupt in countries joining the European Union recently than in its long-standing members. This seems to indicate that EU enlargement is as important a factor in terms of product specialisation as the SMP or EMU. Nevertheless, the usual division between north and central Europe, on the one hand, and the south, on the other, remains valid, with the northern countries more specialised in increasing returns and high-tech industries.

The data on export specialisation – contrary to those on production specialisation – show no clear increase in the 1980s and 1990s. This discrepancy is explained by the rapid growth of intra-industry trade, which has tended to make sectoral trade vectors more similar between countries.

At the aggregate level, the geographical concentration of manufacturing production in the EU has remained more or less unchanged since the early 1980s. However, at the level of individual industries, more significant changes in the degree of concentration are observed. Medical and precision instruments, and radio, television and communication equipment are amongst the industries with the sharpest declines in concentration. In these industries, peripheral countries like Ireland and Finland have made inroads at the expense of Germany, France and the UK. For motor vehicles, on the other hand, the already high level of concentration has risen further, as Germany has reinforced its position at the expense of both France and the UK. Low-tech and labour-intensive industries also show a tendency towards increased concentration. In textiles and clothing, for example, the already important share of the southern European countries has risen further.

Further analysis of the determinants of location in the EU shows that a high proportion of the cross-country variation in industrial structure can be explained by the interaction between country and industry characteristics. The location of R&D-intensive industries, for example, has become increasingly responsive to countries' endowments of researchers. Similarly, backward and forward linkages between industrial sectors are becoming increasingly important determinants of location. Economies of scale, on the other hand, have been steadily declining as a location factor in the European Union.

MACROECONOMIC EFFECTS OF PRODUCT MARKET INTEGRATION

Chapter 6 by Dierx, Pichelmann and Röger looks at the macroeconomic impact of the product market reforms since the early 1990s. Product market reforms are considered as strengthening competition, increasing efficiency, stimulating technological innovation and reinforcing the capacity of the economy to respond to adverse shocks. The authors use macro-model simulation analysis: shocks to price mark-ups and total factor productivity are fed into the European Commission's macro-econometric QUEST II model to assess the effects of product market reforms on macroeconomic performance.

The simulation results suggest a medium-term increase in GDP relative to its baseline level of about 2 per cent. In terms of growth rates, this translates into an acceleration of output growth by almost a quarter of a percentage point annually over a period of seven to eight years. Simulations also show that a macroeconomic policy framework providing medium-term stability allows for better exploitation of the positive effects of structural reforms and that coherence and comprehensiveness of reforms is essential. Thus, structural reform efforts have indeed borne fruit and delivered significant benefits in terms of output and employment levels. However, the growth stimulus from past structural reforms tends to fade away over time. Hence, the authors argue that if reform fatigue were to win the day, Europe would not even attain the baseline medium-term growth rate, which barely exceeds 2 per cent. This would be a significant setback to the European Union's ambition to become the most competitive and dynamic economy in the world. In order to achieve the sustainable 3 per cent annual rate of growth, as formulated at the Lisbon summit, the momentum and the breadth of structural reforms will have to be increased.

Chapter 7 focuses on the likely impact of euro/dollar exchange rate fluctuations on European manufacturing. By looking at the sensitivity to monetary fluctuations of manufacturing sectors and the relative importance of these sectors in the different EU Member States, Fouquin and Sekkat are able to measure the degree of asymmetry between the Member States in terms of exposure to movements in the euro/dollar exchange rate. The degree of sensitivity of a given manufacturing sector depends on its exposure to competition from the dollar zone and on its trade elasticity to exchange rate fluctuations.

The exposure to competition from the dollar zone takes into account both competition from imports in the EU market and competition affecting EU exports in the dollar zone and in third markets. The results show that textile products, leather products, machinery and equipment, electrical optical equipment and transport equipment and, to a lesser extent, chemicals are the sectors facing the most competition from the dollar zone.

In analysing the elasticity of trade to exchange rate fluctuations, two issues are addressed: the difference of elasticities across sectors and the extent to which market structure explains such a difference. The results confirm that the effects of exchange rate movements on trade vary across sectors and that such variations can be explained by market structure. For instance, the higher the degree of concentration in a sector, the lower should be the elasticity of trade with respect to exchange rate fluctuations. The level of the elasticity being affected by other factors such as product differentiation or barriers to trade, one ends up with the following classification: the sectors with a high elasticity are energy, food, paper products, machinery and electrical products for imports, and energy, machinery and transport equipment for exports.

Combining the exposure indicator and the elasticity estimates, the sectors that are most sensitive to euro/dollar fluctuations can be identified as machinery and equipment, electrical and optical products and transport equipment. These sectors together represent about one-third of European manufacturing output. High elasticity–low exposure sectors, that is, energy, food and paper, also represent an important share of the European economy. Low elasticity–high exposure sectors (textiles and leather), on the contrary, make up only a small share of the economy. Except for basic metals, the low elasticity–low exposure sectors (wood and wood products, rubber and plastic products, other non-metallic mineral products and basic metals and fabricated metal products) add up to only a relatively small share of value-added in European manufacturing.

The eighth and final chapter, by Dierx, Ilzkovitz and Sekkat, examines how the changes in the conditions of competition and in the organisation of industry resulting from product market integration affect the exposure of EU Member States to asymmetric shocks originating from the euro/dollar fluctuations. Such shocks are asymmetric as there is a variation between sectors in terms of their sensitivity to exchange rate fluctuations and as there is a difference between countries in the economic weight of these so-called 'sensitive' sectors.

Two channels by which European integration can affect country exposure to the euro/dollar fluctuations are identified in this chapter. First, as the Single Market Programme and EMU are raising the level of competition in some of the least competitive sectors, a reduction in the differences between sectors in terms of competition levels should be expected, which should result in a decline of country differences in terms of exchange rate sensitivity as well. Second, European integration may exacerbate the differences between countries in the economic weight of sensitive sectors. However, the increase in the 1990s of both production specialisation and intra-industry trade leaves doubt about the direction of this specialisation effect. As there are forces working in opposite directions, the chapter concludes that that while euro/dollar fluctuations indeed represent an asymmetric shock, the hypothesis that European integration significantly increases the exposure of the EU Member States to this type of asymmetric shock does not receive support.

THE ROAD AHEAD

This volume investigates how the process of product market integration has affected the conditions of competition, the strategies of European companies and the structure of European industry. These effects appear to have helped to improve the macroeconomic performance of the EU economy. Macro-model simulations show that annual GDP growth rates would have been a quarter of a percentage point lower without this process of product market integration. In addition, empirical evidence does not support the view that changes in industry structure resulting from product market integration have increased the exposure of the EU to asymmetric shocks. Instead, by increasing the capacity of prices to adjust to market conditions, product market reforms help to reinforce the power of the economy to respond to adverse shocks. This illustrates the importance of product market reforms for the competitiveness of the European economy.

In spite of the progress made in the 1990s in terms of product market integration, EU living standards were no longer catching up with those in the US, as had been the case for most of the post-World War II period. Since the mid-1980s EU GPD per capita has fluctuated at around 70 per cent of the level in the US. Moreover, EU labour productivity growth rates, which had been consistently above US levels until the mid-1990s, have come down, while those in the US have increased. One main reason for this is that the EU has been lagging behind in the development and use of new technologies. The contribution of information and communication technologies (ICT) to EU growth in the second half of the 1990s, for example, was only half of that observed in the US.

Such observations led to the decision of European leaders in March 2000 to re-launch and broaden the process of structural reforms in the European Union. Within the framework of the 'Lisbon strategy' the focus is not only on the still needed improvements in the functioning of the Single Market (now renamed as the Internal Market), but also on labour market reforms aimed at raising the employment rate and on measures to accelerate Europe's transition to a 'knowledge economy'. This comprehensive reform effort targets an increase in the medium-term annual growth rate of EU GDP to 3 per cent. Due attention has been paid to the need to ensure the long-term sustainability of the improved growth performance envisaged. This implies tackling social exclusion, improving the natural environment and assuring the sustainability of public finances through pension and health care reform. These concerns are clearly beyond the scope of this book, which is focused on product market related issues only.

Regarding product markets, the lack of dynamism of the EU economy can be attributed to the following main elements. First, despite the SMP and EMU, European markets remain relatively fragmented, at least in comparison with the United States. While progress has been made in integrating goods markets, in services significant obstacles to market entry in other EU Member States remain. Many of these obstacles are of a regulatory nature. Second, even within Member States unnecessary rules and regulation and administrative red tape discourage market entry. Improvements in the regulatory framework would certainly contribute to creating in Europe a more competitive business environment conducive to entrepreneurship and economic dynamism. Third, business investment in R&D is insufficient. While such investments are on a clear upward trend in the United States, they have been more or less stagnant in Europe. Fourth, the EU is also lagging behind in product innovation and the diffusion of new technologies.

This is the reason why European leaders have decided within the framework of the Lisbon strategy to promote new reforms aimed at improving the functioning of the Internal Market, simplifying the regulatory framework, increasing investment in knowledge and stimulating the diffusion of new technologies. In order to identify specific priorities for action European leaders meet annually at the Spring European Council. Discussions at this meeting are based on the European Commission's 'Spring Reports', which provide an assessment of progress made thus far. An overall assessment of the Lisbon strategy, however, would merit another book.

NOTES

1. Two other limitations are worth mentioning. First, the analysis does not consider the impact of changes in labour and capital markets and their interactions with those in product markets. Second, the more dynamic effects of market integration and reform on business investment in R&D and innovation are not analysed as such.

2. Other measures that facilitate market entry, such as the reduction in the administrative burden for company start-ups or the liberalisation of network industries (telecommunications, energy, transport, postal services) will have similar effects (see Blanchard and Giavazzi, 2001). The new Internal Market Strategy encompasses all these elements.
3. See Neary (2001) for a critical but constructive review of this literature.
4. This argument is consistent with the 'New Trade Theory' based on increasing returns to scale and product differentiation (Helpman and Krugman, 1985). Markusen and Venables (2000) extend the theory and predict that multinationals, which tend to be heavily involved in intra-industry trade, are more likely to be operating if countries are more similar in both relative and absolute factor endowments.

REFERENCES

Aiginger, K., Böheim, M., Gugler, K., Pfaffermayr, M. and Wolfmayr-Schnitzer, Y. (1999), 'Specialisation and (geographic) concentration of European manufacturing', Osterreichisches Institut für Wirtschaftsforshung (WIFO) Background Report, *DG Enterprise Working Paper*, July.

Blanchard, O. and Giavazzi, F. (2001), 'Macroeconomic effects of regulation and deregulation in goods and labor markets', *NBER Working Paper*, no. 8120, February.

European Commission (1996), 'Economic evaluation of the Internal Market', *European Economy*, no. 4.

European Commission (1997), 'Trade patterns inside the Single Market', *The Single Market Review*, subseries IV, vol. 2.

European Commission (2001), 'Price levels and price dispersion in the EU', *European Economy*, supplement A.

Fontagné, L. and Freudenberg, M. (1999), 'Endogenous symmetry of shocks in a monetary union', *Open Economies Review*, **10**, 263–87.

Frankel, J. and Rose, A.K. (1997), 'The endogeneity of optimum currency area criteria', *NBER Working Paper*, no. 5700.

Helpman, E. and Krugman, P.R. (1985), *Market Structure and Foreign Trade*, Cambridge, MA: MIT Press.

Krugman, P.R. (1991a), *Geography and Trade*, Cambridge, MA: MIT Press.

Krugman, P.R. (1991b), 'Increasing returns and economic geography', *Journal of Political Economy*, **99**, 483–99.

Markusen, J.R. and Venables, A.J. (2000), 'The theory of endowment, intra-industry and multi-national trade', *Journal of International Economics*, **52**, 209–34.

Neary, J.P. (2001), 'Of hype and hyperbolas: introducing the New Economic Geography', *Journal of Economic Literature*, **39**, 536–61.

PART I

Microeconomic issues

2. The impact of a single currency in Europe on product markets: theory and evidence

**Michael Gasiorek, Russell Davidson,
Steve Davies, Bruce Lyons, David Ulph,
Richard Vaughan and Alan Winters**

INTRODUCTION

A key economic objective of integration in Europe is to increase economic welfare by reducing or eliminating barriers between markets. That process of barrier reduction inevitably leads to structural changes in European markets which impacts upon both allocative and technical efficiency. The (positive) impact on efficiency may yield static welfare gains as well as dynamic welfare gains through engendering a potential increase in growth rates.

The extent and nature of the impact of any process of integration depends to a large degree on the effect that barrier reductions or eliminations have on product markets. Hence the primary impact of the Single Market Programme (SMP) was to reduce the costs of trade or market access between European economies. The mechanisms generating structural changes in product markets are then typically seen to be the following. The reduction in trade costs should in the first instance increase the intensity of competitive interaction in European markets. In imperfectly competitive industries the increase in competition leads to reductions in price–cost margins, potentially reductions in profits, and hence to a degree of industrial restructuring. The direct impact of barrier removal as well as any subsequent restructuring could in turn also lead to a greater exploitation of economies of scale. The welfare gains thus derive from the standard triad of potential gains under imperfect competiton – increased variety, economies of scale and the pro-competitive effect.

The creation of a single currency also involves a direct reduction in trade barriers. This arises through the elimination of the costs of exchange rate transactions themselves, as well as the risks associated with movements in the exchange rate. The mechanisms outlined above are thus likely to be present with the creation of a single currency, though probably to a lesser extent. However, in addition to this, a single currency involves the creation of *transparency* in relation to proposed transactions, that is, the ability of consumers and producers to directly compare prices in terms of a single currency.

It is this impact on price transparency, and through it the effect on product markets, which is potentially the biggest difference between the SMP and the establishment of a single currency. Specifically what we show and then empirically address in this chapter is that the creation of greater price transparency can result in: (a) consumers being more aware of price differences thus creating greater intensity of product market competition; (b) producers being more aware of their competitors' responses which can in turn engender greater coordination or collusion between them; and (c) an increase in the scope for arbitrage activity.

The overall effect on product markets of the single currency will thus depend on the interaction between the impact of greater transparency, and that of cost reductions implied by a single currency. Specifically, four analytically distinct effects on markets arising from such a process of integration can be identified. These are:

1. The *market access effect*: integration means that firms have easier access to each other's markets, hence increasing the intensity of competitive interaction.
2. The *market size effect*: integration can lead to an effective increase in the size of the (integrated) market through increased efficiency (for example, from the reallocation of resources or economies of scale), through the reduction in transactions costs and through the possible impact on growth.
3. The *price transparency effect*: the ability of producers, consumers and arbitrageurs to make price comparisons across markets.
4. The *competition effect*: each of the above and in particular the market access and price transparency effects can lead to a change in the nature of competitive interaction. This could imply, for example, a switch from non-collusive to (tacitly) collusive or more coordinated behaviour by firms, or a switch from Cournot competition to Bertrand competition, or a switch from a segmented market to an integrated market strategy.

Most analyses of economic integration have tended to focus on the first, second and last of these effects. This largely arises from the nature of the integration processes being considered which usually involves the reduction of physical or fiscal barriers to trade. In this chapter, summarised here, we focus on the possible extent and subsequent impact of the third effect – price transparency. We do so in the following manner. The first section outlines the underlying theoretical model which explicitly incorporates transparency and its effects on product markets. The second section provides an evaluation of existing data and focuses on how that data could be usefully employed to analyse the impact of a single currency. The third section details the use of more formal econometric techniques in order to analyse selected indicators of product integration and their changes over time. Again the aim here is to develop practical methodologies which can be used to evaluate the impact of integration. The data and methodologies considered in the two first sections largely focus on what can be learnt from an examination of price statistics. In contrast the fourth section focuses directly on issues of integration and market structure. By focusing on a number of well-defined industries, the discussion here highlights that much can be learnt about the impact of integration on product markets through those developments in market structure. Finally, the fifth section discusses the application of a multi-country multi-sector computable general equilibrium model in order to evaluate the possible impact of transparency across a range of different sectors and to allow for an assessment of the aggregate welfare effects.

2.1   PRICE TRANSPARENCY AND MARKET EQUILIBRIA

A Summary of the Theoretical Model

The underlying theoretical model used in this study encompasses the three principal avenues by which an increase in price transparency may be expected to influence market equilibria. Firstly, via the effect on consumers information availability, by making price comparisons between products easier; secondly by enhancing the coordination between firms, by making price wars less likely; thirdly by increasing the arbitrage possibilities between countries.

We assume that there exists a unit mass of consumers, and n firms each selling a different branded good. Let $d^i(p_i, \bar{p})$ be the demand by the representative consumer for a particular brand i when that brand charges a price p_i and other brands charge prices p_i represented by the $(n-1)$ dimensional price vector $\bar{p}$.

We will sometimes think of this demand being determined as follows:

$$d^i(p_i, \bar{p}) = f_i(p_i, \bar{p}) \cdot x_i(p_i) \qquad (2.1)$$

where $f_i(p_i, \bar{p})$ is the fraction of the consumers who buy good i and $x_i(p_i)$ is the amount of good i that each consumer decides to buy.

Before developing the theory further, for reference purposes we note the conventional Bertrand–Nash equilibrium for this model, which in terms of the Lerner price cost margin is,

$$\frac{p_i - c_i}{p_i} = \frac{1}{\eta_{ii}} \tag{2.2}$$

where $\eta_{ii} = -\dfrac{\partial d^i(p_i, \bar{p})}{\partial p_i} \cdot \dfrac{p_i}{d^i} > 0$ is the own price elasticity of demand.

If $\sigma_{ii} = -\dfrac{\partial f_i(p_i, \bar{p})}{\partial p_i} \cdot \dfrac{p_i}{f_i} > 0$; $\varepsilon_{ii} = -\dfrac{dx_i}{dp_i} \cdot \dfrac{p_i}{x_i} > 0$ are the corresponding

elasticities of market share and individual consumer demand, then $\eta_{ii} = \sigma_{ii} + \varepsilon_{ii}$, so (2.2) can also be written:

$$\frac{p_i - c_i}{p_i} = \frac{1}{\sigma_{ii} + \varepsilon_{ii}} \tag{2.3}$$

Note that conventional theory suggests that both η_{ii} and σ_{ii} will be strictly increasing functions of n – the number of firms/products in the market.

We now turn to our basic extension of the differentiated products model to take account of the introduction of the effects of price transparency on market equilibria.

The consumer price transparency effect

We assume that if firm i decides to cut its price *proportionately* by the amount $z_i \geq 0$, then the proportion of consumers that detect this price change and will react to it is defined by the function $h_i(z_i)$, $h_i(0) > 0$, $h_i'(z_i) > 0$. Thus we assume that some consumers are always monitoring price changes, and a positive fraction will always detect even the smallest change. In this way we can model consumer behaviour in the presence of non-transparency of price change. The proportion of consumers revising their demand is assumed to be an increasing function of the proportionate price change.

Transparency and the trigger strategy

We assume that if firm i decides to cut its price proportionately by the amount $z_i \geq 0$ the probability that other firms will react to this price change is defined by the function $g_i(z_i)$, $g_i(0) = 0$, $g_i'(z_i) > 0$. Notice that, contrary to consumers, firms have no reason to react to infinitely small price changes. If the proportionate price cut is detected by any firm, it is assumed to be detected by all firms; we also assume that all consumers are aware of the proportionate price cut. Prices of other firms are assumed to be reduced to the level p where $p < \bar{p}$ consequent on implementation of the trigger strategy.

Transparency and arbitrage
Increased price transparency may increase arbitrage in any market. Arbitrageurs in this context are simply viewed as additional suppliers to consumers. The number of firms in the market therefore increases, and the price elasticity for firm i's product is assumed to increase with the number of products offered to consumers in the market.

Consider the case where the initial price vector in the market for firm i is $(p_i, \bar{p})$. In order for firm i to wish to stay with this price the expected profits of the firm must be lower either if the firm increases the price or lowers the price. Consider initially the case where price reductions are considered.

As a result of these additional assumptions Ulph and Vaughan (2000) show that the following equilibrium condition results,

$$\frac{p_i - c_i}{p_i} = \frac{1}{\alpha_i \eta_i}\left[1 + (p_i - c_i)\beta_i\right] \tag{2.4}$$

where $\alpha_i = h_i(0)$ and $\beta_i = g'(i) = 0$.

We may immediately note that if we eliminate the transparency effects from the equation, that is if we operate in the conventional textbook world where all consumers fully detect any price change – and so $\alpha_i = h_i(0) = 1$ – while other firms do not react to prices – and so $\beta_i = g'_i(0) = 0$ – then equation (2.4) just reduces to equation (2.3) which is the standard Bertrand–Nash Equilibrium.

As can be seen the comparative static effects of an increase in price transparency work in the way intended in respect of equation (2.4).

- An increase in the perception of price changes by consumers – that is, an increase in α_i – would reduce the RHS of (2.4) and thus reduce the price–cost margin.
- An increase in the responsiveness of firms to a price change – that is, an increase in $-\beta_i$ would serve to increase the price–cost margin.
- An increase in arbitrage, by increasing the number of suppliers, would increase σ_{ii} and hence η_{ii} and so reduce the price–cost margin.

Market Segmentation

In the simplest model we have considered the equilibrium for a single market with a representative consumer. Market segmentation may occur for a number of reasons:

- It may be possible for firms to segment the market according to the demand characteristics of consumers, that is, we drop the assumption of the representative consumer.
- There may be differences in costs in reaching different groups of consumers.

If segmentation exists on the basis of historical precedent, for example, existing national markets within the EU then differences may exist both with respect to the search behaviour of consumers or with respect to strategic considerations and trigger strategies between these groups.

Consider segmentation into k groups; we assume that all prices and costs are defined by a common currency.

By the assumption of independence between the groups, we therefore have k equations to determine the price cost margins for each of the groups as defined by

$$\frac{p_i^k - c_i^k}{p_i^k} = \frac{1}{\alpha_i^k \eta_{ii}^k}\left[1 + \left(p_i^k - c_i^k\right)\beta_i^k\right] \qquad (2.5)$$

where we have assumed that the number of firms existing in each of the market segments is identical. In the assessment of price dispersion across market segments, (EU countries) therefore the following variables are viewed to be of importance:

1. The variability of consumer tastes as reflected in the own price elasticities of demand.
2. Differences in cost structures.
3. Differences in the implementation of implicit cartels through the detection function, and the trigger prices consequent on any price change.
4. Differences in the revision effect of consumer demand consequent on any price change.

Note also that in the theoretical model then, price dispersion within market segments is absent. A clear implication is therefore that inter-country price variability should far exceed intra-country price variation.

The effect of the introduction of a single currency on price dispersion therefore depends on the differential impact of such a currency on the above four effects. One possible outcome is that the differences between the segmented markets of revision effects and trigger strategies disappear; through diffusion of attitudes and responses by consumers and firms. If tastes are then homogenised, although the ability of firms to discriminate prices across segments would still exist, it would be no longer optimal to do so.

The effects on evaluation of consumer welfare have not been formulated in this chapter, however, it may be noted that if price dispersion across segments decreased or disappeared, this is quite compatible with greater welfare losses for consumers if a high price equilibrium across segments is engendered.

It is also worth remarking that it is likely that the parameterisation of the model would be rather different depending on whether a final consumer or intermediate market is being considered. Whilst one might expect the trigger strategy aspects of the model to be important both for final markets and intermediate markets, the demand response functions may indicate a far swifter response in intermediate markets. It may even be postulated that $\alpha_i = h_i(0) = 1$, $\beta_i = g'_i(0) = 0$ for the intermediate market cases.

Overall, we would not expect the introduction of a single currency to increase the variation in the costs of production and distribution across countries. In so far as change is brought about we would expect a convergence in cost structure and hence a reduction in the variance of costs. Similarly with respect to demand, the euro would not be expected to increase demand differences between countries. Likewise, increased variation in the collusion regime across countries is unlikely to result.

Concluding Remarks

The model outlined above may be deemed to have some attractive features in relation to the appraisal of price transparency. It predicts an equilibrium price–cost margin above that of the Bertrand–Nash equilibrium. Factors that make it easier for consumers to detect price changes lower the equilibrium price–cost margin. Factors which make it easier for firms to detect price–cost changes raise the equilibrium price–cost margin. The introduction of a single currency and associated increased transparency of information for both consumers and producers, may therefore have ambiguous effects on the price level within a single market. The effects on price dispersion may also be ambiguous; if increased information leads to homogenisation of consumer and producer behaviour then price dispersion will be reduced; however whether this leads to an improvement in consumer welfare depends on whether increased competitive effects resulting from increased consumer information are not offset by the improved ability for implicit collusion by producers.

2.2   INTERPRETING EUROPEAN PRICE DATA

The previous discussion gives strong theoretical grounds for suggesting that the impact of a single currency on product markets is likely to be reflected in both price levels and in the dispersion of prices. In this section we thus focus on an analysis of price data from ACNeilsen and from Eurostat. A description of these data, as well some of the methodological issues related to their use is given in Appendix 2.A. In so doing we indicate some of the methodological issues and summary statistics which may be useful in considering the impact of integration, and in particular the impact of a single currency.

Analysis of Consumer Price Data from ACNeilsen

The most interesting data are those from ACNeilsen, although the sample is patchy in coverage. Since our main interest was in the evolution of price dispersion we deleted any commodity/country pair for which there was not a full set of thirteen observations (two-monthly from March 1994 to March 1996). We refer to this sample as the *unbalanced sample* – unbalanced because commodities have different country coverage and countries different commodity coverage.

Table 2.1 is constructed from the unweighted coefficients of variation (cv) for each product: 'mean cv' refers to these averaged over time and 'std. dev. of cv' to the standard deviation of the cvs over time, which summarises the variability of these measures of dispersion. Those for the EU-14 – EU-15 less Luxembourg – in the first two columns are supplemented by measures for EU-core (Belgium, France, Germany, Netherlands) and EU-non-core (EU-14 less the core).

Considering the EU-14 columns, it is plain that these coefficients of variation do not vary much through time. The standard deviations are all small. This issue was looked at further but it seems to suggest that price dispersion is permanent and stable, and not the result of random noise to the prices in Member States. It is also plain that extracting Switzerland and

Norway, the two non-member countries, does little to change our perception of European price dispersion.

Figure 2.1 plots the mean coefficient of variation and standard deviation through time. It indicates considerable stability, with a very slight upward trend in price dispersion over 1994–95.

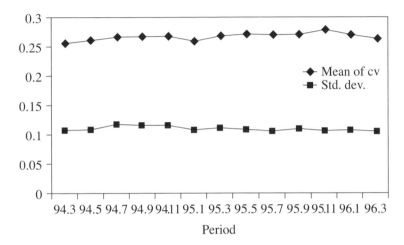

Note: EUR16 = EU15 less Luxembourg plus Switzerland and Norway.

Figure 2.1 Mean coefficient of variation over time, EUR-16, unbalanced sample

A more interesting exercise is to separate EU-14 into core and non-core countries. 'Core' here refers not only to monetary stability, but also to the deep connections that are likely to arise from long-standing connections between the real side of the economies. The latter consideration led us to exclude Austria (usually viewed as part of the Deutschemark zone), while the former led us to include France as well as the other formal DM-zone countries of Germany, the Netherlands and Belgium (–Luxembourg).

In Table 2.1, both the core and non-core columns report mean coefficients of variation and standard deviations only where there are at least three countries in the sample (which implies two degrees of freedom in identifying the coefficient of variation). The numbers of countries in the two samples are reported in the table, as is the F-statistic for testing the equality of the variances of prices within the core and non-core samples against the alternative hypothesis that the non-core has the higher variance. Since the squares of the coefficients of variation are the variance of normalised prices (prices normalised by the mean of their particular sample), the distribution

Table 2.1 Summary statistics of coefficients of variation (cv), unbalanced sample, March 1994–March 1996

	EU-14		EU-core		EU-non-core		F-tests	Signif.*	No. of countries*	
	Mean cv	Std dev.	Mean cv	Std. Dev.	Mean cv	Std. dev.	(Non-core > core)		Core	Non-core
1. Kelloggs Frosties 500g	0.270	0.015	0.105	0.019	0.291	0.016	7.68	S	3	10
2. Kelloggs Corn Flakes 500g	0.268	0.014	0.264	0.028	0.254	0.017	0.93		3	10
3. Uncle Ben's rice (long grain) 500g	0.151	0.044	0.075	0.013	0.172	0.054	5.30	S	4	7
4. Heinz Tomato Ketchup 340g	0.308	0.011	0.129	0.011	0.336	0.014	6.78	S	3	8
5. Danone yoghurt 4 × 125g	0.214	0.012	0.233	0.028	0.194	0.012	0.69		3	5
6. Babybel mini 6-pack	0.228	0.028	0.106	0.009	0.235	0.033	4.92		3	9
7. Whiskas canned cat food 400g	0.202	0.009	0.078	0.005	0.216	0.010	7.63	S	4	10
8. Pedigree canned dog food 400g	0.273	0.027	0.013	0.004	0.291	0.030	480.73	Ss	3	10
9. Sheeba cat food 100g	0.144	0.008	0.127	0.016	0.148	0.013	1.35		4	8
10. Twix (Standard) (1 pack, 2 fingers)	0.320	0.012	0.271	0.012	0.326	0.018	1.45		4	8
11. Toblerone (milk) 100g	0.237	0.025	0.138	0.007	0.236	0.029	2.95	S	3	8
12. M&M 1 pack 45g	0.359	0.014	0.000		0.369	0.017			0	5
13. Nutella Chocolate Spread (hazelnut) 400g	0.446	0.017	0.101	0.025	0.450	0.020	19.98	Ss	4	6
14. Kit-Kat (1 pack, 4 Fingers)	0.283	0.050	0.158	0.011	0.290	0.055	3.34	S	3	9
15. Nescafé instant 100g	0.226	0.012	0.113	0.008	0.233	0.019	4.24	S	4	10
16. Lipton tea bags (Breakfast) (50 bags)	0.225	0.014	0.000		0.245	0.015			0	5
17. Ovomalatine/Ovaltine tin 400g	0.231	0.009	0.251	0.011	0.201	0.016	0.65		4	6
18. Nesquik powder 400g	0.176	0.028	0.061	0.018	0.149	0.050	5.98	S	3	9
19. Coca Cola can 330ml	0.439	0.026	0.103	0.006	0.469	0.030	20.70	Ss	4	9
20. Schweppes Tonic 750ml (plastic bottle)	0.268	0.028	0.000		0.298	0.031			0	9
21. Gatorade (regular) 500ml	0.053	0.017	0.000		0.053	0.017			0	3
22. Perrier bottle 750ml	0.318	0.021	0.185	0.006	0.256	0.023	1.92	S	4	8
23. Evian bottle 2L	0.476	0.028	0.264	0.012	0.509	0.032	3.72	S	3	5

Item										
24. Johnnie Walker Red Label 70cl	0.413	0.043	0.020	0.009	0.485	0.049	595.15	Ss	3	7
25. Bailey's Irish Cream 70cl	0.384	0.025	0.042	0.008	0.424	0.025	99.70	Ss	3	8
26. Heineken cans 4 × 330ml	0.363	0.051	0.000		0.365	0.052			0	7
27. Beck's bottles 6 × 330ml	0.322	0.015	0.000		0.242	0.022			0	5
28. Guinness cans 4 × 330ml	0.239	0.027			0.259	0.030			0	5
29. Ariel washing powder E3	0.269	0.016	0.000		0.277	0.019			0	5
30. Palmolive hand wash liquid 500ml	0.278	0.012	0.116	0.024	0.361	0.019	9.68	S	3	4
31. Ajax 500ml	0.447	0.078	0.390	0.099	0.400	0.018	1.05		3	7
32. Kleenex Tissues regular (1 × 150)	0.289	0.037	0.121	0.010	0.323	0.048	7.07	S	4	7
33. Pampers Ultra Maxi (1 pack 40)	0.082	0.028	0.000		0.000	0.000			0	0
34. Tampax regular (1 pack 32)	0.100	0.020	0.075	0.012	0.107	0.027	2.02	S	3	6
35. Duracell batteries AA 1.5V 4-pack	0.208	0.012	0.086	0.029	0.226	0.015	6.92	S	3	9
36. TDK video tape (VHS180 Hi-grade) 1 unit	0.139	0.020	0.000	0.000	0.000	0.000			0	0
37. Lux soap 4 × 125g	0.129	0.020	0.091	0.019	0.132	0.021	2.11	S	3	8
38. Colgate toothpaste (regular) 100ml tube	0.222	0.053	0.000		0.231	0.053			0	8
39. Nivea face cream 50ml tube	0.219	0.013	0.276	0.012	0.164	0.016	0.35		3	4
40. Oral B toothbrush regular adult (1 unit)	0.146	0.043	0.000		0.161	0.052			0	6
41. L'Oreal Freestyle Mousse aerosol 150ml	0.232	0.018	0.000		0.204	0.030			0	5
42. Plax mouthwash (original) 250ml	0.088	0.018	0.000		0.092	0.020			0	6
43. Gillette Sensor razor blades 5-pack	0.159	0.015	0.110	0.011	0.173	0.021	2.48	S	4	9
44. Impulse Body Spray 75ml	0.203	0.022	0.000		0.180	0.029			0	7
45. Timotei shampoo 200ml	0.155	0.013	0.000		0.139	0.015			0	6

Note:[*] This refers to the number of countries used to calculate the statistics reported in this table. It equals the number of countries for which the price data are available.

of their ratio may be taken to be F-distributed (precisely so if prices are distributed normally).[1] The F-statistics provide only moderate support for the hypothesis that the non-core sample has significantly greater price dispersion than the core sample.

It is also noticeable that the non-core sample shows higher standard deviations. That is, the dispersion of prices over these countries is much less stable over time than in the core, suggesting more shocks. Thus while the non-core sample may not frequently have statistically higher dispersion, it does seem to display greater variability.

Figure 2.2 compares core and non-core dispersion in a different dimension. It plots the mean cvs over time for each commodity (subject to $n \geq 3$). The numbers refer to the commodities defined in the left-hand column of Table 2.1. The figure shows a quite clear tendency for higher dispersion in the non-core sample. The difference is most marked for two alcoholic beverages (commodities nos 24 and 25), presumably because of the dispersion in taxes.

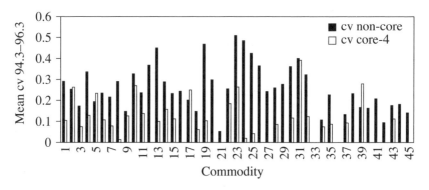

Figure 2.2   CVs for core-4 and non-core

Although we have focused mainly on price dispersion, it is worth thinking a little about how best to characterise price differences between countries. For this purpose we constructed a reduced, compact sample of observations from the ACNeilsen data in which we have complete coverage – that is, no holes. As noted above this required quite drastic surgery because consumption patterns differ strongly across Europe, and left us with 20 commodities, 8 countries and 13 periods.

We subjected this sample to two exercises. First, to isolate any systematic differences in prices across countries we conducted an analysis of variance on normalised prices to separate the variance across countries from that across commodity/time combinations. That is, we first divided each price observation by the mean for that commodity over all time periods and countries, and then decomposed the variance of the resulting data into parts explained by country, by commodity/time combinations and a residual. The commodity/time dimension explained virtually none of the variance. This is not wholly surprising, since commodity variance had essentially been squeezed out by the normalisation. However, the result suggests that in *this time period* the systematic temporal variation of prices is completely insignificant. Systematic country variation, on the other hand, was highly significantly different from zero, explaining around 14 per cent of the total variation of the sample. This result has some parallels with Engel and Roger's (1998) observation that while exchange rate fluctuation explain some of the dispersion in prices between US and Canadian cities, there remains a major component due to real-side factors such as distribution practices and so on. In our case, the latter will be captured by the country effects, whereas *within-sample* exchange rate effects would have shown up in the commodity/time time dimension. If, however, the effects of exchange rate disequilibria extend over the whole of our sample period – by no means an impossibility, given the long adjustment periods identified by other researchers – they would also be captured here in the country effects and we cannot rule them out in this way.

In a second exercise we sought variation in normalised prices in the country/time direction. Again this proved statistically significant overall, explaining about 15 per cent of the variance. However, since 14 per cent of this can be explained by country alone, adding the time dimension is not at all statistically significant. Thus no material part of the observed dispersion of prices comes from time-specific country shocks, common to all commodities sold in the market at that time. Exchange rate changes fall into this last class (unless they are instantly offset by changes in the local currency price of commodities, leaving the ECU price unchanged), so we conclude that *in this sample* exchange rate variability does not directly lead to price dispersion. Note, however, that, as observed above, our sample is really too short to capture the effects of exchange rate variability. Neither does it refute the hypothesis that different currencies are one of the means that firms can use to segment markets and so can be responsible for persistent price dispersion.

Analysis of PLI Data from Eurostat

For this study we examined more formally (than heretofore) the differences in price statistics between the 'EU-core' and 'non-core' regions. As noted above the term core is merely shorthand for the EU-12 DM-zone plus

France and does not imply anything about degrees of commitment to European integration.

We have compared both the price levels and dispersions between core and non-core countries for the 1997 sample. (Given the stability in the data, there is no point in doing this for more years.) There are 268 categories for which we can calculate the statistics. Of these, 144 reported higher mean prices in the non-core than in the core, and there were some regularities in the distribution of these ratios. For example, non-core prices appear to be systematically higher in foods except for fish and fresh meat, transport equipment, audio and related equipment and cultural expenditures, and consistently lower in clothing, leather goods, footwear and all building-related expenditure. Not too much should be made of these differences, however, because in only thirteen cases was the difference between prices statistically significant (and this using a set of assumptions that maximised the probability of rejecting the hypothesis of equality – namely that the variances of prices in the core and non-core were equal and known).

The results on dispersion show more differences – as we might have expected from the analysis of the ACNeilsen sample. The non-core sample persistently showed higher dispersion – 231 cases out of 268 – and in 89 cases the difference was statistically significant. The strongest indications came in fruits, meats, beverages (as above), utilities, insurance and building-related activities.

We repeated these exercises on the Classification of Economic Activities within the European Communities (NACE) 2-digit data derived by combining the category data as described above. Now none of the 40 2-digit groups displayed significant differences in price levels, but 15 of them had significantly larger dispersion outside the core.[2] Figure 2.3 illustrates the core and non-core cvs where it is obvious that dispersion is greater in service sectors than for goods. In part this probably reflects the lower tradability of services (NACE 40 and higher) than goods, but it also presumably arises from the fact that the data for certain services are based on input price data (Eurostat, 1996). The prices for health services, construction and government services (including education) are all costed up from input prices, in which wages will necessarily play a very large part. Whether this biases the results reported here is unclear, although it presumably reduces their statistical significance because it introduces a statistical dependency between the observations for the various service sectors.

Both the ACNeilsen data and the current PLI (Price Level Indices) data suggest that there is less dispersion in prices inside the core than outside it. We do not speculate on why this should be, but clearly it could reflect higher degrees of integration induced by greater relative monetary stability.

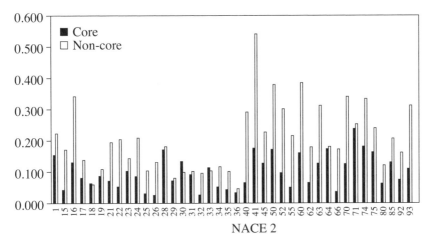

Figure 2.3   Core vs non-core cvs, NACE 2-digit sector, 1997

One cannot simply conclude from this that EMU would reduce dispersion, but it does suggest that further work on the evolution of core-convergence would be worthwhile. If it can be related to changes in the degree of effective monetary integration, then there would perhaps be a case for expecting EMU to have similar effects. Unfortunately, however, there are many non-monetary connections between the core countries – for example, the higher volume of trade, smaller distances, historical mobility between countries – that could just as easily explain price patterns, so it will be no easy task to attribute them confidently to monetary conditions.

2.3   ECONOMETRIC ANALYSIS

The aim of this section was to see the extent to which a more formal analysis of price data can help in understanding the degree to which the markets for specific products are integrated or remain segmented across the different countries of the EU.

The model proposed here is based on two snapshots of prices, for a number of commodities, in the different countries of the Union, at reasonably well separated times. This sort of model is incapable of providing estimates of price dynamics, but it does allow a comparison of price levels in different countries at different times, and, to that extent, it allows one to see to what degree prices have converged over the period separating the two snapshots.

A Cross-Section Approach

The approach developed here is to compare two (or more) snapshots of
the prices of a variety of products at different points in time, with a view to
seeing to what extent overall price levels in different countries have moved,
either together, or in separate directions. The underlying model is a form of
fixed-effects model of the sort used in panel data analyses (see for instance
the first chapter of Baltagi, 1995) but without the time dimension. There
are still two dimensions however, one the cross-country dimension, and
the other the dimension of the different products (or industry product
aggregates) for which price data are available.

The main object of the exercise is to compare the extent of cross-country
dispersion at different time periods, in order to assess to what extent price
levels in different countries have converged over the period of progressive
monetary unification. To that end, results will be compared for the PLI
data in 1993 and 1997.

The data-generating process that is assumed is very simple. The price of a
given product in a given country at the moment the snapshot is taken is the
sum of, first, a fixed effect associated with the product itself, the same across
all countries in the sample; second, a fixed effect associated with the country,
the same for all products considered; and, third, a random error term, which
subsumes all other determinants of the observed price. The Eurostat data
sets provide PLIs for a little more than 250 product aggregates (although
at a rather low level of aggregation) for the 15 countries of the European
Union. In order to obtain as wide a separation in time as possible, snapshots
were treated for 1993 and 1997. A few cases of missing observations made
it necessary to eliminate some of the aggregates from the samples. Actual
sample sizes are reported in Table 2.2.

Various hypotheses suggest themselves as suitable for empirical testing.
The most restrictive of these would be that there are no country-specific
effects, presumably because the European Union constitutes a single,
transparent, market in which costs of transportation can be ignored in the
sense that they do not give rise to price differentials. The data reject that
hypothesis very convincingly indeed.

This being so, it is of interest to see which countries have small effects,
that is, have price levels close to the European average, and which countries
have significantly positive effects (higher prices) or significantly negative
effects (lower prices).

In Table 2.2, the estimated coefficients, and the associated Student's *t*
statistics are presented for all 15 countries for 1993 and 1997. The coefficients
are presented as difference from unity: a value of zero would correspond to
a price level exactly equal to the EU average, while a positive (negative) value

Table 2.2   Snapshots based on PLI data

Country	1993 Parameter estimate	1993 Student's *t*	1997 Parameter estimate	1997 Student's *t*
Germany	0.085141	5.565200	0.011424	0.820495
France	0.084772	5.541043	0.043224	3.104476
Italy	−0.07952	−5.19768	−0.06708	−4.81818
Netherlands	−0.01199	−0.78352	−0.07179	−5.15585
Belgium	0.000388	0.025367	−0.02273	−1.63226
Luxembourg	0.012037	0.786795	0.016415	1.17895
UK	−0.11895	−7.77475	0.012055	0.865840
Ireland	−0.07228	−4.72453	−0.00942	−0.67626
Denmark	0.229348	14.99118	0.216058	15.51786
Greece	−0.16753	−10.95062	−0.12091	−8.68424
Spain	−0.09557	−6.24657	−0.14509	−10.42103
Portugal	−0.16647	−10.88106	−0.20227	−14.52773
Austria	0.098387	6.431019	0.037043	2.660565
Sweden	0.125392	8.196143	0.195890	14.06936
Finland	0.076831	5.021987	0.107181	7.698003

Notes:
1993: Sample size: 251 product aggregates; standard error = 0.015. F statistic for hypothesis that all parameters are zero: 57.751, with degrees of freedom 14 and 3499.
1997: Sample size: 269 product aggregates; standard error = 0.014; F statistic for hypothesis that all parameters are zero: 68.966, with degrees of freedom 14 and 3751.

corresponds to a higher (lower) price level. All 15 countries of the EU are present in the PLI data. In the 1993 snapshot, significantly positive effects are seen for Germany and France (around 8 per cent), and for Austria (10 per cent), Denmark (23 per cent), Sweden (12 per cent) and Finland (8 per cent). Significantly negative effects are seen for Italy (8 percent), the UK (12 per cent), Ireland (7 per cent), Greece (17 per cent), Spain (10 per cent) and Portugal (17 per cent). Effects for the three Benelux countries were insignificant. These results contain no surprises.

In 1997, the positive German effect is no longer significant, the French one remains significant but is smaller (3 per cent), similarly for Austria (4 per cent), Denmark remains almost unchanged (22 per cent), while Sweden and Finland have larger positive effects (20 and 11 per cent respectively). Regarding the negative effects, that for Italy falls a little (7 per cent), the UK effect remains unchanged, Ireland no longer has a significant effect, Greece has a smaller effect (12 per cent), while Spain and Portugal both have larger effects (15 and 20 per cent respectively). Belgium and Luxembourg continue to have no significant effect, but the Netherlands now shows a negative effect of 7 per cent.

These results suggest further possible hypotheses. An interesting one applies only to the original six countries, Benelux, Germany, France and Italy. It can be seen by simple inspection of the *t*-statistics that, with the exception of the later negative effect in the Netherlands, all country-specific effects that were significant in 1993 became less so in 1997 implying that in six countries (Belgium, Germany, France, Italy, Luxembourg and the Netherlands) a convergence of prices towards the EU average took place between 1993 and 1997. For other countries, it is less obvious how best to formulate plausible hypotheses, other than for single countries, for which a comparison of the *t*-statistics is sufficient, but it does seem that Scandinavian prices diverged upwards away from the average over the four-year period, while Iberian prices diverged downwards.

2.4   INTEGRATION AND MARKET STRUCTURE

In this section we focus on the evolution of market structure in response to the process of integration. This approach is complementary to the price-based analysis in the preceding two sections and suggests that the way that integration or transparency impacts upon product markets depends on the underlying characteristics of the market in question.

As discussed earlier the effect of reductions in barriers to trade and competition depends on the impact of these reductions on the four main analytical effects identified – the market access effect (bringing more firms into direct competition with one another), the market size effect (increasing the size of the market), the competition effect (changing the nature of competitive interaction, for example, allowing for more price coordination) and the price transparency effect (allowing consumers and/or professional arbitrageurs to respond to cross-country price differences). In turn the impact via each of these analytical channels will depend on key industry characteristics, namely the extent of economies of scale, the nature of price competition, and the extent of international integration, as well as the nature and scale of investment in endogeneous fixed costs such as R&D or advertising.

For this study we constructed a small sample of seven industry case studies and then examined changes in industry concentration and multinationality over the 1987–97 period. The industries were carefully selected to illustrate the mechanisms discussed above for the sub-set of industries characterised by competition via investment in endogenous sunk costs (notably advertising and R&D). The industries examined include railway stock; soaps, detergents, perfumes, toiletries; rubber products; domestic appliances; alcohol and spirits; wine; and brewing and malting. Railway stock we included as a pronounced example of the effects of removing public procurement bias in an R&D-intensive industry. We included the three sub-industries within the alcoholic drinks sector in order to explore the effects of disaggregation. In a similar way, soaps, detergents and so on comprises two fairly distinct parts: 'soaps and detergents' and 'toiletries and perfume'.

Results

Our findings are summarised in Table 2.3, and the main trends that can be identified are:

- *On average, producer concentration (indicated by the five firm concentration ratio, CR5) at the aggregate EU level has tended to increase* – in four cases substantially, and in one case marginally. The two exceptions are rubber (in which it was already high by 1987) and wine (which remains unconcentrated).
- *In all seven cases, the leading firms have increased the extent of their intra-EU multinational activity.* This is indicated by the number equivalent measure (NM) which normalises across industries by converting each firm's actual distribution of turnover across Member States into a hypothetical number of equal sized operations (note that this measure tends to approach an upper limit of 5 or 6 in industries in which firms are equally distributed across all Member States in rough proportion to the sizes of the Member States).

Both of these findings are interesting from a structural perspective and add some valuable new insights into how market structure is evolving with the ongoing market expansion coming from European integration. The implication of the former is that the escalation in sunk costs has not only kept pace but even outstripped the growth in market size, such that increased concentration is the norm. The only exceptions are rubber (notably tyres) in which concentration was already very high at the start of the period, and wines. Our interpretation of the latter is that wines, unlike the other forms of alcoholic drinks, are characterised by horizontal product differentiation, and are not typically heavily advertised (that is, sunk costs are largely exogenous).

Similarly, the pervasive increase in multinationality is to be expected, given what is known about the rapid growth in intra-EU foreign direct investment (FDI) and cross-border acquisitions since the late 1980s. We would expect this to be especially pronounced in markets, such as those characterised by strong product differentiation and brand images – these are amongst the classic *firm-specific assets* which typically give rise to multinational firms. In this case, however, it is noticeable that the drinks industries have lagged behind, both in the level and rate of growth of the NM index. This implies that, in these cases, market integration is being achieved more by trade or licensing than by cross-border production by owned subsidiaries.

Table 2.3   Changing concentration and intra-EU multinational activity in the sample of industries

Description	C5		NM		
	1997	1987	1997[*]	1997[**]	1987
Soaps, detergents, perfumes, toiletries	42.9	34.4	4.702	4.388	3.778
Rubber products	46.1	48.7	3.851	3.851	2.549
Domestic appliances	43.4	41.6	2.633	2.502	1.753
Alcohol and spirits	52.0	37.3	1.776	1.776	1.401
Wine	17.4	18.4	1.327	1.327	1.176
Brewing and malting	30.3	25.7	1.637	1.637	1.456
Railway rolling stock	77.5	50.6	2.176	2.176	1.0
Arithmetic mean	40.4	36.1	2.858	2.769	2.131

Notes:
C5 is the five-firm production concentration ratio; NM is the number equivalent measure of the Herfindahl-based index of intra-EU multinationality of the five leading firms in each industry (constructed as in Davies and Lyons, 1996, chapter 7).
[*] refers to the case confined to the 12 original Member States; [**] refers to the case where Sweden, Austria and Finland are also included. For comparability with 1987, the former estimates are to be preferred.

Market Structure and Price Transparency

As mentioned earlier, integration and the single currency are likely to lead to an intensification of competitive interaction through the market access effect, as well as through increased transparency. This mechanism was already very advanced for most of our sample even in 1987. The enormous potential impact of this effect can also be seen in the one case where national markets did open up to European-level competition – rail rolling stock.

A key task is to assess the impact of price transparency on the intensity of competition through both increased consumer price transparency and producer price transparency. Start by considering the latter. For most of our sample industries, competition is channelled into advertising and/or R&D,

with price often of relatively less importance. There is typically significant product differentiation, both in vertical quality and horizontal product characteristics. In such industries, individual brands have considerable market power, and even with perfect price information, it is difficult to make quality and characteristic adjusted price comparisons. Thus, increased price transparency as a collusion-facilitating device has much less relevance than in more standardised product industries. Moreover, to the extent that differentiation reduces inter-brand cross-price elasticities, price competition is anyway already relatively soft in such cases.

Consideration of the former requires addressing the question of how the market transaction is effected? More precisely, what is the organisation of the buyers of the industry's products (for example, the retailers)? A key issue here is the ability of manufacturers to price discriminate between Member States, that is, *intra*-brand competition, in contrast to *inter*-brand competition. Of particular significance are the extent to which buyers are organised on a European or a national basis, and the extent of vertical linkages between seller and buyer. These issues can be seen through a closer examination of our sample industries.

Railway rolling stock
Purchasing by rail service operators has become more fragmented in some areas where competition has replaced national monopolies, but wider alliances for international services will concentrate buyers. Significant light-railway buyers are municipal. However, the most important feature is that systems are typically sold by some form of tender, for which there is already perfect transparency as bids must be in a stated currency. It is unlikely therefore that the single currency would result in significant further changes.

Rubber products
First installation tyres for cars and lorries are via bilateral oligopoly. This accounts for 33–50 per cent of sales; the remainder are replacement tyres sold mainly to final consumers through garages and specialist retailers. Some of these are vertically linked to manufacturers. For example, Michelin has 1200 'Euromaster' depots and Continental has 950 in various national chains (NTS in the UK; Vergoelst in Germany). Kwik-fit is Europe's largest independent retailer, but even its geographical breadth is confined to the UK and Benelux. Nevertheless, worldwide procurement of tyres is possible, and car manufacturers can select the cheapest offer, subject to quality and specification. For some consumers, brand loyalty will be important: they may be inclined to buy replacement tyres of exactly the same brand as on the original equipment; and some will be heavily influenced by advertising

and therefore relatively unresponsive to price. However, others will be more price sensitive, which allows wholesalers and retailers some leeway to source competitively, including imports from eastern Europe and the far east, as well as private brands and affiliate brands of the majors. Internet shopping is unlikely to have a significant impact because of the necessity for sales services, including fitting, which can only be done locally (and it is likely that unbundling sales and fitting would increase transaction costs far more than any saving from price competition).

Domestic electrical appliances

The European Competition Commission report on the Electrolux-AEG merger in 1994 suggests that: 'a considerable bargaining pressure is exercised by big stores and by buying groups, of which several are active on a cross-border basis. In addition, private label products are sold under trademarks owned by large retail chains and are mostly produced under tenders by manufacturers.' Cross-border buyer groups are a substitute for the single currency in facilitating international price comparisons and buying where the quoted price is lowest. However, they are only a very imperfect substitute unless they cross all borders, which is organisationally unlikely. It seems that the euro may have a modest impact on prices, as long as the stores remain independent of the manufacturers. Furthermore, there is considerable opportunity for the internet to have an impact on consumer purchasing habits, since the main products are high-value search goods. Manufacturers may develop their own direct sales.

Soaps, detergents, perfumes and toiletries

Soaps and detergents are sold alongside food and drink in increasingly concentrated supermarkets, which are able to exercise buyer power on all but a few 'must stock' brands. Toiletries are still sold through a wider range of retail outlets. In both cases however, as with domestic appliances, in the absence of widespread cross-border buying groups, increased price transparency might have an impact on intra-brand price differentials. Given the nature of the products, it is probably only high-value perfumes which might have a separate internet market, but selective distribution by the manufacturers may prevent this from developing on a significant scale. Beyond this, any internet shopping is likely to be mediated by supermarket chains.

Drinks

Legal cross-border arbitrage sales are still constrained by differential indirect taxes. There is likely to be little impact of price transparency for sales through bars, unless those bars are organised in significant chains. For sales through shops and supermarkets, our comments with respect to soaps and detergents apply equally here. Independent internet shopping is likely to be feasible only for higher quality wines and substantial consumers.

Concluding Comments

The preceding analysis shows that there are clear reasons as to why certain industries may be affected more by integration than other sectors. It also identifies reasons and sectoral characteristics as to why changes in transparency may have a greater effect on either consumer or producer behaviour.

The Single Market Programme (SMP) had a very significant impact on a relatively small group of industries. It was especially strong in those industries characterised by potential competition in endogenous fixed costs (particularly R&D) but which had been artificially constrained within national borders (for example, by strong public procurement bias). A much wider group of industries benefited from more modest injections of competition.

The additional impact of a single currency (full EMU) is likely to be of a different nature because of the role of transparency. Seller price transparency of the type that facilitates collusion may turn out to be important in a few industries. However, where products are heterogeneous, even a single currency will make it little easier to compare the prices of rival differentiated products. Furthermore, producers can often still offer secret price cuts to customers unless they are selling to final consumers (for example, retailers), in which case price transparency is superficial. This begins to focus attention on distribution channels, and it is here that we anticipate a major impact on both competition and structure.

Their importance is even greater when considering buyer price transparency. Even with products that are heavily differentiated between different producers, buyer price transparency becomes important for comparing the same brand sold in different locations. A single currency makes international price comparisons for a particular brand enormously easier (the most famous example is for cars). This potentially allows arbitrage to break down international price discrimination. Thus, EMU can introduce *intra-brand competition*. The extent to which this is actually achieved will depend on: (a) the nature of the product in question (for example, homogeneous or differentiated); (b) the organization of buyers (for example, their concentration); and (c) vertical linkages between buyers and sellers (both through ownership and contracts). Once again, the most famous example is how the car distribution system preserved international price differences.

We believe that there are strong grounds for arguing that the most likely avenue for an impact of the single currency is via a toughening of competition resulting from increased buyer awareness. Even in the presence of different currencies in many (more homogeneous goods) industries the costs to the larger producers (who comprise the majority of the industry) of collecting information on prices across markets are relatively small. For industries with more heterogeneous products even a single currency is unlikely to make it easier to compare prices of rival differentiated products. Transparency for producers is thus not likely to have a large impact. Secondly, other developments (such as the growth of the internet or the possibilities for professional arbitrage) are likely to facilitate responses to price differentials. Clearly, however, the extent to which this materialises will depend on the nature of the product as well as the nature of the buying sector.

In particular just as inter-brand competition brings about a horizontal response in terms of structure (that is, increased EU-level concentration), intra-brand competition can be expected to result in a vertical structural response. In order to protect profits currently achieved through price discrimination, but threatened by a single currency, sellers can be expected to look for contractual or ownership links to preserve their market power.

2.5   THE SINGLE CURRENCY: A CGE ASSESSMENT

In this section we use a computable general equilibrium (CGE) model in order to investigate the relationship between changes in transparency and the consequent impact on industries. The CGE model we use comprises 15 countries and 49 imperfectly competitive manufacturing industries and one perfectly competitive sector.

The theoretical analysis identified key ways in which transparency might impact on product markets. What is clear from that analysis is that the impact on product markets is likely to depend on the extent to which both consumer and producer behaviour is affected. We have incorporated these theoretical insights directly into our modelling structure which thus allows for changes in either consumer or producer transparency (or both).

We also use the results of the earlier sections of this report in order to inform our choice of experiments. A key feature of the modelling procedure then concerns: (a) the base levels of the consumer and producer transparency measures; and (b) the size of the impact (experiment) on these transparency measures. In the calibration procedure we can allow for both symmetric or differentiated levels of transparency. Similarly in the experiments we can allow for either symmetric changes or differentiated changes in transparency.

We thus first conduct some symmetric simulations based on symmetric calibrated transparency measures. The purpose of these experiments is that it allows us to identify the relationships between differing industry characteristics and any changes in transparency. This is important in then interpreting the results of the subsequent experiment. The subsequent experiments are all based on the differential calibrated equilibrium. We start with a symmetric experiment but then move on to consideration of what are the more realistic differential experiments. The differential experiments are then based on underlying information on industry characteristics and on existing levels of price dispersion across industries. The symmetric experiment should thus be seen as providing a framework for interpreting the differential experiments, which in turn can be interpreted as a preliminary assessment of the impact of monetary union in European markets.

The principal aims of this section of the chapter are therefore:

1. To assess the possible impact of EMU and the consequent changes in transparency on output, mark-ups and welfare. Where relevant we report on the results both by industry and by country.
2. To examine the sensitivity of the results to both the size and underlying symmetry of the experiments.
3. To look at the extent to which differing industry characteristics might shed light on the possible sectoral impact of transparency. In so doing we show how transparency is likely to impact upon both mark-ups and industrial structure in identifiable ways.

Model, Calibration and Data

The underlying theoretical model is based on imperfect competition and increasing returns to scale. Full details of the model are given in Gasiorek et al. (1992), who use the same basic model, at a more aggregated level.

The model has 15 countries: each of the EU countries (with Belgium-Luxembourg treated as a single country) plus the rest of the world. Each country is endowed with three primary factors of production – capital, and manual and non-manual labour. Capital is assumed to be perfectly mobile internationally, and available at a constant price. Other factors are internationally immobile, so their prices adjust to equate demands to endowments. The commodity structure is defined by NACE 3-digit industries with the rest of each economy aggregated into a single perfectly competitive composite, which is tradable and which we take as the numeraire. At the 3-digit level there are slightly over 100 manufacturing industries. Each of the manufacturing industries is assumed to be imperfectly competitive, with a number of firms producing differentiated products, production being subject to increasing returns to scale.

Table 2.4 lists the manufacturing industry aggregates we work with, and presents some descriptive information regarding each of these industries. Column (1) gives the average degree of concentration in each industry adjusted for import penetration. The figure reported here is a Herfindahl index, the reciprocal of which gives the number of equivalent sized firms (the larger the index the more concentrated the industry); columns (2) and (3) indicate the extent to which each industry is traded within the EU. The import share gives the weighted average EU share of imports in total domestic consumption, where the weights are each country's share of total consumption of that industry. Hence, for industry 151, of total domestic consumption in the EU, 18.4 per cent is provided by imports from other EU countries. Analogously, the export share gives the weighted average share of exports to other EU countries as a proportion of total production by each country (where the weights are each country's share in total production of that industry). Hence, again for industry 151, the table shows that on average 19.1 per cent of EU production is exported to other EU countries. These two columns thus give some indication of the extent to which each industry is traded in the EU at the base. It can readily be seen that the industries which are traded the most include other textiles (NACE 175), basic precious and non-ferrous metals (NACE 274), engines (NACE 291), and office machinery (NACE 300). Industries which are traded comparatively little include publishing (NACE 221), printing (NACE 222) and metal product (NACE 281–283).

Column (4) gives the calibrated elasticities of substitution where we have allowed the consumer and producer transparency measures to differ by industry and market (these can be interpreted as the elasticities of demand for a given product holding the prices of all other varieties constant). As can be seen from the table these elasticities range from 6.7 (highly differentiated products) to 33.02 (more homogeneous products).

Demand for differentiated products is modelled as a two-stage process, where the demand for a product aggregate depends on a price index for that aggregate, while demand for an individual variety depends on the price of the variety relative to that of the product aggregate. We assume that firms act as price competitors in segmented markets. Each firm chooses price in each country market, taking as constant the price of all its rivals in each market. Optimisation requires the equation of marginal revenue to marginal cost in each market, where the slope of each firm's perceived demand curve depends on the extent of product differentiation, and on the share of the firm in that market. A key feature of the model is that in the fundamental pricing equation we incorporate the insights from the theoretical work we

Table 2.4   Industry characteristics

NACE	Description	Herf. (1)	Import share (2)	Export share (3)	El. (D) (4)
151–153	Meat, fish, fruit & veg	0.006	0.184	0.191	8.52
154–158	Other food products	0.009	0.292	0.258	9.68
159–160	Beverages & tobacco	0.043	0.127	0.111	16.19
171–172	Textile fibres & weaving	0.003	0.309	0.335	14.55
174	Textile articles	0.006	0.166	0.222	18.66
175	Other textiles	0.005	0.389	0.352	12.92
176–177	Knitted textiles	0.008	0.276	0.413	17.31
181–183	Clothes inc. leather & fur	0.003	0.220	0.329	32.9
191–192	Leather products	0.003	0.205	0.271	35.11
201–202	Wood + veneer sheets etc.	0.010	0.211	0.291	18.79
203–204	Builders carpentry + containers	0.004	0.117	0.123	18.06
211–212	Pulp, paper & paper products	0.018	0.263	0.274	9.79
221	Publishing	0.072	0.070	0.071	7.37
222	Printing	0.076	0.046	0.047	7.28
241	Basic chemicals	0.039	0.275	0.282	6.7
242–243	Agro-chemicals, paints etc.	0.059	0.212	0.193	7.85
244–245	Pharmaceuticals, soaps etc.	0.037	0.240	0.220	8.06
246	Other chemicals	0.066	0.291	0.299	6.88
247	Manmade fibres	0.290	0.146	0.172	10.06
251	Rubber products	0.127	0.318	0.349	16.34
252	Plastic products	0.004	0.253	0.245	20.28
261	Glass & glass products	0.118	0.300	0.277	18.03
262–263	Ceramic products	0.019	0.251	0.264	15.99
264–268	Other non-metallic minerals	0.053	0.083	0.082	6.58
271–273	Basic & first processed iron & steel	0.031	0.323	0.310	13.82
274	Basic precious & non-ferr. metals	0.019	0.347	0.443	13.69
281–283	Metal products	0.008	0.101	0.095	13.72
286	Cutlery and general hardware	0.005	0.291	0.307	14.8
287	Other fabricated metal products	0.002	0.274	0.286	14.93
291	Engines, except aircraft etc.	0.013	0.355	0.340	9.12
292–293	Agricultural & other machinery	0.005	0.310	0.278	13.26
294	Machine tools	0.003	0.271	0.298	13.26
295–296	Other machinery	0.007	0.328	0.238	13.95
297	Domestic appliances	0.094	0.278	0.314	13.11
300	Office machinery	0.054	0.344	0.591	10.54
311–312	Electric motors + distribution etc.	0.037	0.185	0.193	6.36
313	Insulated wire & cable	0.058	0.270	0.261	6.36
314–315	Accumulators etc. & lighting	0.024	0.330	0.366	16.02
316	Electrical equipment n.e.c.	0.015	0.272	0.301	6.13
321	Electronic valves etc.	0.096	0.330	0.449	17.94
322	TV & radio transmitters etc.	0.049	0.214	0.203	15.98
323	TV & radio receivers	0.099	0.291	0.391	17.64
331	Medical & surgical equip.	0.062	0.302	0.336	6.72
332–334	Precision instruments	0.012	0.276	0.314	6.33
341–343	Motor vehicles, bodies, and parts	0.038	0.332	0.337	12.09
351–355	Ships, railways, aircraft, motorcycles	0.039	0.253	0.252	12.14
361	Furniture	0.005	0.196	0.198	18.89
362–365	Jewellery, music. ins., sports, games	0.005	0.185	0.273	18.85
366	Manufactured goods n.e.c.	0.048	0.296	0.330	21.2

have done for this chapter and allow for both consumer and producer transparency. Hence, increases in producer transparency serve to increase price-marginal cost mark-ups, while increases in consumer transparency have the reverse effect (see equation (2.4) of the model in section 2.1).

Numerical specification of the CGE model is undertaken first by setting some key parameters and variables, notably those describing concentration and returns to scale on the basis of literature estimates, and then calculating the values of remaining parameters and endogenous variables, including the transparency measures, so that the 1997 base year observations support an equilibrium (for more information on the calibration, see European Economy, 2002, chapter 2).

Transparency, Industry Characteristics and Market Structure

In order to examine more closely the factors which might determine the extent and pattern of the impact of price transparency we have looked at some of the underlying characteristics of the base data set, and related those characteristics to the changes arising from symmetric experiments based on symmetric calibrated transparency measures.

Here we allow first for an increase in consumer transparency, and secondly an increase in producer transparency. The model was calibrated such that the consumer transparency parameter, α (see equation (2.4) in section 2.1), is set equal to 1 with regard to sales by domestic firms in their own market, and is set equal to 0.75 in all other markets. In other words we are assuming that all consumers are aware of any price changes if they originate in the domestic market; and that 75 per cent of consumers are aware of price changes that originate in foreign markets. The producer transparency measure in calibration is simply set equal to zero.

For the first experiment (SS1) we change the consumer transparency parameter in EU markets from 0.75 to 0.85 – that is, we are allowing for a 13 per cent change in consumer transparency. For the second experiment (SS2) we allow for a change in producer transparency from 0 to 0.1. For all these experiments we allow for the free entry and exit of firms but we hold factor prices fixed. The purpose of holding factor prices fixed at this stage is to minimise the factor market general equilibrium effects in order to isolate as clearly as possible the impact of the changes in transparency. Changes in factor prices are allowed for in subsequent experiments.

The results of these experiments are illustrated in Figure 2.4, which graphs the correlation of the impact of changes in consumer and producer transparency respectively on output and mark-ups with respect to key industry characteristics – the calibrated elasticities of substitution, concentration and average import shares.

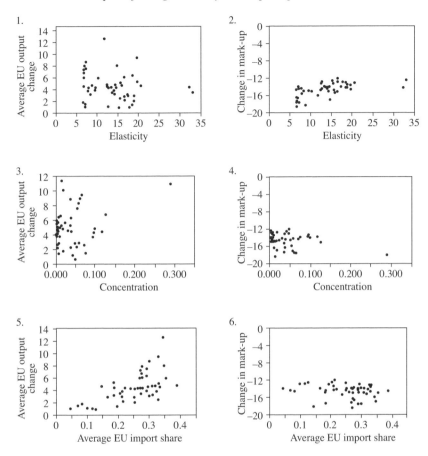

Figure 2.4   Change in consumer transparency: correlation of changes with key characteristics

For example, one might posit that where industries are more imperfectly competitive and hence are characterised by higher price–cost mark-ups an increase in consumer transparency might have a larger impact on those mark-ups and hence also on output. All else being equal, industries that are more imperfectly competitive are likely to be more concentrated and are more likely to have lower calibrated elasticities of demand (reflecting a greater degree of product differentiation). Similarly, the extent to which particular industries are affected is likely a priori to depend on the extent to which the products of that industry are traded. Clearly these factors interact with each other in complex fashions. For example, the calibrated elasticity depends both on the concentration in the industry as well as on the assumed level of returns to scale. At the same time, industries with high economies of scale tend to be more concentrated. We should not therefore expect unambiguous results from such an analysis. The purpose is simply to see whether such correlations can shed any light on the mechanisms at play.

Figures 2.4 and 2.5 each have six panels. Moving from left to right the first two panels in each case show the relationship between the calibrated elasticity and the changes in average EU output and the changes in average EU mark-ups. The middle two panels look at the relationship between base concentration and the output and mark-up changes; and the last two panels focus on the extent to which industry is traded by looking at the average EU import share.

Looking at the impact of changes in consumer transparency: the first two panels show that there is little evidence of correlation between the output changes and the underlying elasticity (which represents the extent to which products are differentiated), but there is clear evidence of the relationship between the change in mark-ups and the elasticity. Those industries which have more homogeneous goods tend to see a smaller impact on the price–cost margins. This in turn indicates that the more homogeneous the goods the smaller the impact of consumer transparency on reducing price dispersion. Note that the more homogeneous goods are more likely to have lower levels of price dispersion at the base because of the underlying higher elasticity. Mark-ups at the base tend to be higher for the more differentiated industries, and consequently integration has a greater impact on those mark-ups.

Panels 3 and 4 show some evidence of a relationship between the results and the degree of concentration in the industry. To a certain degree the more concentrated the industry the larger the output changes, and the larger the changes in price–cost mark-ups. As before the more concentrated industries tend to have more market power (higher mark-ups) at the base, and then the given change in consumer transparency reduces their mark-ups proportionately more. However, these relationships do not appear to be very strong. Finally the last two panels show, particularly in the case of output changes, that there is a clear relationship between the extent to which the industry is traded at the base and the respective levels of impact.

These results would appear to suggest that a given change in consumer transparency is principally likely to have a smaller impact on mark-ups the more homogeneous are the products (the higher the elasticity), and to some extent the less concentrated is the industry. Regarding the changes in output, the impact tends to be larger principally according to the extent to which the good is initially traded, but also to some extent the more concentrated the industry.

A slightly different pattern can be discerned in looking at the impact of changes in producer transparency (see Figure 2.5). The first two panels

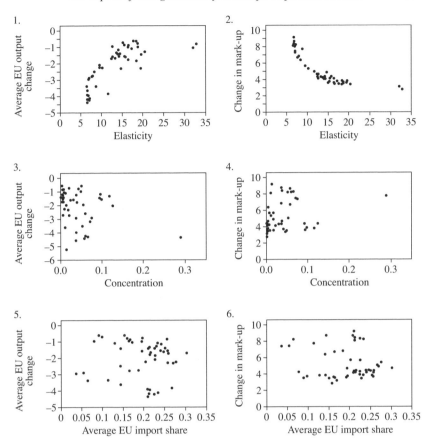

Figure 2.5 Change in producer transparency: correlation of changes with key characteristics

show evidence of a strong relationship between both the changes in output and mark-ups and the base calibrated elasticity. The lower the elasticity, the larger the increase in the mark-up, and the larger the decline in output. This serves to partially reinforce the results derived from looking at the changes in consumer transparency, though of course the direction of change is reversed. There is no strong evidence of a relationship between the base levels of concentration and the output and mark-up changes. To some extent the higher the concentration the bigger the change in output, and the higher the elasticity the bigger the change in mark-up, but these effects are less clear. Finally, the impact of changes in consumer transparency depended to a greater extent on the base traded shares than appears to be the case when looking at the changes in producer transparency, where little relationship can be observed. It does therefore appear that the biggest influence on changes in both output and mark-ups with regard to changes in producer transparency are related to how differentiated the products are.

Finally in Figure 2.6 we show the correlation between the *changes* in concentration, and the output and mark-up changes, for each of the producer and consumer transparency experiments. Panels 1 and 2 show the correlations for the changes in consumer transparency and panels 3 and 4 show the correlations for the changes in producer transparency. It is quite clear that there is a significant relationship, for both transparency parameters, between the changes in concentration and the changes in output and mark-ups. With regard to each of the transparency measures the larger the output changes the larger the changes in concentration, and the larger the change in mark-up the larger the change in concentration. This serves to reinforce the analysis in earlier sections of the chapter where we argued that the examination of changes in market structure can be seen as the dual of the analysis of prices or price–cost mark-ups.

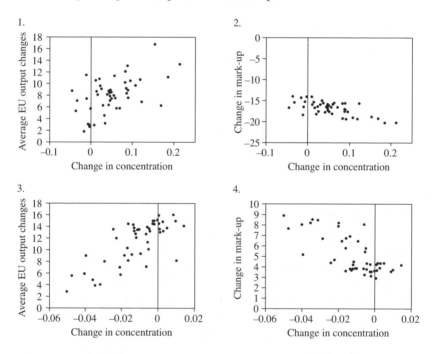

Figure 2.6   Correlation between changes in concentration and changes in output and mark-up

The Single Currency and Price Transparency

We now focus more directly on the possible impact of the single currency on product markets by allowing for a differentiated base calibration and then allowing for more realistic differentiated experiments. For each of the experiments we allow for the free entry and exit of firms and for flexible factor prices.

1. *Symmetric simulation – DS1*　A uniform increase in both the producer and consumer transparency measures. For each industry we allow for a 20 per cent increase in consumer transparency, and a 10 per cent increase in producer transparency.
2. *Differentiated simulations – DD1*　For these experiments we differentiate the size of the transparency impact by sector. This is derived as follows. With regard to producer transparency, we do not expect a large impact on producer transparency nor do we have strong evidence for believing that the impact would differ significantly across sectors. Producer transparency is thus increased by 5 percentage points in each EU market. In contrast changes in consumer transparency are more likely to be substantial and to differ across sectors. The considerations that appear to be important here are the nature of the product in question (for example the extent to which the product is homogeneous or differentiated, the nature of buyer–seller relationships, and the extent to which the products are sold largely to final consumers, or the extent to which they are sold as intermediate inputs). Information on some of the above is available. We have information from the recent work of Davies and Lyons (1996) on industry types. We also have information on the final expenditure share by industry from national accounts statistics. On the basis of this information we therefore allow for a small, medium or high impact on transparency depending largely on these industry characteristics, but also with a degree of judgement where relevant. The rating we have given to each industry is given in the 'Exp. rating' column of Table 2.5 where an H represents a high impact, M a medium impact and L a low impact.[3]
3. *Differentiated experiment with integrated markets – DDint*　The preceding experiments were all based on the segmented markets assumption. For this final experiment we assume that firms change their pricing strategy from one based on segmented markets to one based on integrated markets.

The impacts on output and on mark-ups of the experiments can be seen in Table 2.5 where the columns headed with an 'X' refer to the percentage output changes; and those with 'Mkup' refer to the percentage changes in mark-ups. The first two columns give the output and mark-up changes for the symmetric experiment. All but two industries see an increase in output, with the largest increases being experienced by medical and surgical instruments (8.7 per cent) and by precision instruments (8.1 per cent). The two industries which see a small decline in output are metal products (–0.2 per cent) and printing (–0.1 per cent). All industries see the price–marginal cost mark-ups decline.

It is interesting to compare these columns with columns (3) and (4) where we give the results for the fully differentiated experimented (DD1). The sectoral impact of the changes in transparency are clearly very different where we differentiate the experiment as opposed to where we postulate a uniform impact. Of the 49 industries, 16 experience a decline in output, which comprises all but one of the low impact rated industries plus six of the medium impact rated industries. Clearly the net effect of the relatively smaller consumer price transparency change for these industries, and the producer transparency change, coupled with the general equilibrium interactions results in these declines. Note also that all industries but one (medical and surgical equipment) experience a decline in price–cost margins – including those that see a decline in output. Nevertheless for these industries the decline in price–cost margins is markedly smaller. The largest changes in output are experienced by textile articles (11.22 per cent), other textiles (12.97 per cent), and knitted textiles (9.05 per cent). These results are unsurprising given that these are all high impact rated industries, with fairly high traded shares as well as high elasticities. Not surprisingly also these are among the industries which see the largest changes in price–cost margins.

It is quite clear from these results that if the single currency in Europe does indeed have an impact on consumer transparency, and if the orders of magnitude of that impact are similar to those modelled here, that we can certainly expect a substantial impact on product markets. This is reflected in both the changes in output and in the changes in price–cost margins. Those changes in price–cost margins would then be reflected in the levels of EU price dispersion. In order to assess the extent to which the overall size of the postulated experiments might be reasonable we have compared the changes in price dispersion as a result of these two experiments, with the differences in price dispersion between the core and non-core EU economies reported earlier. It is obviously unlikely that any differences in the latter can be entirely explained by differences in transparency, and therefore such a comparison can perhaps be seen as providing simply an approximate indication for the potential impact of a single currency on transparency and through that on price dispersion. From the comparison, our results suggest that the changes which we report do not appear to generate changes in price dispersion which are greatly different in magnitude to the difference

Table 2.5 *The impact of a single currency in Europe*

Description	Exp. rating	DS1 X (1)	DS1 Mkup (2)	DD1 X (3)	DD1 Mkup (4)	Integrated markets (DDint) X (5)	Integrated markets (DDint) Mkup (6)
Meat, fish, fruit & vegetables	H	3.87	−19.0	7.04	−31.0	7.80	−31.5
Other food products	H	4.25	−18.8	9.04	−37.5	9.46	−37.9
Beverages & tobacco	H	0.53	−16.9	6.38	−46.4	11.09	−48.3
Textile fibres & weaving	H	5.39	−20.5	8.88	−47.2	3.82	−43.7
Textile articles	H	3.68	−18.5	11.22	−46.5	12.08	−46.2
Other textiles	H	5.82	−19.8	12.97	−43.7	10.72	−41.9
Knitted textiles	H	5.97	−20.9	9.05	−48.9	−0.12	−44.9
Clothes inc. leather & fur	M	5.88	−18.6	6.08	−24.9	5.39	−25.0
Leather products	H	4.62	−17.5	7.54	−55.1	2.27	−53.1
Wood + veneer sheets etc.	H	3.67	−17.9	8.00	−36.5	9.57	−37.4
Builders carpentry + containers	M	1.26	−17.0	1.44	−19.6	2.02	−20.1
Pulp, paper & paper products	M	5.85	−19.3	3.76	−21.1	5.83	−22.3
Publishing	L	0.58	−18.4	−1.93	−6.8	7.62	−12.4
Printing	L	−0.08	−18.0	−1.81	−7.2	10.12	−12.7
Basic chemicals	L	8.83	−20.8	−1.60	−4.6	2.70	−7.5
Agro-chemicals, paints etc.	M	4.85	−18.5	1.38	−18.2	9.24	−23.0
Pharmaceuticals, soaps etc.	M	5.1	−19.7	2.46	−21.7	7.22	−24.1
Other chemicals	L	6.89	−20.9	−1.48	−4.6	14.54	−9.4
Manmade fibres	L	6.38	−26.5	−0.19	−9.2	28.26	−18.9
Rubber products	M	7.00	−21.1	6.04	−23.0	31.92	−36.7
Plastic products	M	1.87	−18.4	2.91	−24.9	2.97	−24.8
Glass & glass products	M	4.25	−18.4	5.30	−25.8	21.31	−33.5
Ceramic products	M	3.99	−17.5	2.44	−21.6	4.87	−22.9
Other non-metallic minerals	L	1.10	−17.8	−2.35	−1.1	4.34	−5.9
Basic & first processed iron & steel	L	5.67	−19.0	0.01	−6.3	3.42	−9.0
Basic precious & non-ferrous metals	L	7.81	−20.8	−0.49	−5.0	0.58	−6.7
Metal products	M	−0.22	−17.2	−0.70	−33.1	0.02	−33.3
Cutlery and general hardware	M	4.80	−19.7	2.01	−26.0	0.60	−24.0
Other fabricated metal products	M	3.53	−18.1	3.97	−28.5	4.40	−27.8
Engines, except aircraft etc.	M	4.61	−18.0	−0.96	−5.0	0.26	−6.3
Agricultural & other machinery	M	4.72	−18.5	1.55	−10.7	2.21	−11.1
Machine tools	M	4.84	−18.9	0.52	−9.9	0.75	−9.7
Other machinery	M	3.27	−17.0	0.29	−9.1	0.76	−9.2
Domestic appliances	H	5.93	−19.0	7.48	−27.5	23.91	−35.9
Office machinery	H	5.54	−23.4	2.85	−36.8	6.09	−38.0
Electric motors + distribution etc.	M	4.69	−21.5	−1.52	−6.9	2.28	−9.9
Insulated wire & cable	M	6.45	−20.0	−1.02	−6.1	5.08	−10.1
Accumulators etc. & lighting	M	6.47	−19.6	5.24	−25.6	8.11	−25.5
Electrical equipment n.e.c.	M	4.97	−19.8	−1.89	−5.8	0.27	−6.5
Electronic valves etc.	M	4.54	−17.7	1.64	−15.8	10.25	−21.6
TV & radio transmitters etc.	M	2.95	−16.0	1.56	−14.3	9.90	−18.5
TV & radio receivers	M	6.84	−19.9	3.56	−18.5	21.50	−25.7
Medical & surgical equip.	L	8.67	−21.1	−3.37	0.3	2.70	−3.9
Precision instruments	M	8.06	−20.9	−1.38	−7.7	−0.2	−8.7
Motor vehicles, bodies, and parts	M	6.49	−18.2	2.11	−15.1	6.67	−19.5
Ships, railways, aircraft, motorcycles	L	4.86	−18.4	−1.25	−5.3	2.11	−8.3
Furniture	M	1.89	−17.2	2.44	−20.8	2.92	−21.2
Jewellery, music. instruments, sports, games	M	6.30	−18.8	3.16	−19.7	3.75	−20.3
Manufactured goods n.e.c.	M	6.72	−17.6	6.24	−24.7	12.30	−28.1

in price dispersion between the core and the non-core, and that therefore our results can be seen as providing a preliminary indication of the impact of monetary union on European product markets (for detailed results on this, see European Commission (2002), chapter 2, table 16).

Integrated Market Experiment

The integrated markets assumption is one that has been widely used in the empirical literature as a means of modelling a strong pro-competitive impact arising from deeper integration. When there is national market segmentation, firms set prices in each national market independently; moving to integrated markets means that producers treat the EU market as a single market in which they have to adopt a unified pricing strategy. Earlier work has shown that switching to an integrated markets pricing rule tends to lead to much higher welfare changes, but also much larger sectoral changes especially for the smaller economies. The theory outlined earlier suggests that transparency is likely to impact on consumers, producers and on the activities of arbitrageurs. We do not have an explicit means of modelling arbitrage here. Nevertheless, wide-scale arbitrage, if it occurred, would have a strong pro-competitive impact on EU product markets as well as leading to a narrowing of price differentials (net of transport costs). The integrated markets assumption leads to similar outcomes, and can thus be seen as, in some ways, analogous to the presence of widespread arbitrage. However, it should be emphasised that the two are not identical.

For the integrated market experiment the size of the transparency impacts is exactly the same as in the first of the fully differentiated experiments (DD1), and so the results in columns (5) and (6) of Table 2.5 should be compared with those in columns (3) and (4). It can be readily seen that the pattern of results is quite different. There are now only two industries which see a decline in output (knitted textiles and precision instruments) and neither of these are low impact rated industries. Indeed with segmented markets, knitted textiles was one of the three industries which saw the largest expansion in output; with integrated markets its position changes dramatically. The industries with the largest output changes are now manmade fibres (28.3 per cent), rubber products (31.9 per cent) and domestic appliances (23.9 per cent). Note that of these three industries, while manmade fibres has a large change in output, the change in the price–cost mark-up is relatively lower in comparison to the other industries.

What these results suggest is that there is a significant difference between the impact on product markets of a change in consumer transparency and the pro-competitive impact of integrated markets, and also that as in earlier work the shift to integrated markets does represent a much greater pro-competitive impact which is then reflected in the output and mark-up changes.

The Potential Impact of Monetary Union on Member States

In this section we turn to examining how the different experiments impact upon output and welfare across countries (see Table 2.6). If we consider first the impact by country of the symmetric experiment (DS1) we see that all countries witness an increase in manufacturing output with the biggest changes occurring in Belgium, the Netherlands, Ireland and Denmark, and the smallest changes in France, Germany, Spain and the UK. The differences are quite substantial with Denmark seeing an increase of 14.79 per cent and Spain seeing output go up by just 2.09 per cent. Price–cost margins go down in all countries and the average decline ranges between 16 per cent and 22 per cent.

Table 2.6   The impact of transparency by country

Country	Imp. share	Change in output (%)			Change in mark-ups (%)			Change in welfare* (%		
		DS1	DD1	DDint	DS1	DD1	DDint	DS1	DD1	DDint
France	0.307	4.64	2.58	5.51	–17.59	–13.15	–14.21	0.49	0.05	–0.16
Belgium-Lux	0.454	14.01	15.76	20.77	–21.55	–20.45	–22.35	1.32	2.91	4.79
Netharlands	0.442	13.23	18.41	21.97	–21.10	–21.12	–22.65	1.32	2.67	4.21
Germany	0.242	3.19	0.71	2.22	–16.17	–10.91	–11.43	0.20	–0.14	–0.25
Italy	0.207	4.92	1.61	6.96	–17.94	–12.63	–14.68	0.40	–0.02	–0.14
UK	0.236	3.65	0.51	2.72	–16.93	–12.42	–13.19	0.37	–0.04	–0.23
Ireland	0.459	13.50	21.91	29.93	–20.79	–29.16	–31.31	1.24	3.80	8.64
Denmark	0.445	14.79	21.04	27.41	–21.58	–24.47	–27.03	1.16	3.30	5.21
Greece	0.483	4.40	17.07	27.73	–18.51	–35.09	–37.77	2.01	6.70	9.23
Portugal	0.411	5.55	9.62	26.30	–18.88	–25.02	–30.30	2.44	5.05	13.35
Spain	0.278	2.09	1.42	9.82	–17.22	–17.28	–20.68	0.69	0.37	0.61
Sweden	0.364	7.86	9.93	13.76	–19.30	–21.09	–23.24	0.56	0.78	0.97
Finland	0.317	8.63	3.42	11.89	–19.10	–24.89	–28.13	0.55	0.99	1.64
Austria	0.463	12.67	14.70	20.78	–20.95	–24.30	–26.31	0.99	1.80	2.91

Note: * change in compensating variation as a proportion of manufacturing value-added.

More realistic are the results when we differentiate the experiment according to the underlying industry characteristics (DD1). We now see that while the relative country rankings of the changes are very similar there is a much greater variation in the output changes across country, and correspondingly in the price–cost mark-ups. The biggest change in output occurs in Ireland and Denmark (just over 21 per cent), and the smallest changes in the UK and Germany (~ 0.5 per cent). These results are driven by two factors: (i) countries with the larger output changes tend to be more open, as reflected in the larger import shares; (ii) this is reinforced by the fact that at the base consumer transparency levels are lower in certain countries, and hence the differential impact of transparency in these countries is relatively higher.

Turning now to welfare it can be seen that with experiment DS1 all countries experience an increase in welfare, and the cross-country pattern of changes shows that Portugal and Greece experience the largest increases in welfare (2 per cent and 2.4 per cent respectively), while the smallest changes are for Germany and the UK (0.2 per cent and 0.37 per cent respectively). For all countries these changes in welfare are fairly modest. While the relative cross-country rankings remain fairly constant when we allow for the more realistic differentiated experiment (DD1), the relative magnitudes change considerably. If we consider first the 'smaller' experiment we see that Greece and Portugal see an increase in welfare of 6.7 per cent and 5.1 per cent respectively, Ireland and Denmark 3.7 per cent and 3.8 per cent, Belgium-Luxembourg and the Netherlands 2.9 per cent and 2.7 per cent respectively, while Germany, Italy and the UK all experience a small welfare loss. Once again this is the consequence of the differences in the openness of the economies, but also, and more importantly, of the differences in the base levels of transparency by industry and by country. The impact of the integrated markets assumption results again in larger welfare effects, but the cross-country pattern of changes is very similar.

2.6   CONCLUSIONS

Conceptually there are four key effects on product markets arising from greater economic integration and from the introduction of a single currency: the market access effect, the market size effect, the competition effect and the price transparency effect. The impact of the reduction of barriers to trade, be they physical or fiscal, is largely on the first three of these effects; the main significance on product markets of the single currency is through the price transparency effect. While greater producer price transparency may turn out to be important in a few industries, we argue that there is a prima facie case for the single currency having a relatively small direct impact on producer price transparency, and a greater impact in certain identifiable industries on consumer price transparency. The greater facilitation of international price comparisons gives scope for arbitrage to break down international price discrimination. The extent to which this occurs will depend on the nature of the product in question, the organisation of the industry, and the nature of vertical linkages between buyers and sellers.

Empirically the effects of market integration and greater transparency should, in principle, be observable both through their impact on prices and price dispersion and on key aspects of market structure such as concentration. In order to examine the impact of integration and transparency on product markets, detailed (highly disaggregated) data are required. This applies both to analyses of prices and price dispersion and to analyses of market structure. Given the availability of disaggregated price data, coefficients of variation appear to be one of the most appropriate statistics for the analysis of such data.

The use of a computable general equilibrium model to analyse price transparency again suggests that the impact of transparency across both industries and countries depends crucially on the underlying characteristics described above, as well as on the extent to which industries are traded within the EU. Increases in welfare will depend on the extent that the consumer transparency effect dominates, or on the extent to which integration results in a substantial pro-competitive impact either through arbitrage or through firms switching to an integrated markets strategy.

APPENDIX 2.A   DATA USED AND METHODOLOGICAL ISSUES

Data Used

(A) *The Neilsen Sub-Sample of Consumer Products*   This sample was kindly made available by ACNeilsen as illustrative of the data they could provide for monitoring prices. It comprises information on the prices of 45 non-durable consumer goods between March 1994 and March 1996, converted into ECUs. Sixteen countries are covered – the EU-15 less Luxembourg plus Switzerland and Norway. These data allow a much finer view of consumer prices than the Eurostat PLI data and are probably a more satisfactory way of reviewing the efficiency of markets.

(B) *Eurostat PLI Sample*   These data were made available for the years 1990, 1993, 1995, 1996 and 1997 at the level of the 270 products or product groups, although earlier data also exist. As these data have been extensively analysed elsewhere – for example, DRI (1997), European Commission (1999a and 1999b) – we do not present many calculations on them.

Methodological Issues

Choice of summary statistics
First, pricing decisions are inherently product-specific which makes it very difficult to make meaningful comparisons of price statistics across products at a given point in time. Instead, one needs to look at changes in price statistics for given products over the period in which transparency could have changed. Secondly, firms' pricing is subject to a variety of extraneous shocks – for example, cost and tax changes, new technology, new products and switches in demand. Since these are difficult to quantify accurately it is then difficult to say whether an observed price change is due to changes in transparency or to some other stimulus. At an empirical level, however, it may be easier to identify changes in transparency in terms of changes in price dispersion rather than changes in price levels. This is because price dispersions may be more robust to many of the extraneous shocks than price means, and second, the formulae for dispersion derived from the theoretical model suggest that changes in transparency enter price dispersion quadratically and so might generate more observable movements there.

Following previous work (for example DRI, 1997; European Commission, 1999a, 1999b) we use the coefficient of variation (standard deviation ÷ mean) as our basic measure of price dispersion. The coefficient of variation (cv) is unit-free, and reports on the proportionate variance across countries and is thus comparable across commodities. This is also the statistic that falls most naturally out of the theoretical analysis. It is worth reiterating, however, that dispersion is strictly only an intermediate variable. The ultimate objective is to see if the SMP or EMU lowers average prices to consumers and so increases real income.[4]

Aggregation
On the basis of the theory it seems most natural to use statistics at the level of individual products, because summary statistics entail the loss of information. However, data are not always available at the most detailed level and if they were, would be almost overwhelming in their volume. Hence it is also necessary to think what could be usefully done with more aggregated series.

If the focus is on compiling cost of living indices (price level indices – PLI), one wishes to take account of the fact that relatively high prices for one commodity can be offset by relatively low prices for another. Some averaging over commodities is then desirable, and the dispersion of these PLI aggregates can be considered across countries. When it comes to assessing the effectiveness of commodity markets greater detail is desirable. Even if price differences between commodities are offsetting, their existence speaks of frictions in the arbitrage between markets, and there is at least a presumption that eliminating these frictions will lower prices and improve consumer welfare.[5] Although ultimately the objective is to assess (and eventually minimise) the PLI, the difficulties of identifying the various determinants of the PLI mean that studying only the aggregates is likely to miss developments in market structure.

Weighting
Although detailed data are best for assessing market performance, in practice most data refer to aggregates of individual products. For examining the *phenomenon* of price collusion, price dispersion treating all products and markets symmetrically in the aggregation procedure would be appropriate (as each observation is a separate drawing from the distribution of prices and to a first order it does not matter if it pertains to a 'large' product or market, or a small one). If interest extends to the *significance* of collusion or price dispersion, the case for symmetry is much weaker. If theory suggests consumer costs to dispersion, it becomes important to know how many consumers purchase at each price. In this case it is more appropriate to weigh prices by population in calculating the statistical moments.

NOTES

1. However, the exact degrees of freedom for the test are unclear. If we had data for only one period the correct degrees of freedom would be (n_n-1) and (n_c-1) where n_n is the number of non-core countries and n_c the number of core countries. If we view periods as identical – the polar extremes of our observations above that pattern were very stable – these would remain the correct degrees of freedom for the actual exercise. Significance on this basis is indicated by a lower-case 's' in the significance column, of which there are five in all. The alternative is that periods are wholly independent, in which case we have $13(n_n-1)$ and $13(n_c-1)$ degrees of freedom, leading to upper-case 'S's in the column. There are 22 of these (out of 45) in all. In truth the answer probably lies closer to identical information than to independent observations.
2. The significant cases were: NACE 15, 16, 21, 22, 25, 26, 32, 40, 41, 52, 55, 62, 66, 70, 93.
3. For H industries, we move the consumer transparency measure 50 per cent of the way towards complete transparency, for M industries 25 per cent of the way, and for L industries 10 per cent.
4. There is a theory that suggests the welfare advantages of uniform prices, but it is equally well known that price discrimination can be welfare improving if it increases the total volume of sales (output). The implicit assumption of our and the Commission's analysis is that reductions in dispersion due to improved transparency will be welfare improving even though, for quite different reasons, the optimal dispersion could be greater than zero.
5. It is possible that contestability keeps the profits of incumbent firms at normal levels, while allowing random differences in the prices of individual products; in this case product-level price dispersions will not be informative. However, this does not really explain why entry cannot undercut the prices of those products that have relatively high price drawings in the random distribution.

BIBLIOGRAPHY

Allen, C., Gasiorek, M. and Smith, A. (1996), 'Trade creation and trade diversion' European Commission, Brussels.

Bagwell, K. and Ramey, G. (1992), 'The diamond paradox: a dynamic resolution', Northwestern University Discussion Paper No. 1013.

Baldwin, R.E. (1990), 'The growth effects of 1992', *Economic Policy*, **9**, 247–81.

Baldwin, R.E. and Venables, A.J. (1994), 'Methodologies for the ex post evaluation of the single European market', unpublished report to DG II, European Commission, Brussels.

Baltagi, B.H. (1995), *Econometric Analysis of Panel Data*, Chichester: Wiley.

Banerjee, A., Dolado, J., Galbraith, J.W. and Hendry, D.F. (1993), *Co-integration, Error-Correction, and the Econometric Analysis of Non-Stationary Data*, Oxford: Oxford University Press.

Ben David, D. (1993), 'Equalizing exchange: trade liberalization and income convergence', *Quarterly Journal of Economics*, **108** (3), 653–79.

Berndt, E.R. and Savin, N.E. (1975), 'Estimation and hypothesis testing in singular equation systems with autoregressive errors', *Econometrica*, **43**, 937–58.

Brenton, P.A. and Winters, L.A. (1992), 'Bilateral trade elasticities for exploring the effects of 1992', in L.A. Winters (ed.), *Trade Flows and Trade Policy after '1992'*, Cambridge, Cambridge University Press/Centre for Economic Policy Research.

Buigues, P., Ilzkovitz, F. and Lebrun, J.-F. (1990), 'The impact of the internal market by industrial sector: the challenge for the Member States', *European Economy*, Special Issue.

Burdett, K. and Judge, K.L. (1983), 'Equilibrium price dispersion', *Econometrica*, **51**, 955–69.

Chang, W. and Winters, L.A. (1999), 'How regional blocs affect excluded countries: the price effects of MERCOSUR', Centre for Economic Policy Research discussion paper series, no. 2179, June, and The World Bank policy research working paper, no. 2157, August.

Chen, N.A. (1999), 'The behaviour of relative prices in the European Union, a sectoral analysis', mimeo, ECARE, Brussels, May.

Cooper, R.J. and McLaren, K.R. (1992), 'A system of demand equations with effectively global regularity conditions', University of Western Sydney, Working Paper 92/06.

Davidson, R. and MacKinnon, J.G. (1993), *Estimation and Inference in Econometrics*, New York: Oxford University Press.

Davies, S. and Lyons, B. (eds) (1996), *Industrial Organisation in the European Union*, Oxford: Oxford University Press.

Diamond, P. (1971), 'A model of price adjustment', *Journal of Economic Theory*, **3**, 156–68.

DRI (1997), 'Price competition and convergence', European Commission, Brussels.

EAG (1996), 'Study on the extent of realization of economies of scale due to the internal market programme', European Commission, Brussels.

Engel, C. and Rogers, J.H. (1998), 'Relative price volatility: what role does the border play?', International Finance Discussion Paper 623, Board of Governors of the Federal Reserve System, Washington DC.

Engle, R.F. (1982), 'A general approach to Lagrange multiplier model diagnostics', *Journal of Econometrics*, **20** (1), 83–104.

European Commission, Directorate-General for Economic and Financial Affairs, (1995), 'The impact of exchange rate movements on trade within the single market', *European Economy, Reports and Studies*, no. 4.

European Commission, Directorate-General for Economic and Financial Affairs (1996), 'Economic evaluation of the Single Market', *European Economy, Reports and Studies*, no. 4.

European Commission (1996), *The Single Market Review*, London: Kogan Page.

European Commission (1999a), 'Market integration and differences in price levels between EU member states', Study 4 in *Annual Economic Report*, European Commission, Brussels, 212–34.

European Commission (1999b), 'Economic and structural reform in the EU (Cardiff II)', COM(1999) 61 final, European Commission, Brussels.

European Commission (2002), 'European integration and the functioning of product markets', *European Economy, Reports and Studies*, special report no. 2.

Eurostat (1996), 'Comparison in real terms of the aggregates of ESA: results for 1994', European Communities, Luxembourg.

Gasiorek, M., Smith, A. and Venables, A.J. (1992), '"1992": trade, factor prices and welfare in general equilibrium', in Winters (ed.), pp. 35–63.

Ginsbergh, V. and Vanhamme, G. (1989), 'Price differences in the EC car market', *Annales d'Economie et de Statistique*, **15/16**, 137–49.

Green, E.J. and Porter, R.H. (1984), 'Noncooperative collusion under imperfect price information', *Econometrica*, **52**, 87–100.

Hague, A.A. (1995), 'The power of cointegration tests: does the frequency of observation matter?', mimeo, York University, Canada, presented at 7th World Congress of the Econometric Society.

Haskel, J. and Wolf, H. (1999), 'Why does the law of one price fail: a case study', CEPR Discussion Paper, 2187, CEPR London.

Jacquemin, A. and Sapir, A. (1991), 'Competition and imports in the European market', in Winters, L.A. and Venables, A.J. (eds), *European Integration: Trade and Industry*, Cambridge: Cambridge University Press and CEPR.

Kirman, A.P and Schueller, N. (1990), 'Price leadership and discrimination in the European car market', *Journal of Industrial Economics*, **39**, 69–91.

Klemperer, P. (1995), 'Competition when consumers have switching costs: an overview with applications to industrial organisation, macroeconomics and international trade', *Review of Economic Studies*, **62**, 515–39.

Marston, R.C. (1990), 'Pricing to market in Japanese manufacturing', *Journal of International Economics*, December 1990, **29**, 217–36.

Martínez, C. (1996), 'The European Union's competitiveness in the Triad. Methodological issues and analyses of indicators', typescript II/705/95-EN, European Commission, Brussels.

Mertens, Y. and Ginsbergh, V. (1985), 'Product differentiation and price discrimination in the European Community: the case of automobiles', *Journal of Industrial Economics*, **34**, 151–65.

OECD (2000), *EMU One Year On*, Paris: OECD.

Porter, R. (1983), 'Optimal cartel trigger price strategies', *Journal of Economic Theory*, **29**, 314–38.

Pratten, C. (1988), 'A survey of the economies of scale', in *Studies on the Economics of Integration, Research on the 'Cost of Non-Europe': Basic Findings*, vol. 2, Brussels, Commission of the European Communities.

Reinganum, J.F. (1979), 'A simple model of equilibrium price dispersion', *Journal of Political Economy*, **87**, 851–8.

Rob, R. (1985), 'Equilibrium price distributions', *Review of Economic Studies*, **52**, 487–504.

Rotemberg, J. and Saloner, G. (1986), 'A supergame-theoretic model of business cycles and price wars', *American Economic Review*, **76**, 390–407.

Rubinstein, A. (1993), 'On price recognition and computational complexity in a monopoly model', *Journal of Political Economy*, **101**, 473–84.

Salop, S. and Stiglitz, J. (1977), 'Bargains and ripoffs', *Review of Economic Studies*, **44**, 493–510.

Salop, S. (1977), 'The noisy monopolist:imperfect information, price dispersion and price discrimination', *Review of Economic Studies*, **44**, 393–406.

Salop, S.C. (1986), 'Practices that (credibly) facilitate oligopoly co-ordination', in J.E. Stiglitz and G.F. Mathewson (eds), *New Developments in the Analysis of Market Structure*, London: Macmillan.

Scitovsky, T. (1950), 'Ignorance as a source of monopoly power', *American Economic Review*, **40**, 48–53.

Sleuwagen, L. and Yamawaki, H. (1998), 'The formation of the European Common Market and changes in market structure and performance', *European Economic Review*, **32**, 1451–75.

Smith, A. and Venables, A.J. (1988), 'Completing the internal market in the European Community: some industry simulations', *European Economic Review*, **32**, 1501–25.

Smith, A. and Venables, A.J. (1991), 'Economic integration and market access', *European Economic Review*, **35**, 388–95.

Stahl, D.O. (1989), 'Oligopolistic pricing with sequential consumer search', *American Economic Review*, **79**, 700–712.

Ulph, D. and Vaughan, R. (2000), 'Price transparency and market equilibria', mimeo, University College London, March.

Varian, H.R. (1980), 'A model of sales', *American Economic Review*, **70**, 651–9.

Verboven, F. (1996), 'Price discrimination in a common market', *Rand Journal of Economics*, **27**, 240–68.

Williamson, K. and Porter, F. (1994), 'UK visible trade statistics – the Intrastat system', *Economic Trends*, 490, August, 38–49.

Winters, L.A. (1984), 'British imports of manufactures and the Common Market', *Oxford Economic Papers*, **36**, 103–18.

Winters, L.A. (ed.) (1992), *Trade Flows and Trade Policy after '1992'*, Cambridge: Cambridge University Press and Centre for Economic Policy Research.

Wolinsky, A. (1986), 'True monopolistic competition as a result of imperfect information', *Quarterly Journal of Economics*, **101**, 493–511.

3. Changes in the industrial and geographical diversification of leading firms in European manufacturing

Laura Rondi, Leo Sleuwaegen and Davide Vannoni*

INTRODUCTION

For a long period the industrial policies of national governments in Europe aimed at reinforcing the position of leading firms in the country in order to face the rapidly growing competition from US and later from Japanese firms (Cox and Watson, 1996). The privileged position of these firms offered them substantial monopoly power within their markets, which, unfortunately, also often resulted in the use of many inefficient practices. Most governments sustained the privileged position of these national champions through the erection of various kinds of non-tariff trade and investment barriers directed against foreign competitors and creating strong borders protecting national markets.

The recognition that these policies failed and were partly responsible for slow growth, high unemployment and inflation after the first oil shock in 1973 led the European Commission to formulate and implement an ambitious integration programme eradicating all the various barriers to trade and investment. The Single Market Programme came into effect in 1987 and was largely completed by the mid-1990s. The programme concerned mainly the manufacturing industries. Services sectors have more recently become the subject of integration measures. The macroeconomic and sectoral consequences of the integration programme have been intensively discussed in the literature. Surprisingly, the consequences for individual firms have hardly been documented.

The present chapter represents an original attempt to trace the changing industrial and geographical diversification strategies of firms as the integration process moves forward. The analysis is based on a unique database covering the product structure and geographical distribution of the leading European firms in the manufacturing sectors for three years characterising different moments in the integration process, 1987 (start), 1993 (half-way) and 1997 (near completion). Before analysing the data, Section 3.1 offers some theoretical perspectives on the consequences of the European market integration programme for the international strategies and structures of European firms.

3.1 EUROPEAN MARKET INTEGRATION: THE SINGLE MARKET PROGRAMME

The Economic Consequences

The process of European market integration involves primarily a reduction in trade and investment costs of doing business across borders of EU Member States, and a displacement of fragmented national markets by a single (EU) market. Market integration was triggered by the Single Market Programme (SMP) in 1985, comprising a wide variety of measures to harmonise regulations and open up public procurement markets in the EU. The integration process has since then been systematically changing the nature of competition, and therefore the structure and performance of industries and firms. The 'official' European Commission view (summarised in the Cecchini Report on the 'Costs of Non-Europe' (Cecchini, Catinat and Jaquemin, 1998) anticipates four main effects from the SMP, each having implications for the structure of industries and firms:

- direct cost savings due to the elimination of non-tariff barriers, such as fewer customs delays and costs of multiple certification;
- cost savings derived from increased volumes and more efficient location of production (scale and learning economies and better exploitation of comparative advantage);
- tightening of competitive pressures, reduced prices and increased efficiency as more firms from different member states compete directly in the bigger market place; and
- increased competitive pressures generating speedier innovation.

Besides the direct effects, strong industry and firm restructuring effects are expected to follow from market integration. Unfortunately the research on the latter point is rather limited (Sleuwaegen, 1995). From a macroeconomic point of view, the most extensive evaluation of the SMP is that of the

European Commission itself (1996) based on a large body of commissioned research, using mainly fairly aggregate Eurostat databases. Following the results of a macroeconomic model it was estimated that the level of EU GDP in 1994 was about 1.1 per cent to 1.5 per cent above the level that would have prevailed in the absence of the Single Market Programme.

The Impact of the SMP on Industrial and Geographical Diversification of Firms

The ex-ante expectations of the effects of the Single Market on the product structure of individual firms mostly relied on the hypothesis of 'return to core business' (Davies et al., 2001a and 2001b). Increased European competition involves the widening of competition to a European-wide set of players in all industries which, if no strategic action were taken, would lead to a deterioration of the competitive position of the firm in all of its product-market combinations. The competitive threat spurs the firm to reallocate resources into its core activities and related products, such that the firm's set of distinctive competencies becomes more focused towards those businesses in which it has excelled before. As a result the firm is likely to reduce the level of industrial diversification and also, stimulated by the reduced costs of doing business across national borders, to expand geographically. Moreover, the wider European Single Market creates more possibilities to specialise and reduce the level of vertical integration in line with Adam's Smith adage, 'Specialisation is limited by the extent of the market'. Firms will divest activities and opt for outsourcing those activities for which they now find suppliers offering better conditions within the EU. As a result industrial diversification across vertically related stages of production and distribution is expected to decline as market integration progresses.

Considering geographical diversification, beyond the need to expand the core business across borders, increasing market integration makes it easier for firms to enter other EU Member States. The costs connected with entering the market of another Member State are comparatively low for established European firms. This gives rise to major cross-entries of markets within the EC (frequently through mergers and acquisitions (M&A)). This not only applies to established firms, but also to small or new firms that are no longer interested in penetrating a national market but wish to launch themselves on the single European market. The competitive pressure caused by firms entering the market is often reinforced by firms outside the EC. These firms fear that the completion of an internal market will inexorably lead to an increase in Community protectionism. With these forces at work, the level of geographical diversification of EU as well as non-EU firms across Member States is expected to rise substantially.

Market integration also improves coordination possibilities for larger established firms and drives firms better to exploit scale and scope economies within Europe. This improvement changes the configuration of firm activities, such that certain sub-activities will become more geographically concentrated in some Member States. The geographical concentration process goes together with the development of more efficient logistics systems made possible by further deregulation of the transportation and telecommunications sectors in Europe. Vandermerwe (1993) discusses the formation of Euro-networks within Europe in view of the ongoing market reconfigurations on a European and global scale, with the structure and location of activities of firms no longer based on specific countries.

A recent UN Report (United Nations, 1993) identifies a similar shift in strategy of multinational enterprisess (MNEs). As stand-alone strategies with multi-country structures become too costly due to duplications, transnational firms reorganise to a structure that allows a complex strategy. The restructuring leads to so-called new global and regional networks, where firms concentrate on their core activities and build close relationships with suppliers and distributors. In this process of organisational restructuring, the location of every part in the supply chain becomes a strategically important element. The way in which the development of such a network structure is expected to affect the geographical diversification of firms remains an empirical question. This chapter will provide a first assessment of the possible impact of market integration on the geographical diversification of large firms as well as on other firms' characteristics.

3.2   CHANGES IN INDUSTRIAL AND GEOGRAPHICAL DIVERSIFICATION OVER THE PERIOD 1987–97

The MSM Data

The analysis uses firm-level data from the Market Share Matrix (MSM).[1] This matrix identifies the set of 'leading firms' in European manufacturing industries and disaggregates their turnover data, extracted from individual company accounts, according to NACE 3-digit product lines and production centres located in the EU. A firm qualifies as a 'leader' if it is one of the five largest EU producers in at least one manufacturing industry. For every such firm, the matrix includes estimates of its EU turnover in each industry in which it operates (not only in those where it is a 'leader'), and disaggregates firm turnover, according to its production across industries and across production centres in EU Member States. The MSM has been constructed for the years 1987, 1993, 1997.

The matrix built on these principles provides measures of industrial diversification and intra-EU geographical diversification of the matrix firms.

Changes in Diversification Patterns over the Decade 1987–97

A comparison of the basic dimensions of the time comparable matrices 1987, 1993, 1997 provides a quick guide to the major changes in firm diversification over this period, as reported in Table 3.1. The evidence suggests that EU firms have reduced their industrial diversification at the expense of industries in which they are not leaders (non-leading diversification). Reduction in diversification occurred between 1993 and 1997 in particular, after the completion of the Single Market Programme, and not between 1987 and 1993 when the removal of non-tariff barriers was in progress and most expected to exert its influence over corporate restructuring. This non-linearity suggests that the de-diversification process may have continued in the years after 1997. Recent anecdotal evidence is consistent with the idea that firms are still pursuing strategies of return to the core. With all the caveats that these comparisons deserve, 1993 appears as a transition year, with firms tentatively undergoing rationalisations, first increasing and then decreasing their range of operations across industries. The analysis of firm diversification when survival, entry and exit (within the MSM) are taken into account will throw more light on this issue.

Turning to geographical diversification, we first notice that although the number of EU firms in the matrix decreased over time, the number of transnational EU firms increased in that same period. Whereas in 1987 only 61 per cent of all EU firms in the matrix were active in more than one Member State, this significantly increased, to 83 per cent in 1997. In 1987 EU firms were on average active in three countries only. This number continuously increased over the period to an average of 4.5 countries in 1997. The percentage of total production occurring outside the home country has also increased: from, on average, 19 per cent to 30 per cent. Although this is a remarkable increase, it indicates that more than two-thirds of total production is still produced in the home country. Thus, for the average EU firm, the location strategy seems to be still very much home country oriented, but geographical diversification across EU member states is strongly increasing. Non-EU firms were much more geographically diversified before market integration, and still increased the number of countries in which they are active. The larger diversification reflects the fact that most of these firms do not have a home basis in any of the European countries and have typically been more transnational before any market integration took place.

Table 3.1   Changes in the structure of the MSM between 1987, 1993 and 1997

	1987	1993	1997
Number of industries	67	67	67
Number of firms	223	218	223
Industrial diversification			
Number of diversified firms	175	176	170
Number of industry entries	1079	1016	810
Leading	335	335	335
Non-leading	744	681	475
Number of industry entries per firm	4.84	4.66	3.63
Leading	1.50	1.54	1.50
Non-leading	3.34	3.12	2.13
Geographical diversification			
Number of EU transnational firms	117	124	138
Number of non-EU transnational firms	32	43	57
Country entries per EU firm	3.06	4.01	4.53
Country entries per non-EU firm	4.94	5.21	5.23
Average % home country production EU firms	81	76	70

Changes in the Distribution of Diversification across Firms

Table 3.2 presents the distributions of diversification indices across firms, by comparing the quartiles and extreme deciles of the distributions of our two measures for industrial and geographical diversification (D_I and D_G, respectively): the 'Number equivalent of entropy' and the 'Output share in secondary industries/countries' (with firms ranked by diversification). The higher the entropy,[2] the more diversified the firm's operations are across industries or countries. The second measure is part of the entropy measure and looks at the share of output that the firm is producing in secondary industries outside its most important industry. For geographical diversification, the output measure looks at the share of EU production outside the most important production country in the EU. For EU firms the most important country is defined as the home country where they are based.

The return to the core (industrial de-diversification) in the 1987–97 period is only partially reflected in the decline of the mean values of the two measures of industrial diversification. The evidence of de-diversification is clearly evident only when the entropy index is used, which suggests a retreat

Table 3.2   *Distribution of industrial and geographical diversification across firms, 1987, 1993, 1997*

	Number equivalent of entropy				Output share in secondary industries/countries*			
	1987	1993	1997	Change 1997–87	1987	1993	1997	Change 1997–87
Industrial diversification								
Arithmetic mean values of D_I								
All matrix firms	2.62	2.60	2.25	–0.37	0.27	0.29	0.25	–0.02
Std. dev.	1.95	1.72	1.44	–0.51	0.24	0.24	0.23	–0.01
Survivors	2.68	2.76	2.46	–0.22	0.28	0.31	0.29	0.01
Distribution of D_I *across firms*								
Decile 9	4.74	4.77	4.33	–0.41	0.59	0.64	0.61	0.02
Quartile 3	3.23	3.37	2.72	–0.51	0.46	0.49	0.43	–0.03
Median	2.05	2.03	1.79	–0.26	0.25	0.30	0.22	–0.03
Quartile 1	1.20	1.26	1.13	–0.07	0.04	0.06	0.03	–0.01
Decile 1	1.00	1.00	1.00	0.00	0.00	0.00	0.00	0.00
Geographical diversification								
Arithmetic mean values of D_G								
All matrix firms**	1.89	2.37	2.76	0.87	0.17	0.26	0.33	0.16
Std. dev.	1.17	1.42	1.51	0.34	0.21	0.25	0.24	0.03
Survivors	2.23	2.73	3.00	0.77	0.23	0.32	0.35	0.12
Distribution of D_G *across firms*								
Decile 9	4.88	5.22	5.34	0.46	0.70	0.71	0.72	0.02
Quartile 3	3.51	4.37	4.88	1.37	0.60	0.63	0.65	0.05
Median	2.26	3.00	3.49	1.23	0.41	0.53	0.52	0.11
Quartile 1	1.27	1.87	2.36	1.09	0.25	0.33	0.37	0.12
Decile 1	1.00	1.00	1.40	0.40	0.13	0.19	0.25	0.12

Notes:
*   Industries applies to industrial diversification, countries to geographical diversification.
**   For EU firms secondary countries are all EU countries except the home country. For non-EU firms the 'EU home country' is the EU country in which they have the largest production, secondary countries are all the remaining EU countries.

by firms from marginal industries. While the mean value of the entry index remained stable between 1987 and 1993, it decreased between 1993 and 1997. The decline of the standard deviation of both indices of industrial diversification confirms a general convergence of corporate structures.

Measured by the number equivalent of entropy, EU leading firms had operations in 2.25 sectors in 1997, as opposed to 2.62 in 1987. Firms in the top decile of the distribution were operating in 4.74 industries in 1987 and in 4.33 ten years later. Looking through the indices in Table 3.2, we find that highly diversified firms decreased diversification more substantially, although the trend is non-linear, with firms displaying first an increase and then a reduction in the mean values. At this level of aggregation, these preliminary findings are nonetheless suggestive of rationalisations that eliminated operations in unrelated or marginal industries.

A separate row in the table looks at firms that have survived in the MSM as leaders in at least one industry over the period 1987–97. We would expect that the increasing competitive pressure would be more in favour of less diversified firms than of high diversifiers. Hence, we should find that survivors are either less diversified or refocusing over the period. Overall, the empirical findings appear to be consistent with the return to the core hypothesis. The survivors (120 firms) display relatively high diversification, which appears to be associated with the fact that they tend to be amongst the largest firms in the sample (see Section 3.3). Nevertheless, they reduced their degree of industrial diversification by the end of the period as measured by the entropy index. The mean value of the output share in secondary industries, on the other hand, remained virtually unchanged, which suggests that de-diversification has mainly affected marginal, secondary activities.

Summarising the results for product diversification, the comparisons across indices allow us to partially confirm and better qualify the former preliminary results. Firms have readjusted their corporate structure around a lower number of industries, but have not re-focused the output share in their primary industries in any remarkable way. In other words, instead of a *return to core business*, we are documenting a *return to core businesses*.

The strong expansion outside the home country in the 1987–97 period is reflected in the increase of the mean values of the distribution of geographical diversification. This holds true for the entropy index as well as for the output measure. The standard deviation of the indices has not increased to the same degree, confirming a general tendency of wider geographical corporate structures crossing the borders of Member States. The output share in secondary countries, on average, almost doubled over the decade.

Measured by the number equivalent of entropy, EU leaders had operations in 2.76 countries in 1997, as opposed to 1.89 in 1987. Firms in the top decile of the distribution were operating in 4.88 countries in 1987, and in 5.34 countries ten years later. The biggest changes appear to have happened at the centre of the distribution, shifting the distribution substantially over time. As to the output share in countries outside the base country, the largest shift occurs at the lower half of the distribution. The combined findings for the two measures suggest that heavily diversified firms have increased diversification by spreading their activities more equally across borders, while the less diversified firms have increased diversification by investing more outside the base country.

The firms that survived in the MSM as leaders in at least one industry over the period 1987–97 (120 firms) displayed a relatively high geographical diversification, which increased further by the end of the period. This result is consistent with the overall shift in the distribution of all leading firms, including the entrance of new leaders after 1987.

3.3 DIVERSIFICATION IN RELATION TO CHARACTERISTICS OF LEADING FIRMS

Firm Size

A stylised fact in the empirical literature on diversification is the positive correlation between industrial and geographical diversification and firm size (see, among others, Davies et al., 1996; Davies et al., 2001a and 2001b; Sembenelli and Vannoni, 2000; Vannoni 1999a). The theoretical literature provides several motivations for this well-documented evidence: scale and scope economies, intangible and proprietary assets, managerial hubris, risk diversification.[3] In particular, the resource theory of diversification argues that, in the growth process, firms accumulate resources which can be profitably employed to enter new markets, if transaction costs make it costly to sell the services of such resources through the market mechanism (Penrose, 1959; Rubin, 1973; Teece, 1980 and 1982).

While the empirical literature suggests that industrial and geographical diversification are basically different growth strategies of firms exploiting firm-specific assets, their exact relationship – complements or substitutes – is still largely unexplored (but see Davies et al., 2001b). The evidence on the EU leaders diversification after 1993 suggests that both diversification strategies need not to go in the same direction. In Section 3.4 we analyse this relationship at a somewhat deeper level.

In addition to common factors, some arguments point to a specific relationship between firm growth and either industrial or geographical diversification.

According to the agency view of diversification, managers pursue their own objectives (private benefits deriving from empire-building and risk diversification) in conflict with shareholders' interests for profit maximisation (Marris, 1964), and over-invest in growth projects that reduce the firm's value (Jensen, 1986). A side effect of the positive relationship between size and product diversification is that large corporations are most likely to exhibit a considerable amount of unrelated and industrially illogical diversification. Empirical and theoretical literatures converge in predicting that this 'golf-course' diversification is eliminated as soon as competition in the core industry toughens. In Table 3.3 we explore whether this prediction applies to EU leaders.

Table 3.3   Diversification by firm size, 1987, 1993, 1997

	Number equivalent of entropy				Output share in secondary industries/countries[*]			
	1987	1993	1997	Change 1997–87	1987	1993	1997	Change 1997–87
Industrial diversification								
Arithmetic mean values of D_I								
Top 50		3.72	3.86	3.11	−0.61	0.36	0.40	0.36	0.00
Top 100		3.42	3.22	2.69	−0.73	0.37	0.37	0.32	−0.05
Firms outside top 100	1.96	2.08	1.89	−0.07	0.20	0.23	0.20	0.00
Geographical diversification								
Arithmetic values of D_G								
Top 50		2.56	2.97	3.47	0.91	0.27	0.31	0.39	0.12
Top 100		2.40	2.83	3.40	1.00	0.25	0.32	0.40	0.15
Firms outside top 100	1.47	1.98	2.24	0.77	0.11	0.21	0.27	0.16

Note: [*] Industries applies to industrial diversification, countries to geographical diversification.

By comparing the mean values for the top 50, the top 100 and the remaining matrix firms, we find evidence that firm size is positively related with diversification levels at every point in time. Medium and small firms outside the top 100 display, on average, lower levels of diversification, only marginally decreasing between 1987 and 1997. Within the largest size classes, we find that the top 50 firms do reduce diversification, on average, over the decade. We have counted that, from 1987 to 1997, five firms drop down from the top 50 list to a lower ranking as a result of the return to the core. But the most sizeable reduction is in the top 100 class, in which the output share of the secondary industries falls by 5 percentage points in the 1993–97 sub-period. Necessarily, therefore, the medium–large firms ranked 51 to 100 appear to have de-diversified more substantially than the largest firms that are ranked in the top 50.

Looking at the timing of the return to the core, we find an interesting pattern. Changes in the mean values display a monotonicity in de-diversification only for medium–large firms. In contrast with the ex-ante expectations of the effects of the SMP, the largest firms increased diversification in the run-up to 1992, and appear to have responded to the increased competitive pressures only in most recent years. Firms outside the top 100 display a similar trend, but the motivations behind the lag in the response to increased competition may differ across size classes, and is clearly a matter for further research.

The link between the process of firm growth and the transnationalisation process has been examined in several studies. In combination with the evidence pointing at the importance of intangible assets, empirical research has shown that when firms grow in their home market, the opportunities on the national market shrink and firms are pushed or pulled into international markets (Horst, 1972; Caves and Pugel, 1980). When firms decide to go abroad, they must incur a fixed cost of learning how things are done abroad. Moreover, establishing a subsidiary abroad implies a considerable sunk cost, which can better be incurred by large firms. Oligopolistic reaction theories also predict that larger firms in loose-knit oligopolistic industries are also likely to follow each other in expanding abroad (Knickerbocker, 1973).

From Table 3.3, it is clear that there is a strong difference in geographical diversification between the top 100 firms and the firms outside this top 100, and this difference becomes even stronger over time. In 1987, top 100 firms were already much more internationally active than firms outside the top 100. From the entropy measure, the firms inside the top 100 increased their geographical diversification substantially more than the firms outside top 100 firms. The latter group of firms, however, showed a more marked increase in the output share in secondary countries. Again, this evidence is consistent with the finding that larger firms have rationalised production by spreading it more equally across EU Member States while the smaller leaders have focused on catching up in the transnationalisation of production, be it in a less balanced structure than the one observed for larger firms. All in all, the evidence suggests, for geographical diversification as well as for industrial diversification, a tendency toward growing convergence in the geographical production structure of leading EU firms over time.

Country of Origin

In 1987, firms with origins in the UK, Germany and Italy exhibited a relatively high degree of industrial diversification (see Table 3.4). German firms remained appreciably more diversified in 1997. Italian firms, on the contrary, showed the largest decrease in the first sub-period, 1987–93 (partly due to the privatisation of several subsidiaries of the state holdings IRI and ENI), while British firms de-diversified more intensely between 1993 and 1997. Firms originating in Germany, on average, exhibited a different pattern, as industrial diversification increased quite remarkably in the first

sub-period and declined thereafter. But the overall reduction, only reflected
by the entropy index, is marginal. French firms were only moderately
diversified in 1987, and they tended to remain so at the end of the period.
The Netherlands and Sweden, with 8 and 6 leaders respectively in the
1997 matrix, are both characterised by high diversification, but the former
displays an increase and the latter a decrease over the decade. The intra-EU
operations by non-EU transnationals are less diversified on average than
their European rivals, but as we do not account for their operations at home,
nor in the rest of the world, we have only a partial view of the extent and
trend of their diversification. Contrary to European firms, they increased
their level of industrial diversification within EU manufacturing.

Table 3.4   Diversification by country of origin 1987, 1993, 1997

	Number equivalent of entropy			Output share in secondary industries/countries[*]		
	1987	1993	1997	1987	1993	1997
Industrial diversification						
Germany	2.85	3.32	2.77	0.29	0.37	0.33
UK	2.95	2.60	2.27	0.34	0.33	0.27
France	2.39	2.39	2.20	0.25	0.28	0.27
Italy	2.90	2.38	2.18	0.26	0.23	0.23
Belgium/Luxembourg	2.16	1.42	1.91	0.40	0.09	0.21
Netherlands	2.55	2.55	2.60	0.29	0.37	0.31
Denmark	–	1.27	1.84	–	0.05	0.15
EU-12	2.71	2.64	2.33	0.28	0.30	0.27
Other countries[**]	1.34	1.72	1.96	0.13	0.19	0.20
Geographical diversification						
Germany	1.40	1.63	2.15	0.08	0.11	0.21
UK	1.78	2.31	2.54	0.16	0.27	0.31
France	1.69	2.44	3.10	0.12	0.26	0.33
Italy	1.37	1.77	1.76	0.10	0.17	0.18
Belgium/Luxembourg	2.04	2.63	3.67	0.15	0.32	0.47
Netherlands	2.85	3.35	3.82	0.33	0.38	0.45
Denmark	–	1.33	2.06	–	0.08	0.17
EU-12	1.64	2.06	2.44	0.12	0.20	0.27
Other countries[**]	3.37	3.62	3.75	0.46	0.50	0.51

Notes:
[*]   Industries applies to industrial diversification, countries to geographical diversification.
[**]   Austria, Finland, Sweden, US, Japan, Australia, Canada, Switzerland and Norway.
Given the low number of diversified/transnational firms in Ireland, Greece, Portugal and
Spain, no entropy measure is presented for these countries.

Overall, although there is still evidence of systematic differences and country specificity, the changing pattern of industrial diversification shows some indication of convergence between firms originating in the different EU Member States. While in 1993 German firms were the very significant exception to the more general trend of a return to the core, this appears to be no longer the case.

Firms originating from smaller countries reach their limits of growth in the home market much faster than firms originating from larger countries, and thus it is natural that they show a higher level of geographical diversification. However one caveat when interpreting the empirical data is that, within the Market Share Matrix, firms originating from smaller countries are likely to be under-represented. Therefore, any inference based upon the average corporate structure for those countries is distorted by a selection bias. All the firms originating from smaller Member States, with the exception of those of Spanish origin, are transnational, that is, producing in at least one country other than the home country. Danish firms show the lowest and Belgian and Dutch firms show the highest level of geographical diversification.

Among the firms originating from the larger Member States, French firms showed a high level of geographical diversification in 1997; over the period 1987–97 French firms also increased the level of geographical diversification most drastically. Italian firms appear to be the least geographically diversified and show the smallest increase in entropy as well as in output share in secondary countries. Some of this appears to be due to a relatively higher percentage of smaller leaders amongst the Italian firms in the MSM. Non-European firms, not having a real home country basis in the EU have continued to expand more equally across Member States and show as a result a higher entropy as well as a larger output share in secondary countries.

Summarising, the results for geographical diversification show that the tendency to expand across EU borders generally holds for all firms, irrespective of their country of origin, suggesting a growing convergence of corporate structures. This is similar to the results obtained for industrial diversification.

Industry Type

In this section, we explore the influences of product market factors by grouping firms according to the nature of their primary industry. Table 3.5 reports the mean values of the usual diversification indices for two industry typologies. The first one distinguishes homogeneous product industries (Type 1) from those producing differentiated products (Type 2). Type 2 industries, in turn, may be further split up depending on whether product differentiation is achieved mainly by advertising expenditures (2A), by investment in R&D (2R) or by both (2AR). The second typology identifies the set of industries that were supposed to be most affected by the implementation of the SMP, that is, the so-called sensitive industries. Chapter 4, section 5 of this volume provides further detail on the definition and characteristics of the different types of industries.

In the first part of the table, the industrial diversification results for Type 1 and Type 2 industries clearly indicate that there has been a convergence of corporate structures. In 1987, firms originating from differentiated product industries were more diversified than those originating from homogeneous product industries. By 1997 Type 2 firms had re-focused to the point that they had become much less diversified than Type 1 firms. This is not exactly what we would have expected, since firms in differentiated product industries are usually thought to enjoy more market power than firms in homogeneous industries, and therefore to be more 'protected' from the tougher competition associated with the opening up of EU markets. However, it appears that the competitive escalation in R&D and advertising expenditure in the larger and more integrated EU markets has led firms to divest from secondary industries and to concentrate their efforts on strengthening their position in their core businesses.

Within the differentiated group, firms originating in research-intensive industries were, and remain, the most diversified, but they reduced their levels of diversification quite substantially (for example, the output share in secondary industries dropped from 35 per cent to 28 per cent). The return to the core has been particularly intense between 1993 and 1997. Advertising-intensive firms and, to a lesser extent, 2AR firms started from lower levels of diversification, but they also have reduced their diversification, mostly in the first sub-period.

The theoretical literature predicts that research, and advertising-intensive firms tend to be more diversified because they have intangible assets (technological know-how, brand name, research or marketing skills) that can be used as public good and easily transferred to new (related) industries, or countries. Moreover, technological know-how and research expertise (and much less so advertising and marketing skills), can be also profitably exploited through vertical integration, which is captured, but not separately identified, by our indices of diversification. The evidence of net de-diversification that we document in this section suggests that, in this period, the unlimited use of such intangible assets may ultimately have been restrained by the increasingly competitive pressure within the EU, leading firms to refocus on fewer industries where the price–cost margins are higher, and to exit from marginal industries where a leading position cannot be obtained.

Table 3.5   Diversification by industry type, 1987, 1993, 1997

	Number equivalent of entropy			Output share in secondary industries/countries[*]		
	1987	1993	1997	1987	1993	1997
Industrial diversification						
All manufacturing	2.62	2.60	2.25	0.27	0.29	0.25
By type of product						
Type 1 – homogeneous products	2.42	2.66	2.32	0.25	0.31	0.27
Type 2 – differentiated products	2.77	2.56	2.20	0.29	0.28	0.24
2A – Advertising-intensive industries	2.45	2.18	2.17	0.27	0.23	0.23
2R – Research-intensive industries	3.21	3.08	2.43	0.35	0.36	0.28
2AR – Advertising and						
research-intensive industries	2.22	2.00	1.82	0.20	0.18	0.19
By SMP sensitivity (Non-tariff barriers)						
High-tech public procurement	3.30	2.81	2.21	0.35	0.32	0.21
Regulated public procurement	2.08	1.52	1.85	0.26	0.17	0.24
Traditional public procurement	2.05	2.70	2.06	0.24	0.34	0.26
Moderate non-tariff barriers	2.90	2.69	2.22	0.30	0.30	0.24
Non-sensitive industries	2.51	2.60	2.33	0.26	0.29	0.27
Geographical diversification						
All manufacturing	1.79	2.08	2.46	0.21	0.28	0.34
By type of product						
Type 1 – homogeneous products	1.30	1.65	1.87	0.10	0.22	0.30
Type 2 – differentiated products						
2A – Advertising-intensive industries	1.77	2.31	2.33	0.22	0.38	0.35
2R – Research-intensive industries	1.64	1.95	2.26	0.17	0.22	0.29
2AR – Advertising and						
research-intensive industries	2.02	2.21	2.62	0.21	0.29	0.35
By SMP sensitivity (Non-tariff barriers)						
High-tech public procurement	2.02	2.25	3.11	0.19	0.25	0.42
Regulated public procurement	1.76	2.15	2.65	0.22	0.28	0.36
Traditional public procurement	1.75	2.01	2.11	0.26	0.36	0.28
Moderate non-tariff barriers	1.63	1.92	2.11	0.15	0.24	0.29
Non-sensitive industries	1.43	1.82	2.03	0.13	0.24	0.31

Note: [*] Industries applies to industrial diversification, countries to geographical diversification.

This interpretation is confirmed when we look at the de-diversification trend for industries classified according to their sensitivity to the Single Market Programme. The removal of non-tariff barriers was expected to have a particularly strong effect on high-tech public procurement industries (such as computers, telecommunications and medical instruments) and on a sub-set of traditional or regulated public procurement industries (such as pharmaceuticals, wires and cables, railways and shipbuilding, soft drinks and beer and pasta). In Table 3.5 we find that diversification steadily came down in high-tech industries only, and much less so in traditional and regulated industries. Amongst the industries where the removal of non-tariff barriers was expected to have a moderate effect, the reduction of diversification was also quite substantial. Finally, the remaining group of non-sensitive industries displayed a weak tendency to reduce diversification.

Concerning geographical diversification, Table 3.5 shows that, as expected from the intangible assets hypothesis, firms active in Type 1 industries, that is, homogeneous goods industries, are less transnational than firms active in Type 2 industries. However, while firms of all types increased their geographical diversification over time, the increase in output produced in secondary countries was most significant in Type 1 industries, indicating that the relevant market for these firms has become EU-wide, with a real need to expand operations throughout Europe. Within Type 2 industries, the firms competing on the basis of both advertising and R&D show a higher and increasing level of geographical diversification. In contrast to Type I homogeneous industries, production is more equally spread across countries, as implied by the higher entropy value, suggesting a greater decentralisation of activities across Member States, in line with the need to be closer to customers.

Dividing the data sample into those firms active in non-SMP-sensitive industries versus those firms active in SMP-sensitive industries, the table shows that the non-SMP-sensitive group has strongly caught up in transnational production, especially with respect to the traditional public procurement and the moderate non-tariff barriers clusters of the SMP-sensitive group of industries. This observation suggests that the market integration process has provided, in general, a stimulus for all firms to internationalise. The firms that were strongly affected by market fragmentation through non-tariff barriers were already highly transnationally organised before the Single Market, especially those firms from high-tech public procurement cluster industries, characterised by high technology and a relatively high percentage of public procurement. This latter group of firms continued to increase its geographical diversification and build up strong European-wide positions, at the same time specialising in core businesses, as revealed by their reduced industrial diversification. The latter observation suggests a possible trade-off between geographical expansion and industrial diversification.

3.4 ALTERNATIVE CORPORATE STRATEGIES: INDUSTRIAL AND GEOGRAPHICAL DIVERSIFICATION, AND FIRM GROWTH

In this section we extend our analysis by considering industrial diversification jointly with geographical diversification as growth strategies available to the firm.[4] In particular, using very simple statistical tools, we aim to respond to the question of whether industrial diversification and geographical diversification have been complementary or substitute routes to growth for leading firms in the EU.

We start by comparing, for 1987 and 1997, the simple count of firms which are both industrially and geographically diversified against those who choose only one option (see Table 3.6). The first things we note is that both industrial and geographical diversification have become increasingly important in achieving the status of an EU leader in this period. The number of firms that were uninational and specialised has halved, and the number of firms both transnational and industrially diversified has increased by almost 20 per cent. The two groups represent 6.7 per cent and 68 per cent of the firm total in 1997, thus suggesting complementarity between industrial and geographical diversification. Interestingly, however, while the number of uninational firms that are only diversified at home dropped from 47 to 18, the number of specialised transnationals increased from 19 to 38. This, in turn, suggests that the industrial diversification route to growth, especially when confined to the domestic market has lost appeal amongst EU leaders. Finally, the rows and columns totals of these matrices show that in 1987 industrial diversification occurred more frequently than geographical diversification (175 versus 147), but that the opposite was true in 1997 (170 versus 190).

Table 3.6   The incidence of industrially diversified and transnational firms in 1987 and 1997: simple frequencies

| | Number of firms | | | | | |
| | 1987 | | | 1997 | | |
	Specialised	Diversified	Total	Specialised	Diversified	Total
Uninational	29	47	76	15	18	33
Transnational	19	128	147	38	152	190
Totals	48	175	223	53	170	223

It appears from this evidence that industrial diversification was perceived as an easier route to follow than transnationality in 1987, at the start of the implementation of the SMP, but not in 1997. We can only speculate that the entry barriers raised by country specificity due to cultural and institutional differences have been lowered, and that the trade-off between entering another Member State or a new industry has been re-balanced in favour of the transnational option.

Armed with this impressionistic view of a re-balancing of corporate strategies, we turn to Table 3.7 where we present the correlation matrix of levels and changes in industrial diversification, geographical diversification and firm size.[5] Our purpose is to provide some preliminary evidence of whether industrial and geographical diversification are complementary or substitute routes to firm growth. Correlations are calculated between the 1987 levels and the growth rates of the sub-sample of 123 leaders that survived in the MSM from 1987 to 1997. Industrial and geographical diversification in 1987 are shown to be moderately complementary (0.15). More interesting though is the strong positive correlation between output growth and the increase in industrial diversification for surviving leading firms in the EU (0.41). The correlation between firm growth and growth in geographical diversification is also positive, although it is perhaps somewhat lower than we expected (0.22). In contrast with the findings for the full sample of firms in Table 3.6, which suggested substitutability between the two strategies, surviving leaders appear to have pursued both industrial and geographical diversification as routes to growth. This is in line with the positive, although weak, correlation between the changes observed in both types of diversification (0.05). The correlation between the *levels* of geographical diversification and the *growth* of industrial diversification, on the other hand, is negative (−0.19), which suggests that firms that were most geographically diversified in 1987 showed a tendency to reduce industrial diversification over the 1987–97 period. The reverse is not true, however, as the correlation between the *levels* of industrial diversification and the *growth* of geographical diversification is (weakly) positive (0.10).

Table 3.7   Correlation matrix of levels and changes in firm size, industrial and geographical diversification

	Δ Size	Δ Div.	Δ Mult.	Div87	Mult87	Size87
Δ Size	1					
Δ Div.	0.41	1				
Δ Mult.	0.22	0.05	1			
Div87	−0.22	−0.39	0.10	1		
Mult87	−0.05	−0.19	−0.34	0.15	1	
Size87	−0.25	−0.13	−0.13	0.29	0.17	1

Note: Size = change in firm size between 1987 and 1997; Div. = change in industrial diversification between 1987 and 1997; Mult. = change in geographical diversification (or multinationality) between 1987 and 1997; Div87 = industrial diversification in 1987; Mult87 = geographical diversification (or multinationality) in 1987; and Size87 = firm size in 1987.

To test the assertion that there has been a general convergence of corporate structures across size classes, with 'smaller' firms expanding via industrial diversification and 'larger', more mature firms moderately de-diversifying, we report in Table 3.8. the average growth rates of size, industrial diversification, and geographical diversification for firms distributed in quartiles based on their initial levels of industrial diversification. Comparisons of the mean values across the quartiles show that the least industrially diversified firms grew most rapidly, experienced the largest increase in industrial diversification, but increased their geographical diversification relatively slowly. In contrast, the most industrially diversified firms grew less rapidly, but appear to have rationalised their corporate structures the most, as they displayed the highest rate of geographical diversification and the highest rate of industrial de-diversification of the four quartiles. Taken together, this multi-faceted evidence suggests that substitutability between industrial and geographical diversification as routes to corporate growth may be present more frequently than accounted for by the previous findings. This is clearly an issue for future research.

Table 3.8   Growth rates of firm size, industrial and geographical diversification by initial (1987) level of industrial diversification, arithmetic mean values

Percentile	Div87	Δ Size/Size87	Δ Div./Div87	Δ Mult./Mult87
75th – 100th	3.41	0.45	−0.25	0.65
50th – 75th	2.15	0.59	0.03	0.54
25th – 50th	1.36	0.73	0.10	0.32
1st – 25th	1.00	0.86	0.13	0.36

Note: Size = change in firm size between 1987 and 1997; Div. = change in industrial diversification between 1987 and 1997; Mult. = change in geographical diversification (or multinationality) between 1987 and 1997; Div87 = industrial diversification in 1987; Mult87 = geographical diversification (or multinationality) in 1987; and Size87 = firm size in 1987.

3.5   CONCLUSIONS

This chapter has explored the diversification strategies of EU leading firms. Its main purpose was to verify if, following the ex-ante expectations of the impact of the SMP as well as a variety of theoretical explanations, 'return to the core' and geographical concentration in production had occurred over the decade 1987–97.

We have found evidence of a tendency for firms to refocus on their leading business. Industrial diversification is decreasing on average and firms who are either very large or very diversified appear to reduce their initial levels of diversification more than smaller or less diversified firms do. In a similar vein, the decade under investigation witnessed a convergence of corporate structures between EU Member States. Countries that in 1987 were hosting the most industrially diversified leading firms, such as Germany, the UK, Italy and Sweden, have undergone a considerable reduction in diversified operations. The entropy index of industrial diversification shows a greater decline than the output share in secondary industries, which suggests that firms' operations in marginal industries have been scaled back more than proportionally. This is consistent with our finding that those firms that were able to survive as leading firms in the MSM displayed a relatively high degree of industrial diversification, which however had declined by 1997.

At the same time firms have increasingly expanded and/or rebalanced their geographical operations across Member States, thereby strongly increasing their geographical diversification of production over time. French firms in particular have substantially increased the geographical scope of their operations within the EU.

The SMP was expected to impact asymmetrically across industries. In particular, firms in the sectors defined as most sensitive to EU integration were expected to react more strongly. Our analysis confirms this for industrial diversification. Amongst the SMP-sensitive industries, leading firms in high-tech industries characterised by a high percentage of public procurement strongly reduced their industrial diversification, while at the same time strongly increasing their geographical diversification. Moreover, separating firms by type of product (homogeneous or differentiated), we find that industrial diversification declined quite remarkably in industries where either advertising or R&D expenditures were important strategic weapons. This suggests that in these sectors competitive pressures induced firms to refocus towards the core business and to abandon non-leading activities. Firms in homogeneous industries expanded strongly outside their base country, albeit in a less balanced way than firms in differentiated industries.

The last issue we investigated is whether geographical and industrial diversification are substitutes or complements in the growth strategies of firms. The results highlight the facts that the number of firms which are both industrially and geographically diversified has increased (suggesting complementarity), but also that geographical diversification has become the preferred route to growth as compared to industrial diversification (suggesting substitutability). Further evidence in favour of complementarity comes from the sub-sample of surviving leading firms, for which we report a positive correlation between growth in industrial and geographical diversification. However, within this sub-sample, firms that were most industrially diversified in 1987 reduced industrial diversification by 25 per cent and increased geographical diversification by 65 per cent over the period, which would seem to be an indication of substitutability.

The above patterns are not linear through time. While industrial diversification for some categories of firms appears to be still on the rise between 1987 and 1993, it is only in the period 1993–97 that we find clear evidence of a return to the core. This is an intriguing result, since the completion of the Single European Market was expected to persuade firms to reorganise their corporate structures by the end of 1992. The lag in the firms' responses to the EU-wide shock suggests that the return to the core may still be in progress in the years after 1997 and that the process of European market integration has not necessarily slowed down.

Contrary to some ex-ante theories of the impact of market integration on the geographical diversification of firms, this chapter provides no evidence of a decrease in the level of geographical diversification by leading firms in the EU over the period 1987–97. On the contrary, both the number of transnational firms and the level of geographical diversification of the average firm have continuously increased over that period, irrespective of the country of origin or industrial sector. These findings as well as the evidence of a growing convergence in industrial diversification and geographical diversification of leading firms in European manufacturing industries strongly suggest that the relevant market in which firms compete has increasingly become European-wide.

NOTES

*   The authors would like to thank An Van Pelt and Silvana Zeli for research assistance.

1. The principles, methodology and data sources for the 1987 exercise are explained in Chapter 4, section 2 of this volume, and further detailed in Davies et al. (1996) and for the time comparison 1987, 1993, 1997 in Veugelers et al. (2002).
2. The entropy index is defined as $D_I = -\Sigma p_i \log(p_i)$, where i stands for all industries in which the firm is active and p_i for the relative share of the firm's production belonging to industry i. It measures the degree of production size disparity between industries in which the firm is active. If all industries have an equal share of a firm's production, entropy equals $\log n$, where n is the number of industries in which the firm is active. If production is concentrated in only one industry, the entropy index is at its minimum and equals zero. The entropy index of geographical distribution (D_G) is defined in an analogous way except that the index i stands for country instead of industry.
3. For surveys of the theories of diversification and of the empirical evidence, see Montgomery (1994) and Vannoni (1999b).
4. Davies et al. (1996, Ch. 12) and Davies et al. (2001b) made earlier attempts to investigate this issue when only the data for 1987 were available.
5. For simplicity, we use only the entropy measure of industrial and geographical diversification in this table.

BIBLIOGRAPHY

Berry, C.H. (1971), 'Corporate growth and industrial diversification', *Journal of Law and Economics*, October, 14, 371–83.

Buigues, P. and Jacquemin, A. (1989), 'Strategies of firms and structural environments in the large internal market', *Journal of Common Market Studies*, **XXVIII** (1), September.

Buigues, P., Ilzkovitz, F. and Lebrun, J.-F. (1990), 'The impact of the internal market by industrial sector: the challenge for the Member States', *European Economy*, special edition.

Caves, R.E. (1996), *Multinational Enterprise and Economic Analysis*, Cambridge: Cambridge University Press.

Caves, R.E. and Pugel, T.A. (1980), 'Intra-industry differences in conduct and performance: viable strategies in US manufacturing industries', Monograph Series in Finance and Economics, no. 1980–2, Graduate School of Business Administration, New York University, New York.

Cox, A. and Watson, G. (1996), *Industrial Enterprise and European Integration – from National to International Champions in Western Europe*, Oxford: Oxford University Press.

Davies, S.W., Lyons, B.R., Matraves, C., Rondi, L., Sembenelli, A., Gual, J., Sleuwaegen, L. and Veugelers, R. (1996), *Industrial Organisation in the European Union*, Oxford: Clarendon Press.

Davies, S.W., Rondi, L. and Sembenelli, A. (2001a), 'European integration and the changing structure of EU manufacturing, 1987–1993', *Industrial and Corporate Change*, **10**(1), 37–75.

Davies, S.W., Rondi, L. and Sembenelli, A. (2001b), 'Are multinationality and diversification complementary or substitute strategies? An empirical analysis on European leading firms', *International Journal of Industrial Organization*, **19**(8), 1315–46.

Douglas, S. and Craig, S. (1992), 'Advances in international marketing', *International Journal of Research in Marketing*, 9, 291–318.

Dunning, J.H. (1980), 'Toward an eclectic theory of international production: some empirical tests', *Journal of International Business Studies*, Spring/Summer, 9–31.

European Commission (1988), 'The economies of 1992', *European Economy*, no. 35 (Cecchini Report), Office for Official Publications of the European Communities, Luxembourg.

European Commission (1996), 'Economic evaluation of the internal market', *European Economy*, no. 4.

Horst, T. (1972), 'Firm and industry determinants of the decision to invest abroad', *Review of Economics and Statistics*, **54**(3), 258–66.

Jensen, M.C. (1986), 'Agency costs of free cash flow, corporate finance and take-overs', *American Economic Review*, 76, 323–9.

Knickerbocker, F.T. (1973), *Oligopolistic Reaction and the Multinational Enterprise*, Cambridge, MA: Harvard University Press.

Marris, R. (1964), *The Economic Theory of Managerial Capitalism*, New York: Free Press.

Montgomery, C. (1994), 'Corporate diversification', *Journal of Economic Perspectives*, **8**(3), 163–78.

NIESR (1996), 'The Single Market review 1996: capital market liberalization', Office for Official Publications of the European Communities, Luxembourg.

Penrose, E.T. (1959), *The Theory of the Growth of the Firm*, Oxford: Oxford University Press.

Rubin, P.H. (1973), 'The expansion of firms', *Journal of Political Economy*, 81, 936–49.

Sembenelli, A. and Vannoni, D. (2000), 'Why do established firms enter some industries and exit others? Empirical evidence on Italian business groups', *Review of Industrial Organisation*, **17**(4), 441–56.

Sleuwaegen, L. (1995), 'Competition, strategic management and industrial restructuring of Europe after 1992', in A.M. Rugman and A. Verbeke (eds), *Research in Global Strategic Management*, vol. 5, Greenwich, CT: JAI Press Inc. Connecticut.

Teece, D. (1980), 'The diffusion of an administrative innovation', *Management Science*, **26**(5), 464–70.

Teece, D. (1982), 'Towards an economic theory of the multiproduct firm', *Journal of Economic Behaviour and Organisation*, 3, 39–63.

United Nations (1993), World Investment Report, 'Transnational Corporations and Integrated International Production', New York/Geneva: United Nations.

Vandermerwe, S. (1993), 'A framework for constructing Euro-networks', *European Management Journal*, **11**(1), 55–61.

Vannoni, D. (1999a) 'Entries and exits in foreign markets: Italian multinationals' expansion in the European Union', *International Journal of the Economics of Business*, 2, 181–96.

Vannoni, D. (1999b), 'Empirical studies on corporate diversification', *Rivista Italiana degli Economisti*, 1, 107–35

Vannoni, D. (2000), 'The diversified firm: non formal theories versus formal models', *Economia e Politica Industriale*, 106, 85–104.

Veugelers, R., Sleuwaegen L., De Voldere, I., Reynaerts, J., Rommens, K., Rondi, L., Vannoni, D., Benfratello, L., Davies, S., Egger, P. and Pfaffermayr, M. (2002), 'Determinants of industrial concentration, market integration and efficiency in the European Union', Chapter 3 in 'European integration and the functioning of product markets', *European Economy*, Special Report, no. 2.

4. Industrial concentration, market integration and efficiency in the European Union

Reinhilde Veugelers[*]

4.1 THE IMPACT OF MARKET INTEGRATION ON INDUSTRY CONCENTRATION

During the last decade markets have become increasingly globalised and national production systems more and more globally integrated. Many elements have positively influenced the level of industry globalisation during the late 1980s and 1990s, such as convergence in demand, advances in transportation and globalisation of business services, to name a few (Yip, 1995). In this process of world market integration, the formation of regional economic blocs such as the EU has played an important role. Regional market integration within the EU was critically influenced by the 1992 Single Market Programme (SMP), and further strengthened by monetary integration.

The process of market integration systematically changes the nature of competition, and therefore the structure and performance of industries and firms. Following Smith and Venables (1988), market integration can be seen as (i) a reduction in trade costs between national markets, and/or (ii) a complete displacement of segmented national markets by a single aggregate market (in which price discrimination is no longer possible). The beneficial effects of market integration on the EU economy come from lower prices and increased production. Amplified competitive pressure is an important catalyst for beneficial effects, not only directly, by reducing market power, but also indirectly, by eliminating cost inefficiencies. Hence, a cornerstone in the evaluation of market integration is the effect on competition and market concentration.

Within the academic literature, most of the rigorous analysis of the impact of market integration on industry structure was due to Smith and Venables (1988).[1] They applied an extended Krugman (1979) approach, involving trade with monopolistic competition, to ten industries across six countries. Their results suggest that industrial structure does matter: the most dramatic effects on welfare are likely in industries in which national market concentration is high and pre-integration behaviour is less competitive.

Focusing more explicitly on the theoretical implications for industrial concentration from an industrial organisation perspective, one can argue (see Davies et al., 1996) that as the fixed and variable costs of exporting within the EU decline, segmented national markets will be replaced by a larger single market. Prices will fall, especially if there is a toughening in the competitive regime. High cost producers will exit, leaving survivors who will have typically increased their scale to exploit production scale economies. Within product markets characterised by product differentiation, where first stage competition is conducted through advertising and/or R&D, the trend towards larger scale would be even stronger (Sutton, 1991). In such markets, enlargement encourages escalation of these sunk costs by the market leaders in pursuit of higher 'vertical' quality, accentuating the scale disadvantage of small firms. All in all, the expectation from market integration is fewer firms that are larger in size. Of course, this stylised story is essentially short-run, abstracting from possible second-round effects in which market enlargement encourages entry of new low cost producers. A likely source of entry of new firms comes from firms located outside the EU who are attracted to operating inside the larger integrated EU market.

In drawing out the empirical implications of market integration for concentration, the appropriate market dimension needs to be identified. Within an enlarged relevant market, there will be more and larger relevant sellers to take into consideration than was previously the case in each of the individual (more or less) segmented national markets. In that sense, seller concentration in the effective marketplace will be lower. However, with high cost producers exiting, leaving firms who have typically increased their scale of operations, the number of producers will decline, both at the aggregate EU level, and within individual Member States. The expectation must be for increased firm size and higher producer concentration. It should be stressed, however, that this is not necessarily a sign of reduced competition. To the extent that integration also leads to tougher competition among the large players, this will lower margins further, and lead to even greater exit of marginal firms, and increased concentration.

In summary, the tightening of competitive pressure, the shake-out of firms unable to produce innovations and exploit scale economies, leads to a smaller number of more efficient producers, which typically will increase production concentration. Coordination among a smaller number of players may also lead to more coordinated behaviour in the sector.

4.2 THE MARKET SHARE MATRIX MEASURING INDUSTRY CONCENTRATION IN EU MANUFACTURING

A number of studies have appeared, attempting to assess the actual impact of SMP. The most extensive evaluation of the SMP programme is that of the European Commission itself (1996), based on a large body of commissioned research, using mainly fairly aggregate Eurostat databases. The main drivers behind the economic gains were found to be an increase in efficiency and a rise in total factor productivity. But the effects on industrial concentration of market integration in general and the SMP in particular remain relatively unexplored.

Rather than drawing on official aggregate data, our empirical analysis allows us to assess changes in industry concentration by using more disaggregated firm-level data from the Market Share Matrix. Briefly,[2] the basic idea of the Market Share Matrix (MSM) is to identify a set of 'leading firms', and disaggregate their turnover data, extracted from individual company accounts, using a common industrial classification scheme at a meaningful level of disaggregation. A firm qualifies as a 'leader', if it is one of the five largest EU producers in at least one manufacturing industry. For any such firm, the matrix disaggregates its EU production into all industries in which it has operations – not only those in which it is a 'leader'. The matrix furthermore disaggregates for every firm its total EU production within each industry across the different Member States in which the output is produced.

A matrix built on this basis allows us to look into a range of structural dimensions of industries and firms. For any leading firm, we can discuss multinational production and firm diversification (as in Chapter 3). For the purpose of the current chapter, the MSM data when coupled with published Eurostat data on aggregate industry production will allow us to identify, for every considered industry, production concentration at the EU level. Since the Market Share Matrix was constructed so as to include the shares of at least the five largest producers in each industry, the five firm concentration ratio C5, being the shares of the five largest matrix firms in total EU industry production, comes out naturally from the matrix and this will be the index we will be using in the analysis to discuss concentration. At the overall manufacturing sector level, since the matrix will include most large EU firms in manufacturing, it also enables us to estimate aggregate concentration of EU manufacturing.[3]

To avoid confusion, we must define our measure of firm size very precisely. The size of firms and industries is measured by the value of sales of goods produced in the EU. Firm size is therefore confined to production within the EU. It differs from sales in the EU at the firm level because it includes the firm's extra EU exports and excludes any EU sales which are coming from outside the EU. At the industry level, there is an additional difference, because it excludes all imports from non-EU producers. Thus the use of the term 'market share' in the analysis is somewhat loose and must be excused on the grounds of convenience. Pragmatic reasons make sales-based measures almost impossible. While it is simple to adjust industry-level production data by subtracting extra-EU exports and adding extra-EU imports, there are two problems in identifying the share of the leading sellers by sales: company accounts do not always report the existence of non-EU sourcing and there is no systematic source of information on the market shares of leading importers not producing in the EU. This implies that data-driven constraints force us to use production concentration rather than seller concentration in the analysis, although of course, sales concentration data would be better to measure market power. Nevertheless, production concentration is less likely to be very different from sales concentration for the EU than for a typical Member State. Indeed, if it wasn't for extra-EU trade, sales and production concentration ratios would be identical at the EU level.

This matrix has been constructed for 1987, first reported in Davies et al. (1996), and first updated in 1993 (Davies et al., 1998). Veugelers et al. (2002) updates the mapping to 1997 and examines how certain aspects of structure have changed amidst a process of ongoing market integration, while Van Pelt et al. (2002) reports on the 2000 results. While the MSM data are extremely valuable in sharpening our understanding of the changes in EU industries that have occurred over the critical period 1987–2000, the task is not trivial, not least because it necessarily involves identifying an appropriate counterfactual for a period in which major global changes were underway. It is important to keep in mind that the comparison over time cannot solely be attributed to the SMP, although it is a major factor of change in the considered period.

4.3 AGGREGATE RESULTS FROM THE MSM (1987–2000)

Table 4.1 provides a time comparison of the aggregate concentration of the EU industry as measured by the MSM. Although the number of sectors is fixed over the time period, with $66 \times 5 = 330$ leading positions to be filled in the matrix, the number of matrix firms can vary over time since firms can take leading positions in more than one sector.[4]

Table 4.1   Industry concentration in 1987–93–97 and 2000 matrices

	1987	1993	1997	2000
Number of matrix firms (NM)	221	212	214	222
Total matrix production (TMP)	655.8	788.3	918.5	1181.0
Total leading production (TLP)	485.0	597.8	723.6	931.5
Total manufacturing production* (TP)	2091.1	2485.0	3216.0	3773.1
Average firm size (TMP/NM)	2.97	3.72	4.29	5.32
Average matrix coverage (TMP/TP)	0.31	0.32	0.29	0.31
Average C5-concentration (TLP/TP)	0.23	0.24	0.23	0.25

Notes: * Production figures are expressed in billion euro and in current prices. Total manufacturing production (TP) is provided by the European Commission on the basis of Eurostat (New Cronos database). Total matrix production (TMP) includes the sum of all EU production by all matrix firms. Total leading production (TLP) includes the sum of EU production accounted for by the top five producers in their industry.

The average size of matrix firms is large. Obviously, the size distribution of matrix firms, being highly skewed towards larger firms, given the selection of leading firms only, is not representative for EU manufacturing. It is more interesting to discuss the evolution of the production size for the leading firms over the considered period.

Over time the number of matrix firms has remained substantively stable, but their identities may well have differed between the years. Nevertheless, the identity of the biggest firms in the matrix has remained remarkably stable. The top four positions in 1987, 1993 and 1997 were shared between Fiat, Volkswagen, Daimler-Benz and Siemens. In the top four of 2000, the American car manufacturer Ford replaced Siemens. Top position was shared between Fiat (in 1987 and 1997) and Daimler-Benz (in 1993 and 2000). The size distribution of matrix firms has remained relatively stable as well, even if the relative importance of the biggest firms has increased slightly over time. The top five matrix firms represented 17.3 per cent of total matrix sales in 1987, 18.4 per cent in 1993, 19.3 per cent in 1997 and 18.2 per cent in 2000.

The average size of the matrix firms increased from 2.97 billion euro in 1987 to over 3.72 billion euro in 1993, 4.29 billion euro in 1997 and finally to 5.32 billion euro in 2000 (in current prices). This confirms the expectation of firms increasing their size to exploit production scale economies in integrating markets.

The matrix firms accounted for 31 per cent of total EU manufacturing production in 2000. This gives a broad indication of the extent of aggregate concentration in Europe: about 222 firms account for nearly one-third of

EU production.[5] Aggregate turnover of matrix firms, expressed as a share of total EU manufacturing, remained almost unchanged, indicating a relatively stable matrix coverage. When expressing leading turnover of matrix firms as a share of total EU production, we have in effect a weighted average $C5$-concentration ratio. The sum of the firms' leading shares account for 25 per cent of total manufacturing in 2000.[6] These numbers suggest that in a typical EU industry, the top five firms account for nearly one-quarter of EU production in the considered period. The average $C5$ producer concentration shows an increase between 1997 and 2000.

4.4   CHANGES IN INDUSTRY CONCENTRATION BY SECTOR

The previous section has provided a bird's eye view on changes in industry concentration following market integration, using aggregate MSM statistics. To sharpen our understanding of the changes that have occurred in EU industries over this critical period, an inter-industry component of the analysis is extremely valuable. The disaggregated firm-level data from the MSM project allows us to concentrate on explaining not only changes in the population averages, but also differences between industries.

Table 4.2 details the distributions of industries in terms of concentration changes over the considered period 1987–2000 and also in the latest time period 1997–2000. While on average the concentration was quite stable over time (see Table 4.1), Table 4.2 reveals considerable inter-industry differences.

Table 4.2   Frequency distribution of changes in C5 concentration per industry

	Range percentage point change	1987–2000 number of Industries
Largest increase	> + 0.25	7
Considerable increase	[+ 0.10 + 0.25]	16
Minor increase	[+ 0.02 + 0.10]	14
Stable	[− 0.02 + 0.02]	12
Minor decrease	[− 0.10 − 0.02]	8
Considerable decrease	[− 0.25 − 0.10]	7
Major decrease	< − 0.25	2

Over the period 1987–2000 we find 32 out of the 66 industries where concentration changes by as much as 10 percentage points, sectors which can therefore hardly be described as 'stable'. Nine industries witnessed a decrease in concentration by more than 10 percentage points. These include industries like manmade fibres, lighting, aerospace, motor vehicle parts, confectionery and steel tubes. In more than one-third of the industries we find an increase in concentration by more than 10 percentage points. These include musical instruments, clocks and watches, tobacco and railway. Hence, when zeroing in on individual sectors, we find considerable cross-industry variation, both in terms of the size of changes in concentration, but also in the direction of change in concentration, with some sectors witnessing considerable decreases in producer concentration in the EU, while most manage to increase producer concentration. The next section will try to further unravel the cross-industry variation in the change in $C5$ concentration.

4.5   INDUSTRY CHARACTERISTICS AFFECTING CHANGE IN CONCENTRATION

Industry Size

There is a broad tendency for concentration to fall in larger industries, but to rise in smaller industries. For instance in basic chemicals, market concentration fell from 27 per cent in 1987 to 19 per cent in 2000, in motor vehicles market concentration fell from 54 per cent in 1987 to 52 per cent in 2000. Also, telecom and electronic equipment saw its market concentration fall from 33 per cent in 1987 to 23 per cent in 2000. As reported in Veugelers et al. (2002), this size effect is confirmed by a simple regression of the change in concentration on the 1987 turnover of the industry, where the regression coefficient is negative and (just) significant.

Homogeneous versus Differentiated Industries

While larger industries seem to have a larger tendency for concentration to fall, industrial organisation theory suggests that the link between market size and concentration depends on the nature of product competition (Sutton, 1991). Rather than seeing concentration as exogenously determined by basic market conditions such as economies of scale, more recently economists have viewed industrial concentration as the outcome of the competitive process. The way firms compete and the instruments they use to compete will influence the industrial structure in which they operate.

In industries where products are homogeneous and competition is basically through prices, the so-called Type 1 (homogeneous, exogenous fixed costs) industries, competition can be very fierce, with firms only making sufficient profits to keep themselves in the market. In such industries, the larger the market, the more firms can be sustained in the market, and hence the lower the concentration. The lower bound to concentration decreases as market size increases. The dynamics of market integration will put downward pressure on prices as more firms compete with each other, shifting the lower bound to concentration. An important result here is that this process can continue with the lower bound to concentration even approaching zero as market size increases.

This contrasts sharply with industries where products can be differentiated and where firms can engage in fixed outlays to differentiate their products, such as R&D and/or advertising. Since these sunk costs are endogenous, and can be used as entry barriers to smooth competition, Type 2 industries will tend to be more concentrated than Type 1 industries. If market size increases, this will – as is the case in Type 1 industries – lead to more competition by existing firms driving down concentration. However, with more competitors firms will also be encouraged to engage in higher spending on R&D and advertising, creating barriers to entry which will put an upward pressure on concentration. To summarize, the key difference as compared with Type 1 industries is that the lower bound to concentration will decrease less with increasing market size and may even increase. The main theoretical results are summarised in the following hypotheses (see also Davies et al., 1996, p. 99):

- For Type 1 (homogeneous, exogenous fixed costs) industries, the lower bound to concentration as a function of market size is monotonically decreasing, while for Type 2 industries (differentiated, endogenous fixed costs), the lower bound to concentration as a function of market size need not be monotonically decreasing, and may even increase.
- For Type 1 industries, the lower bound to concentration approaches zero as market size increases, while for Type 2 industries, the limiting level of concentration is strictly positive.

We operationalise the distinction between homogeneous and heterogeneous industries using data on what a 'typical' industry spends on advertising and R&D: product differentiation is equated with 'high' expenditures on advertising and/or R&D. Within the differentiated group, industries are disaggregated further according to the method of differentiation: advertising versus R&D. Broadly speaking, Type 2A includes industries mainly in food, drink and tobacco, Type 2R are industries in engineering, broadly defined, without significant sales to final consumers, and Type 2AR are often consumer durables.[7]

Table 4.3   Concentration in homogeneous and differentiated industries

	Number of industries	Average $C5_{87}$	Average $C5_{93}$	Average $C5_{97}$	Average $C5_{00}$
Type 1: Homogeneous products	29	16.2	17.1	17.3	19.7
Type 2: Differentiated products	37	31.1	33.8	33.9	37.3
Type 2A: Advertising intensive	12	24.0	30.7	30.8	38.2
Type 2R: R&D intensive	17	35.1	35.9	34.9	33.3
Type 2AR: Advertising and R&D intensive	8	33.2	34.2	36.4	44.6

If we first focus on the level of concentration, Table 4.3 shows that – conforming to expectations – differentiated industries are indeed more concentrated than homogenous industries, a difference which is statistically significant at <1 per cent significance level for all years considered. This result is entirely consistent with the standard theory on the determinants of concentration (see Davies et al., 1996). Sectors with a high level of concentration are typically associated with a combination of R&D and advertising.

For the dynamic analysis, there are no strong differences in the rate of change of concentration between homogeneous (Type 1) and differentiated product (Type 2) industries. Both types of sectors increased concentration by about 20 per cent on average over the period 1987–2000. This increase in concentration is mainly observed in the last sub-period 1997–2000. Contrary to expectations, we find no evidence for decreases in concentration in Type 1 industries, which on average have managed to increase concentration as measured by $C5$, albeit less marked than in the differentiated sectors. Overall, the level of concentration continues to be significantly higher in Type 2 industries.

On the other hand, there is some evidence of marked differences within the differentiated set of industries. Concentration is typically higher when product differentiation is driven by R&D or by a combination of advertising and R&D, as compared to concentration in advertising-intensive industries. But over time concentration has tended to rise fast where advertising was more important, but fall where R&D was the primary source of differentiation. The end result is a smaller divergence between concentration in R&D sectors and advertising-intensive sectors in 2000. The sectors combining R&D and advertising show the highest concentration levels.

SMP Sensitivity

Another important difference between industries is how integrated they already were prior to 1992. The level of initial market integration is likely to affect how further developments will affect industry concentration. The sectors which are sensitive to market integration forces are typically more concentrated, as documented in Davies et al. (1996). Hence, we expect the forces of market integration to affect the changes of concentration, if only because of non-linearities in the relationship.

This implies including as an industry dimension for classification how sensitive industries were likely to be to further reductions in trade impediments. Buigues et al. (1990) identify a set of industries which were anticipated to be most sensitive to the effects of the SMP. This anticipation was based on a variety of statistical criteria (for example, dispersion of prices, public procurement, trade flows and so on).[8]

Table 4.4   Concentration in SMP-sensitive industries

	Number of industries	Average $C5_{87}$	Average $C5_{93}$	Average $C5_{97}$	Average $C5_{00}$
SMP-non-sensitive industries	40	21.1	23.7	23.5	28.1
SMP-sensitive industries	26	29.9	30.8	31.5	31.8
Groups 1–2–3: public procurement	12	31.0	34.4	37.0	37.3
Group 1: High-tech	3	37.6	41.5	40.6	34.2
Group 2: Regulated	4	27.1	33.3	33.9	45.0
Group 3: Traditional	5	30.1	30.9	37.2	33.1
Group 4: Moderate non-tariff Barriers	14	28.9	27.7	26.8	27.1

Table 4.4 illustrates that SMP-sensitive industries tend to be more concentrated, with a $C5$-concentration ratio in 1987 almost 10 percentage points above that in non-SMP-sensitive industries. But over the period 1987–2000 the non-SMP-sensitive industries increased their concentration levels considerably, again mostly in the last sub-period, 1997–2000, closing the gap with the SMP-sensitive industries in 2000. If we zoom in on the different types of SMP-sensitive industries, we find that the group of moderate non-tariff barriers has witnessed on average a modest decline in concentration, while the high-tech public procurement industries show a significant decrease in the last sub-period.[9] The other public procurement industries have witnessed on average an increase in concentration, especially

the regulated public procurement. As a consequence, while the difference in concentration between groups 1–3 versus 4 was not statistically significant in 1987, the public procurement type of industries had obtained by 2000 a significantly larger concentration than the moderate non-tariff barrier industries ($\alpha = 6$ per cent).

Initial Level of Concentration

When examining the sectoral characteristics related to the nature of product market competition and SMP sensitivity, these factors were found to influence both the changes in concentration and the level of concentration. The relationship between the level of concentration and the changes in concentration can be examined in more detail. Does the initial level of concentration matter? Do we expect a regression towards the mean with high concentration sectors showing a decline in the level of concentration and low concentration sectors managing to increase concentration? Or does the opposite hold, with high concentration sectors being able to further increase concentration?

Table 4.5   Changes in concentration for high concentration sectors

	All sectors	High $C5_{87}$	Low $C5_{87}$
$C5_{87}$	0.25 (0.16)	0.40 (0.12)	0.13 (0.06)
$C5_{00}$	0.30 (0.18)	0.41 (0.14)	0.21 (0.16)

Note: Arithmetic unweighted averages/standard deviations in brackets.

Table 4.5 shows that on average both high and low concentration sectors have witnessed an increase in concentration. However, the low concentration sectors have witnessed on average a much higher increase in concentration. This suggests a regression towards the mean only for the low concentration sectors. But the standard deviations are quite substantial, indicating an important cross-sector variation. Tables 4.6 and 4.7 further describe this cross-sector variation.

Table 4.6 details for the sectors with the highest initial concentration levels in 1987 the changes in concentration in the period 1987–2000. Interesting to note is that most sectors that were highly concentrated in 1987 have witnessed a decline in concentration, indicating the difficulty of maintaining large leading production shares. Only tobacco and cycles and motorcycles have managed to increase their concentration levels, most spectacularly the tobacco sector. Nevertheless, despite the fact that most of the highly concentrated sectors have witnessed decreases in concentration, these sectors have typically maintained an above average concentration level. Note that some 'heavyweight sectors' such as motor vehicles and aerospace are included in this list.

Table 4.6   Changes in concentration for high concentration sectors

Sector	$C5_{87}-C5_{00}$
Lighting	0.61–0.41
Manmade fibres	0.61–0.39
Aerospace	0.60–0.42
Computers and office equipment	0.57–0.44
Motor vehicles	0.54–0.52
Optical instruments	0.52–0.43
Rubber and tyres	0.52–0.43
Tobacco	0.49–0.84
Cycles and motorcycles	0.42–0.48
Confectionery	0.42–0.26
Average of all sectors	0.25–0.30

When we examine the lower tail of the distribution we find substantial cross-industry variation and no clear evidence for low concentration sectors to revert to the mean. Only footwear, leather and clothing and knitwear have managed to substantially increase their level of concentration, but they still remain, on average, at rather low levels of concentration. Plastics and wood manufacturing have seen their low level of concentration decrease even further.

Table 4.7   Changes in concentration for low concentration sectors

Sector	$C5_{87}-C5_{00}$
Clothing, made-up textiles and knitwear	0.03–0.07
Furniture	0.03–0.04
Textiles	0.04–0.05
Metal products	0.05–0.04
Wood sawing	0.05–0.04
Footwear	0.06–0.12
Meat products	0.06–0.07
Leather	0.07–0.19
Plastics	0.07–0.04
Wood manufacturing	0.08–0.06
Average of all sectors	0.25–0.30

This concentration trajectory of reversion to the mean has been examined in more detail in Veugelers et al. (2002). Regressing end-period concentration against start-period concentration reveals a coefficient significantly lower than unity, implying that sectors which are highly concentrated are less likely to increase their concentration levels as compared to less concentrated industries. This is however against a background of considerable turbulence. The period after the 1992 project displays most turbulence. This is contrary to the more typical expectation that most of the dramatic changes would have occurred in the period before 1992 but confirms that market integration forces continue to be important after 1992. Turbulence will be further examined in the next section.

4.6   PERSISTENCE IN DOMINANCE

A high market concentration classically worries policy makers since a high share enjoyed by the top five firms in an industry usually makes it easier for these firms to collude, leading to welfare inferior monopolistic outcomes. But concentration as measured by the $C5$ ratio is not a perfect proxy for collusive conduct. The ability to collude also depends on other characteristics such as the homogeneity among leading firms and the stability within the group of leading firms. Collusion is expected to be easier when there are a limited number of similar leading firms, which face not too many changes. That the link between high concentration and collusion is not so straightforward is also reflected by the structural conditions in the EU where in most sectors there are very few large firms – typically around three or four firms with an aggregate market share of at least 60–70 per cent – and also a relatively symmetric market share.

From a dynamic perspective, we need to understand what determines the likelihood that collusive agreements are sustained over longer periods of time. Turbulence is one factor that may limit the leading firms' capability to maintain collusive agreements. As Caves and Porter (1978, p. 289) already noted:

> The instability of market shares, especially among an industry's leading firms, provides a measurable indicator of rival behaviour in oligopolistic markets. The stability of shares reflects the stability and completeness of the oligopolistic bargain, as well as the size and nature of exogenous disturbances to that bargain.

When the leading firms face less changeable conditions, it is easier for these firms to collude. Hence when high concentration is observed together with high stability, this is associated with more collusive potential. Consequently, the combination of high concentration and low turbulence will be more detrimental for welfare than when high concentration is associated with high turbulence. In order to better establish the link between concentration, as measured through $C5$, and collusion, the MSM methodology, being able to trace the individual leading firms over time, allows examinination of the stability of market share dominance in several dimensions:

- a change in the identity of leading firms (that is, entry of new leading firms and exit of old leaders) and/or
- a change in leading firms' dominance (that is, evolution over time of production shares of the incumbent leaders).

Changes in the identity of leading firms are due to the entry of new firms into the club of leading producers. These 'new' firms can be incumbent firms already producing in the industry, but joining the leading top five producers for the first time. They could also be new firms to the industry, possibly diversifying from other sectors. Entry into the top five can be through internal growth or through acquisitions. The production share obtained by entrants is the complement of the change in shares of the old leaders, as the following equality shows:

$$C5_{t+1} \equiv PS5^{Lt}_{t+1} + PS5^{ENT}_{t+1} \tag{4.1}$$

With $PS5^{Lt}_{t+1}$ = production share at $t + 1$ of the firms in the top five at both time t and time $t + 1$.

We will use as a measure of persistence of the leading five the market share of the old leaders relative to the new leaders: $PS5^{Lt}_{t+1}/ C5_{t+1}$. Following (4.1) the measure in its complement can also be considered as assessing the force of new matrix firms entering into the top five $(1 - PS5^{ENT}_{t+1}/C5_{t+1})$. The maximum value of 1 is obtained if the same firms are in the top five, that is, when there is no new matrix entry in the top five. In this case we have stability in terms of the identity of the leading firms. Nevertheless, these leading firms may not have stable production shares, as their position relative to the other non-leading firms in the industry may improve or deteriorate. The change in dominance through changing shares is in this case perfectly reflected in the change in the $C5$ concentration ratio.

As soon as there is a new player in the top five, the value for our measure $PS5^{Lt}_{t+1}/C5_{t+1}$ will be lower than 1. In this case, the more the old leaders have lost position relative to the new leading firms, the closer the value will be to zero. The measure $PS5^{Lt}_{t+1}/C5_{t+1}$ is therefore the inverse of leadership turbulence. It measures, in case there are new leading firms, how important this entry is.

With the MSM allowing us to measure whether there is persistence in the dominance of the five leading firms, we can examine the hypothesis that highly concentrated sectors are more likely to stay concentrated or even increase their concentration if entry among the leading firms is low and persistence is high. This means linking levels of concentration to persistence and changes in concentration.

We will first study the persistence in dominance of the top five firms, to be followed by an examination of persistence in dominance of the leading firm.

Persistence in Top Five Leadership

As Table 4.8 shows, on average the value for $PS5^{L87}_{00}/C5_{00}$ is 46 per cent (std 0.27), which suggests that over a period of 13 years, the leading top 5 companies have lost more than half of their production position relative to newcomers (arithmetic non-weighted averages across sectors).

Table 4.8   Decomposition of the average C5 in 2000

	All sectors	High $C5_{87}$	Low $C5_{87}$
$PS5^{L87}_{00}/C5_{00}$	0.46	0.60	0.37

If we focus only on high concentration sectors, that is, those sectors that in 1987 have above average concentration levels (that is, higher than 25 per cent), the average value for $PS5^{L87}_{00}/C5_{00}$ rises to 60 per cent, while for low concentration sectors the value drops to 37 per cent (a difference which is statistically significant below the 1 per cent level) (see Table 4.8). This confirms that high concentration sectors witness less turbulence among leading five companies. Also Caves and Porter (1978) found that stability tends to rise with concentration.

Table 4.9 reports the change in concentration for sectors that are among the ten highest in terms of persistence. Over the period 1987–2000 there were only two industries (glass and alcohol and spirits) where there was no change in the five leading companies over the considered period (that is, $PS5^{L87}_{00}/C5_{00} = 1$). It is interesting that these are also industries with above average concentration levels and relatively small changes in concentration, which seems the first evidence in favour of our hypothesis. Also the industries where there is a change in the leading five companies, but with very low levels of turbulence in terms of production shares, have above average concentration in 1987 (excluding soft drinks, bread and biscuits, and other foods, which score around average). Nevertheless, despite the low turbulence most of these sectors all witnessed a decrease in concentration by 2000, with the exception of soft drinks, soap and toiletries, and first processing of steel.

Table 4.9 Concentration for sectors with no or little turbulence

Sector	$C5_{87}$	$PS5^{L87}_{00}/C5_{00}$	$C5_{00}$
Glass	0.38	1	0.37
Alcohol and spirits	0.27	1	0.35
First processing of steel	0.36	0.91	0.52
Soap and toiletries	0.31	0.91	0.47
Soft drinks	0.23	0.87	0.36
Rubber and tyres	0.52	0.86	0.43
Motor vehicles	0.54	0.85	0.52
Bread and biscuits	0.23	0.83	0.22
Aerospace	0.60	0.75	0.21
Other foods	0.21	0.75	0.21
Average of all sectors	0.25	0.46	0.30

Source of Entry into the Top Five Leadership

With on average more than half of leading production in a sector accounted for by firms who were not among the top five leading producers in 1987, it is interesting to examine where these new leading positions come from. New leading positions in the top five within an industry can come from diversifying matrix firms who had a leading position in another sector in 1987, or from 'de novo matrix firms' who were not previously in the matrix in 1987 (but could have been active in the sector in a non-top five position).

$$C5_{t+1} = PS5^{Lt}_{t+1} + PS5^{\text{DIV ENT}}_{t+1} + PS5^{\text{DE NOVO ENT}}_{t+1}. \qquad (4.2)$$

Table 4.10 reports the average values (arithmetic unweighted averages across sectors).

On average, new leading entry accounts for 15 per cent of the production share in a typical sector, while incumbent leaders also account for 15 per cent. Hence, new leading firms account for half of $C5_{00}$. Decomposing this market share of new leading entry, we can observe that most of the entry is coming from 'de novo matrix firms': these hold on average 10 per cent of industry production in 2000, while diversifying incumbent firms hold only half of this, namely 5 per cent. The small production share of diversifying incumbents, 5 per cent, can be correlated to the general trend of diminishing diversification and a return to the core activities in most of the sectors, as discussed in Veugelers et al. (2002).

Table 4.10   Decomposition of the average C5 in 2000

$C5_{00}$	$PS5^{L87}_{00}$	$PS5^{ENT}_{00}$	$PS5^{DIV\ ENT}_{00}$	$PS5^{NOV\ ENT}_{00}$	$PS5^{ENT}_{00}/C5_{00}$
0.30	0.15	0.15	0.05	0.10	50%

We can also split the entry according to geographical origin. Non-EU firms (including Austrian, Finnish and Swedish firms) entering into the leading top five positions after 1987 on average account for 5.9 per cent of total industry production in the EU (arithmetic average). While this is rather modest on average (there are 23 sectors with zero non-EU entry), there are some sectors where this entry is very substantial. Examples of such sectors are: musical instruments (57 per cent), clocks and watches (33 per cent) oils and fats (29 per cent), and pasta (22 per cent).

Linking Turbulence to Changes in Concentration

Finally, we test whether in industries where concentration is high and at the same time turbulence is low, concentration is more likely to increase or at least to be maintained at a high level, while if there were new leading firms in a highly concentrated industry, whether this 'entry' would reduce the producer concentration. This requires linking initial levels of market concentration and turbulence to changes in concentration. When splitting the high concentration sectors into high and low turbulence we find important and significant differences in changes in concentration (see Table 4.11). But the results do not entirely support the proposed hypothesis: highly concentrated sectors that have little turbulence in concentration (that is, relatively little, or less important, entry among the top five) witness on average a stable level of concentration (that is, a very small decline of less than 1 per cent). The highly concentrated sectors where turbulence is high (that is, there is important new entry among the leading firms) witness on average an increase in concentration by 7 per cent. However, the difference between the two subgroups is not statistically significant. All this seems to suggest that, on average, entry of new leaders in the top five position, replacing older leaders, seems to lead to similar production share positions of the leading five firms, hence leading to a stable concentration. The new leaders seem to be able to obtain more or less the same production share as the firms they are replacing in the top five.

Table 4.11   Average change in concentration 1987–2000[*]

	Total	High $C5_{87}$	Low $C5_{87}$	High $C5_{87}$ + High $PS5/C5$	High $C5_{87}$ + Low $PS5/C5$	Low $C5_{87}$ + High $PS5/C5$	Low $C5_{87}$ + High $PS5/C5$
$\Delta C5$	0.050	0.016	0.076	−0.003	0.072	0.041	0.103

Note: [*] Change in concentration is defined relative to the level of concentration. High and low turbulence are defined on values for $PS5^{L87}_{00}/C5_{00}$ smaller/larger than 60 per cent, which is the average value for $PS5^{L87}_{00}/C5_{00}$ for high concentration sectors.

When zeroing in on individual industries, namely the high concentration sectors with the highest and lowest turbulence, the same picture emerges (Table 4.12). Motor vehicle parts and sugar are illustrations of the proposed hypothesis, namely that highly concentrated sectors with high turbulence have problems maintaining their high concentration level. In these sectors the force of new leading entry reduces the dominance of the leading firms. Non-ferrous metals, oils and fats and pasta increased their concentration despite a high level of turbulence. Also confirming the hypothesis, but at the other end of the spectrum, is that four of the five sectors with the lowest turbulence managed to increase (or at least retain) their concentration level. These sectors are alcohol and spirits, glass, first processing of steel and soap and toiletries. The only exception is rubber and tyres, which shows a decline in concentration, despite the low turbulence. In summary we only find some support for one part of the hypothesis, namely that high concentration sectors in an environment of low turbulence on average retain or increase their concentration levels. But most of the high concentration–high turbulence sectors also manage to increase producer concentration. This result requires further investigation. It should be checked whether turbulence is the major explanatory variable for the changes in concentration occurring. This requires a multivariate analysis correcting for other correlated factors that may be driving the relationship. Most notably the importance of external shocks related to shifts in demand or costs, have to be included in the analysis. If the result proves to be robust, it is important from a policy point of view to assess whether the increase in production share of the leading firms reflects an improvement in the efficiency among leading firms, with less efficient incumbents being replaced by more efficient new leaders or whether it results from increased collusion. This requires looking at the impact on productivity and performance (compare Section 4.7).

Table 4.12   Linking turbulence and changes in concentration for selected
*   sectors*

	$C5_{87}$	$PS5^{L87}_{00}/C5_{00}$	$C5_{00}$
Sectors with high initial concentration and low turbulence			
Glass	0.38	1	0.37
Alcohol, spirits and wine	0.27	1	0.35
First processing of steel	0.36	0.91	0.52
Soap and toiletries	0.31	0.91	0.47
Rubber and tyres	0.52	0.86	0.43
Sectors with high initial concentration and high turbulence			
Motor vehicle parts	0.37	0	0.20
Non-ferrous metals	0.25	0.20	0.31
Oils and fats	0.26	0.22	0.53
Sugar	0.42	0.22	0.28
Pasta	0.36	0.34	0.38
Average of all sectors	0.25	0.46	0.30

Turbulence in Top Leadership

Price leadership is often suggested as a mechanism used by firms to coordinate their (pricing) decisions. Dominant-firm price leadership, with one single firm setting prices that are followed by the other firms in the industry, can support a monopolistic solution to the oligopolists pricing coordination problem, as already identified by Markham (1951). Hence, having a dominant and persistent firm in an industry can be associated with a higher probability of the leading firms reaching and maintaining collusive outcomes. The MSM allows the identification of the dominant firm as the firm which not only holds the largest production share but also has a considerable production share. This means an above average leading production share, that is, $C1>9$ per cent which is the average value across all industries in 1987. About one-third of the sectors classify accordingly. The most notable sectors with a dominant firm are lighting, with Philips as leader having a production share of 38 per cent, computers and office equipment, where IBM holds the leadership with 33 per cent, and rubber and tyres, where Michelin holds 26 per cent.

Stable leadership
For the 23 industries with a dominant firm, we can check the stability in leadership in Table 4.13. In only four sectors (that is, 17 per cent of all

sectors) with a dominant leader, the same leader persisted over the time period considered. The MSM further allows tracking the production share of the persistent leader over the time period considered, $\Delta PS1$.

Table 4.13   Changes in leading share in sectors with a dominant and persistent leader

	Cl_{87}	$\Delta PS1^*$	Cl_{00}
Rubber and tyres	0.26	-0.60	0.14
Glass	0.19	0.06	0.20
First processing of steel	0.12	0.08	0.13
Confectionery	0.10	−0.25	0.07
Average (std. dev.) for all sectors	0.17	−0.17	0.14
with high Cl_{87} and same leader	(0.08)	(0.32)	(0.05)

Note: * To calculate the change in production share of the leader in 1987 over time, defined as $\Delta PS1$, we used the following equation:

$$\Delta PS1 = (PS1^{L87}_{00} - PS1^{L87}_{87})/((PS1^{L87}_{00} + PS1^{L87}_{87})/2)$$

With $PS1^{L87}_{00}$ = the production share which the old leader from 1987 still holds in 2000 and $PS1^{L87}_{87}$ = the production share which the old leader from 1987 had in 1987 (= Cl_{87}). Cl_{87} = production share of leading firm in 1987; $\Delta PS1$ = change in production share of 1987 leading firm between 1987 and 1997; Cl_{00} = production share of leading firm in 2000.

On average, over the 13-year period considered, there was a decline of 17 per cent in the production share of the leading firm. But at the same time the large standard deviation shows that there is considerable variation around the mean. In rubber and tyres and confectionery, the leaders lose extensively in $PS1$ (their $\Delta PS1$ is substantially above the average of −17 per cent). In glass and first processing of steel, on the other hand, the leader has managed to slightly increase its leading position. All this indicates that on average even if a firm is able to maintain leadership, maintaining a solid position as leader is difficult, on average.

Changes in leadership
The difficulty of maintaining leadership is brought out even more by the large number of sectors in which there was a change in leadership. In 19 out of the 23 sectors where a dominant leader could be identified in 1987, this firm no longer holds the top position in 2000 and is hence replaced by a new leading firm. In most of these sectors, the new leader originates from the top three in the industry in 1987 or at least from the top five (see Table 4.14). Only in oils and fats, pasta and sugar did the new leader not

Microeconomic issues

hold a top five position in 1987 in the industry. Only for pasta was this new leader (Nestlé) already present in the matrix in 1987 with a leading position in another sector. In motor vehicle parts, railway and motor vehicles the new leader managed to move from a top five position in 1987 into the top position in 2000 by acquiring a firm not present in the matrix of 1987. In aerospace the top two in 1987, British Aerospace and Aerospatiale merged with Casa to attain the number one position in 2000. Finally, in steel tubes, a firm not yet present in the matrix, Salzgitter, got into the top position in 2000 by taking over the former number one, Mannesmann.

For the sectors where there was a change in the identity of the leading firm, we next checked the position of the old leader ($\Delta PS1$).

Table 4.14   Changes in C1 and PS1 for sectors with a high $C1_{87}$ and a new leader in 2000

	Cl_{87}	$\Delta PS1$	$PS1^{L87}_{00}/C1^{L00}_{00}$	Cl_{00}	
Average (std. dev) for all sectors	0.16	−0.86	0.49	0.15	
with a high Cl_{87} and a new leader	(0.08)	(0.82)	(0.35)	(0.06)	
Sector	Cl_{87}	$\Delta PS1$	$PS1^{L87}_{00}/C1^{L00}_{00}$	Cl_{00}	Origin of new leader	MA/JV*
Lighting	0.38	−1.16	0.56	0.18	Top 3	No
Computers and office equipment	0.33	−0.96	0.95	0.12	Top 5	No
Optical instruments	0.21	−2	0.00	0.14	Top 3	No
Aerospace	0.18	−1.02	0.26	0.23	Top 3	Yes
Pasta	0.18	−0.58	0.48	0.21	New	No
Cycles and motorcycles	0.17	−0.39	0.90	0.13	Top 5	No
Manmade fibres	0.17	−2	0.00	0.19	Top 5	No
Motor vehicle parts	0.16	−2	0.00	0.05	Top 5	Yes
Sugar	0.15	−0.91	0.79	0.07	New	No
Motor vehicles	0.13	−0.15	0.72	0.15	Top 5	Yes
Oils and fats	0.13	−0.27	0.48	0.20	New	No
Railway	0.12	−2	0.00	0.24	Top 5	Yes
Medical instruments	0.12	0.08	1	0.13	Top 3	No
Domestic appliances	0.11	−0.79	0.41	0.12	Top 5	No
Insulated wires and cables	0.11	0.18	0.72	0.18	Top 3	No
Tobacco	0.11	0.28	0.54	0.27	Top 5	No
Steel tubes	0.11	−2	0.00	0.07	Top 3	Yes
Telecom and electronic equipment	0.10	−0.79	0.66	0.07	Top 3	No
Soap and toiletries	0.10	0.23	0.84	0.14	Top 3	No

Note: * Only mergers and acquisitions and joint ventures among leading firms are considered.

On average there is a considerable decline in market share of the 1987 leader ($\Delta PS1$). As a consequence, if the dominant firm in 1987 loses its leading position to a new leader, there is a substantial loss in position of the old leader relative to the new leader as witnessed by a relatively low $PS1^{L87}_{00}/C1^{L00}_{00}$ measure, which indicates the production share in 2000 which the old leader of 1987 holds, relative to the production share which the new leader of 2000 holds in 2000. But again there is considerable variation across sectors.

In five sectors (optical instruments, railway, steel tubes, motor vehicle parts and manmade fibres), the old leader dropped out of the top five ($\Delta PS1$ = –2). For Bayer (optical instruments), Alcatel (railway) and Hoechst (now Aventis) (manmade fibres) this fitted into their strategy of refocusing on other sectors. In steel tubes Salzgitter acquired the top position by taking over Mannesmann, the leader in 1987. In motor vehicle parts, Bosch lost its position in the top five due to the entry of US firms (TRW and GM) and M&A activity (Faurecia). The sectors where the $PS1/C1$ ratio is higher than average (51 per cent) are all sectors where the $C1$ declined substantially. Hence, these are the sectors where the new leading position is less dominating, tempering the loss in position of the old leader relative to the new leader. This pattern is for instance observed in computer and office equipment, sugar and lighting. But there are also sectors where the new leader emerges as stronger than the old leader, such that $C1$ is much larger in 2000 than in 1987 (aerospace and oils and fats). In these cases the loss of position of the old leader, although relatively modest in absolute terms, is exacerbated when considered relative to the new stronger leader, resulting in a low value for $PS1/C1$, despite the modest loss in $PS1$.

Linking (Stability in) Leadership to (Stability in) Concentration

Finally in Table 4.15, we analyse to what extent having a dominant and persistent leader in an industry helps to establish and maintain collusion in the industry, as measured by the $C5$ ratio.

When a sector has a dominant leader which is also persistent (as defined by a high $C1$, and the same leader over the considered period) this sector tends to have a higher than average $C5$ concentration in 1987. Examples are rubber and tyres, first processing of steel and glass. For these sectors we find that not only is concentration $C5_{87}$ high, it is also stable or increasing over time. In rubber and tyres the concentration declined to about the average level in 2000.

In the sectors where the old leader did not manage to maintain its leading position, we find, on average, a high $C5$ in 1987 and in 2000. Since we know that in most cases the new leader was at least as dominant as the old leader, it seems that dominance suffices to maintain concentration, while stability seems less important, as long as the new leader is at least equally dominant. Nevertheless the variance in concentration in 2000 is higher in the sectors with changing leaders, where some sectors have witnessed a considerable decline in $C5$ – such as manmade fibres, aerospace, lighting and motor vehicle parts – while others have managed to increase concentration, such as tobacco, oils and fats and railway.

Table 4.15 Linking (stability in) leadership to (stability in) concentration

	$C5_{87}$	$C5_{00}$
All sectors	0.25	0.30
	(0.16)	(0.18)
Sectors with high Cl_{87} and stable leader	0.42	0.40
	(0.07)	(0.11)
Sectors with high Cl_{87} and new leader	0.43	0.44
	(0.12)	(0.16)

Note: $C5_{87}$ = total production share of five leading firms in 1987; $C5_{00}$ = total production share of five leading firms in 2000.

Although this crude analysis seems to suggest that dominant leadership is a catalyst for strong and stable collusion, any conclusion should await a full multivariate analysis of (changes in) concentration. The analysis only suggests an interesting possible explanatory variable to consider in such a full analysis.

4.7 CONCENTRATION, EFFICIENCY AND MARKET POWER

The MSM data have demonstrated the increasing size of leading firms, with a consequent increasing effect on producer concentration, especially in the last sub-period observed, 1997–2000. But there is considerable cross-industry variation. High concentration industries were found on average to be more likely to have decreasing production concentration. The MSM data also revealed a considerable turbulence among leading firms, both in the number of new firms in the top five and in the production shares of the old leaders. While these results may suggest pro-competitive effects from market integration, the cross-section evidence also suggests that, especially in the last sub-period there is a marked trend towards an increase in producer concentration on average and even in those sectors where concentration is decreasing, these decreases are modest. Furthermore, when there is turbulence due to new leading firms in highly concentrated sectors, these new leading firms typically succeed in maintaining and even increasing the leading production share.

While the MSM has allowed us to discuss changes in concentration in a period of ongoing market integration, the final goal of such analysis is to assess the impact of changes in concentration (or the lack thereof) on EU welfare. The SMP through a more competitive environment, 'will translate into a combination of a reduction in mark-ups and a reduction in costs, where those were due to the presence of X-inefficiency or inefficiently small scales of operation' (European Commission, 1996, p. 128). Using data up to 1996, in a first assessment the European Commission (1996) found that the SMP indeed had had an impact on productivity, prices and cost margins. In addition, the Commission concluded that 'the completion of the internal market following the elimination of non-tariff barriers between EU countries, will ... lead to a higher degree of price convergence as far as it promotes a competitive pressure by imports and decreases the disparity in consumers' preferences between countries' (European Commission, 1996, p. 161). In fact, there has been a convergence in EU-15 price levels, which continues beyond the SMP period (European Commission, 2001).

Using the MSM data for 1997, in the following we provide a rough exploration of the link between concentration and market efficiency. Since the MSM does not collect information on firm costs or profits, efficiency and profitability is assessed at the industry level. Specifically, we ask whether (changes in) concentration are correlated with changes in labour productivity and price–cost margins at the industry level. We measure these effects for the period after the implementation of the SMP, that is, 1993–96/7. A full treatment of the effects of concentration on market efficiency is beyond the scope of the current chapter, since it would require much richer data and econometric analysis. Here we will report the univariate results, which have been further tested in a multivariate analysis, reported in Veugelers et al. (2002).

(Changes in) concentration matter because of their effect on market power and efficiency. We start with efficiency, as measured by labour productivity growth of the industry. The correlation coefficient for productivity growth and concentration is positive and significant (see Table 4.16). But the numbers already indicate that the relationship is, at least, not simply linear. Although low concentration sectors have the slowest increase in labour productivity, the highest concentration sectors have a smaller increase in labour productivity when compared with the medium concentration groups. When relating changes in concentration to productivity growth, no significant effect shows up in the univariate statistics. However, in an econometric analysis of productivity growth à la Barro, correcting for other determinants, Veugelers et al. (2002) find a negative and significant coefficient for change in concentration. Hence, productivity growth appears to be higher in sectors where concentration is declining. Since we know from the previous section that the highly concentrated sectors are also the ones with the largest decreases in concentration, both univariate and multivariate results point in the same direction, namely that the high concentration sectors witness the largest decreases in concentration and have the higher productivity growth.

Table 4.16   Linking concentration (1987) to changes in labour productivity and price–cost margins (1993–96/7)

Quantiles of concentration	Average concentration	Average annual growth of labour productivity	Price–cost margin[a]	Speed of price convergence
First quantile 0–25	0.08	2.04	0.15	0.50
Second quantile 25–50	0.18	3.69	0.16	0.43
Third quantile 50–75	0.30	3.21	0.15	0.36
Fourth quantile 75–100	0.56	2.87	0.14	0.26
Total	0.24	2.82	0.15	0.44
Spearman Rank Correlation		0.18**	0.06*	

Notes:
** significant at 1%; * significant at 5%.
For data availability reasons, not all 72 sectors are included for price–cost margins (n = 53) and speed of convergence (n = 49).
[a] Defined as (value added – wage costs)/gross production.

As is well known from standard industrial economics theory, higher concentration should be positively related to profits. The effect of concentration on price–cost margins (PCMs) encompasses an efficiency effect and a market power effect. When correlating concentration levels to industry price–cost margins as an imperfect proxy for profits, we find a positive, but only weak link (see Table 4.16). Also in an econometric analysis linking PCMs to industry concentration, Veugelers et al. (2002) find a weak, but positive sign. Since this positive effect could be due to the efficiency effect (see above), this is by no means a proof of market power associated with concentration.

A final piece of information we can use to assess market power is price dispersion within the EU, across Member States. We would expect price differentiation to prevail in highly concentrated markets, where firms enjoy market power. Increasing market integration would reduce the scope for price differentiation if it reduces market power.

Using as input the standard deviation of the price level index (source: European Commission), Veugelers et al. (2002) estimate the speed of convergence in price levels using the concept of σ-convergence as formulated by Barro and Sala-i-Martin (1995). They find that concentration is uncorrelated with the average level of price dispersion, but that the speed of the decline in price dispersion depends on the level of concentration. As the last column in Table 4.16 shows, the estimated speed of adjustment is much lower in concentrated industries. Although this result does not necessarily indicate the existence of market power, it is consistent with it.

4.8   CONCLUSIONS

An analysis of the Market Share Matrix data over time (1987–2000) provided a rich and detailed mapping of how industry concentration has changed within EU manufacturing in a period of ongoing market integration. The results suggest that production concentration initially did not change very much on average, but has increased in the last sub-period considered (1997–2000). However, this average hides a rich diversity across industries – in many cases, there have been dramatic changes over the decade as a whole, and especially in the post-1993 period. Highly concentrated sectors in particular have witnessed a decline in concentration, but nevertheless remain at above average concentration levels. At the same time, there has been considerable turbulence in market leadership in EU manufacturing industries. Over a period of 13 years, the leading top five companies from 1987 have lost more than half of their production share position in 2000 relative to new leading firms. Also, among the leading top five firms there is considerable turbulence. In most of the sectors with a dominant leader in 1987, a new leader had emerged in 2000.

When zeroing in on sectors, high concentration sectors witness more persistence in top five leadership. We find no support on average for the hypothesis that stability works positively for concentration levels. On the contrary, highly concentrated sectors that have little turbulence in leadership, relatively little or less important entry among the top five leading producers, witness on average a loss in concentration. The highly concentrated sectors where turbulence is high, that is, sectors where there is important new entry among the leading firms, witness on average an increase in concentration. The new leaders seem to be able to obtain a higher production share than the firms they are replacing in the top five. A further characteristic to predict high concentration is the presence of a dominant leader in the industry. Our crude analysis seems to suggest that a catalyst for strong and stable industry concentration is the presence of a dominant leader in the industry, which does not necessarily need to be the same firm over time.

When linking our concentration measure to industry performance measures, the results, although preliminary, are in line with previous research. We find that productivity growth is significantly higher in industries exhibiting a tendency of decreasing concentration. Additionally, productivity and profitability are higher in concentrated industries, while the process of the decrease in price dispersion is slower.

All in all, while the time comparison of the MSM results have generated interesting results, they call for further work. In-depth multivariate analysis fully taking into account the interdependence between structural characteristics in a dynamic framework is clearly needed to confirm the tendencies discovered in the data and to identify the true drivers of the observed trends.

But further work is also clearly needed to expand the MSM data over time. Always keeping in mind the fragility of the data, the MSM data have uncovered an acceleration in turbulence during the later periods considered. This confirms that market integration forces continue to be important beyond the 1992 project. This ongoing process of market integration on a global scale and the acceleration in dynamics in the later years of the observation period, which was uncovered in the chapter, call for a continued updating of the matrix and a constant monitoring of the effects of changes in concentration on market performance.

NOTES

*   The author would like to express her gratitude for (financial) support received from the European Commission and Ernst & Young. The author would also like to thank the contributors to the MSM research project (KUL, CERIS, UEA and WIFO) and more particularly Steve Davies, Peter Egger and Michael Pfaffermayr for their input into this chapter. The research assistance of An Van Pelt (Ernst & Young Researcher at KUL) is gratefully acknowledged.
1. See also Smith and Venables (1991), Venables (1990a), Venables (1990b), Baldwin and Venables (1995).

2. The principles, methodology and data sources of the 1987 MSM are detailed in Davies et al. (chapter 3). For the 1987–97 MSM, see Veugelers et al. (2002).
3. Although the list of matrix firms is not likely to differ much from a list of the largest European firms, there are some differences. On the one hand the matrix will include some small firms which have qualified to be leader in a smaller industry. On the other hand, it will exclude some firms of large size which because they are diversified, never attain a top five position in any particular industry or because they lie just outside the top five in a very large industry such as cars or aircraft.
4. In fact dividing the number of potential leading positions by the actual number of matrix firms gives a rough indication of the extent of diversification with strong market power implications.
5. Since some large firms will not appear on the matrix, as explained before, this figure understates aggregate concentration.
6. While the $C5$ measure is based on the five leading firms' production only, the coverage also includes production by non-leading firms, which hold a leading position in other matrix sectors. The divergence between coverage and concentration is typically associated with inward diversification from firms who have a leading position elsewhere.
7. See Davies et al. (1996) for more detail.
8. Within the set of sensitive industries, four groups were defined. Group 1 consists of industries that are associated with public procurement and are industries in which demand is growing strongly (including information technology, office automation, telecommunications, medical equipment). Group 2 comprises more traditional industries (electric boilers, railway equipment, pharmaceutical products) characterised by high non-tariff barriers with little openness. In group 3 (including shipbuilding, electrical and electronic equipment, certain food-processing activities) industries are structurally similar to those of group 2, except that price dispersion is much smaller (shipbuilding, electrical engineering). Group 4 comprises industries characterised by moderate non-tariff barriers, such as different national standards and administrative controls. Many of the products in this group are consumer goods (radios, televisions, domestic electrical appliances, clothing, footwear, toys).
9. But note that there are only three industries included: ICT, telecom and medical equipment.

REFERENCES

Baldwin, R.E. and Venables, A.J. (1995), 'Multinational firms and the new trade theory', National Bureau of Economic Research, Working paper series 5036, Cambridge, MA.

Barro, R.J. and Sala-i-Martin, X. (1995), *Economic Growth*, New York: McGraw-Hill.

Buigues, P., Ilzkovitz, F. and Lebrun, J.-F. (1990), 'The impact of the internal market by industrial sector: the challenge for the Member States', *European Economy*, special edition.

Caves R.E. and Porter M.E. (1978), 'Market structure, oligopoly and stability of market shares', *Journal of Industrial Economics*, **26**(4), 289–313.

Davies, S.W., Lyons, B.R., Matraves, C., Rondi, L., Sembenelli, A., Gual, J., Sleuwaegen, L. and Veugelers, R. (1996), *Industrial Organisation in the European Union*, Oxford: Clarendon Press.

Davies, S., Rondi, L. and Sembenelli, A. (1998), 'S.E.M. and the changing structure of EU manufacturing, 1987–1993', CERIS Working paper N.5/1998.

European Commission (1996), 'Economic evaluation of the Internal Market', *European Economy: Reports and Studies*, no. 4.

European Commission (2001), 'Price levels and price dispersion in the EU', *European Economy: Supplement A*, no. 7.

Krugman, P. (1979), 'Increasing returns, monopolistic competition and international trade', *Journal of International Economics*, **9**(4), 469–79.

Markham, J. (1951), 'Nature and significance of price leadership', *American Economic Review*, **41**, 891–905.

Smith, A. and Venables, A.J. (1988), 'Completing the internal market in the European Community: some industry simulations', *European Economic Review*, **32**(7), 1501–25.

Smith, A. and Venables, A.J. (1991), 'Economic integration and market access', *European Economic Review*, **35**(2–3), 388–95.

Sutton, J. (1991), *Sunk Costs and Market Structure*, Cambridge, MA: MIT Press.

Venables A.J. (1990a), 'The economic integration of oligopolistic markets', *European Economic Review*, **34**(4), 753–69

Venables A.J. (1990b), 'Trade policy under imperfect competition: a numerical assessment', Centre for Economic Policy Research Discussion Paper 412.

Van Pelt, A., Devoldere, I., Veugelers, R. and Sleuwaegen, L. (2002), 'Sources of leadership in EU manufacturing', KUL-VLGMS-E&Y, mimeo.

Veugelers, R., Sleuwaegen L., De Voldere, I., Reynaerts, J., Rommens, K., Rondi, L., Vannoni, D., Benfratello, L., Davies, S., Egger, P. and Pfaffermayr, M. (2002), 'Determinants of industrial concentration, market integration and efficiency in the European Union', Chapter 3 in 'European integration and the functioning of product markets', *European Economy: Special Report*, no. 2.

Yip, G. (1995), *Total Global Strategy: Managing for Worldwide Competitive Advantage*, Englewood Cliffs: Prentice-Hall.

5. The location of European industry

Karen-Helene Midelfart, Henry G. Overman, Stephen J. Redding and Anthony J. Venables*

INTRODUCTION

Closer European integration is likely to bring with it major changes in industrial location. Industries will move to exploit differences in countries' comparative advantages and, even if such differences are small, integration may change the attractiveness of central areas relative to peripheral ones and may facilitate the clustering of activities that benefit from linkages with each other.

There are many reasons to welcome such changes. The gains from exploiting comparative advantage can only be achieved by industrial relocation, and clustering brings economic benefits as firms gain better access to suppliers and other complementary activities. But relocation will typically involve short-run adjustment costs before the long-run benefits are achieved. Specialisation may also make countries more vulnerable to the effects of shocks in particular industries, which will be costly if cross-country adjustment mechanisms are inadequate.

The objectives of this chapter are to describe the changes in industrial location that have occurred in Europe in recent decades; to establish whether these are associated with countries' economic structures becoming more or less similar, and industries becoming more or less spatially concentrated; to compare industrial location patterns in Europe and the US; and to identify the underlying forces that determine industrial location and assess the extent to which these have changed in recent years.

Our main findings are as follows.

- Most European countries showed significant convergence of their industrial structure during the 1970s, but this trend was reversed in the early 1980s. There has been substantial divergence from the early 1980s onwards, as countries have become increasingly different from the average of the rest of the EU and, in bilateral comparisons, from most of their EU partners.

- The most dramatic changes in industry structure have been the expansion of relatively high-technology and high-skill industries in Ireland and in Finland. However, the specialisation process has occurred more generally, with nearly all countries showing increasing difference from the early 1980s onwards.
- Many, although not all, industries have experienced significant changes in their location. Key features of these changes include:

  – A number of industries that were initially spatially dispersed have become more concentrated. These are mainly slow growing and unskilled labour-intensive industries whose relative contraction has been accompanied by spatial concentration, usually in peripheral low-wage economies.
  – Amongst industries that were initially spatially concentrated, around half stayed concentrated. Significant dispersion has occurred in a number of medium and high-technology industries and in relatively high growth sectors, with activity typically spreading out from the central European countries.

- Econometric analysis identifies the underlying forces that determine industrial location, and we show that a high proportion of the cross-country variation in industrial structure can be explained by a combination of factor cost and geographical considerations. Four main results come from the econometrics:

  – The location of R&D-intensive industries has become increasingly responsive to countries' endowments of researchers, with these industries moving into researcher abundant locations.
  – The location of non-manual labour-intensive industries was, and remains, sensitive to the proportion of countries' labour forces with secondary and higher education.
  – The location of industries with strong forward and backward linkages has become increasingly sensitive to the centrality/ peripherality of countries. Thus, central locations are increasingly attracting industries higher up the value added chain (that is, industries which are highly dependent on intermediate inputs).
  – Industries which have a high degree of increasing returns to scale tend to locate in central regions, but this effect has diminished markedly over the period.

- Services are in general more dispersed than manufacturing. Two trends – the general shift from manufacturing to services, and catch-up by poorer countries with small initial services sectors – have reinforced this spatial dispersion of services.

• While the industrial structures of EU countries are diverging, those of US states are converging. However, in so far as it is possible to make any comparison of levels of industrial concentration between the EU and the US, we find that EU industries are still less concentrated than are those in the US.

Our results on specialisation and concentration indices are broadly consistent with other studies in the area (for example, Brülhart and Torstensson, 1996; Amiti, 1999; OECD, 1999; WIFO, 1999), although differences arise due to differences in data, time periods and measurement techniques. We go beyond existing studies in a number of different ways. First, we draw out the relationship between the characteristics of industries and the characteristics of the countries in which they are located. Thus, we trace out how the industrial composition of each EU country has become more or less biased with respect to a set of industry characteristics, including capital intensity, skill intensity and technology intensity. Second, we introduce a new measure of spatial dispersion that takes into account the relative locations of clusters of industries. Using existing concentration measures, two industries may appear equally geographically concentrated, while one is predominantly located in two neighbouring countries, and the other split between Finland and Portugal. By taking into account the relative locations of concentrations of industries our measure allows us to discriminate between these two alternatives. We use the measure to study the evolution of location patterns in the EU. It also allows us to carry out a meaningful comparison of the EU and US economic geographies, something which has not been possible with the measures available hitherto.

Our econometric analysis breaks new ground by developing a specification which systematically relates the location of production to industry and country characteristics. We developed our empirical model by constructing a simulation model which incorporates both comparative advantage and new economic geography forces and allowing that model to guide our choice of econometric specification. Estimating our empirical model using EU data allows us to show how some factors have become more important in determining location, and others less. We find that skilled and scientific labour abundance are becoming more important considerations in determining industrial location, and that the pull of centrality is becoming more important for industries that are intensive users of intermediate goods, although less important for industries with high returns to scale. This suggests that a new pattern of industrial specialisation is developing, and that the changes we map out in descriptive sections of the chapter are the manifestations of this change.[1]

The structure of the chapter is as follows. In the next section we briefly outline our data sources and the main variables that we use. Section 5.2 looks at EU countries, showing how their industrial structures differ, and presenting evidence of increasing difference in recent years. Section 5.3 turns to industries, and shows how their location patterns have changed. We present evidence that a number of sectors have become more spatially concentrated, while others have become more dispersed.

In both sections 5.2 and 5.3 we link the changes to industrial characteristics using graphical techniques and descriptive statistics. Section 5.4 undertakes a full multivariate econometric analysis of the way in which characteristics of countries interact with characteristics of industries to determine the pattern of industrial location. Both factor supply and geographical variables drive location patterns, although the importance of different factors has changed markedly over time.

Sections 5.5 and 5.6 change focus, looking respectively at the location of service industries, and at a comparison of the EU with the US. We show that the available evidence shows a slight dispersion in service sector activity. The US is continuing a process of industrial de-concentration, although the data suggests that many US industries are still more concentrated than their EU counterparts. Section 5.7 concludes and offers some preliminary predictions and a discussion of policy implications.

5.1 DATA AND MEASUREMENT

Our main data source is the OECD STAN database. This provides production data for 13 EU countries and 36 industries, from 1970 to 1997. We combine this with production data for Ireland from the UN UNIDO database, giving us data on a set of 14 EU countries (the EU-15, excluding Luxembourg). The production data are complemented by trade data from the UN Com-Trade database for 14 countries and 104 industries, for the years 1970 to 1996. The level of aggregation provided by STAN might mask changes in national specialisation and industrial concentration occurring at the intra-sectoral level. Hence, in addition we use production data from Eurostat's DAISIE database. This provides a level of desegregation that is finer than STAN, but there are a significant number of missing observations and the data only covers the much shorter time period 1985 to 1997. We use it to cross-check the generality of our results. More detailed information on all three data sources is provided in Appendix 5.A.

The basic unit of analysis is the activity level – measured, when using the production data, by the gross value of output – of industry k in country i

at time t, which we shall denote $x_i^k(t)$. We usually want to work with this expressed as a share, either of activity in the country, or total EU activity in the industry. We call these shares

$$v_i^k(t) \equiv x_i^k(t) / \Sigma_k x_i^k(t) \qquad (5.1)$$

$$s_i^k(t) \equiv x_i^k(t) / \Sigma_k x_i^k(t) \qquad (5.2)$$

Thus $v_i^k(t)$ is the share of sector k in the total activity of country i, which forms the basis of our analysis of countries in Section 5.2; $s_i^k(t)$ is the share of country i in the total activity of industry k, which is the basis of the industry analysis of sections 5.3 and 5.4.

Previous studies on the location of production in Europe have used value-added instead of gross production value as measure of activity level. However, the use of value-added makes the analysis much more vulnerable to structural shifts in outsourcing to other sectors. Over the period we study there have been large changes in outsourcing, particularly increased outsourcing of service sector intermediates (see section 5.5 for a more detailed discussion), and it is this that motivates our use of gross production value.[2]

We link industrial activity levels to industrial characteristics (such as factor intensities and returns to scale) and to country characteristics (such as factor endowments and market potential). Data for these measures were collected from a variety of sources, including the OECD and Eurostat, and are described in detail in Appendix 5.B.

While the major part of this chapter focuses on manufacturing industries, we also consider services using data from the OECD services database. The comparison of the economic geography of Europe with that of the US, draws on US state-level data for manufacturing employment, 1970–97.

5.2   THE SPECIALISATION OF COUNTRIES

In this section we look at the production structures of EU countries, and address three questions. How specialised are countries? How similar are the industrial structures of different countries? What are the characteristics of industries located in each country? We trace out changes through time and show that the picture is one of growing differences between countries, at least from the early 1980s onwards.

How Specialised are Countries?

We begin by considering a key question – how specialised are EU countries? Our approach is to construct a measure which allows us to compare each country's industrial structure with that of the average of the rest of the EU. In the next section, we then use the same type of measure to compare the production structures of different countries, and report a full set of bilateral comparisons for all fourteen countries with each other country.

To construct the measure of specialisation we proceed as follows. For each country, we calculate the share of industry k in that country's total manufacturing output (gross production value). As outlined in Section 5.1, we call this variable $v_i^k(t)$. Corresponding to this, we can calculate the share of the same industry in the production of all other countries, denoted $\bar{v}_i^k(t)$. We can then measure the difference between the industrial structure of country i and all other countries by taking the absolute values of the difference between these shares, summed over all industries,

$$K_i(t) = \Sigma_k abs[v_i^k(t) - \bar{v}_i^k(t)] \tag{5.3}$$

with $\bar{v}_i^k(t) \equiv \Sigma_{ji} x_i^k(t) / \Sigma_k \Sigma_{ji} x_i^k(t)$.

We call this the Krugman specialisation index, or K-spec (see Krugman, 1991). It takes value zero if country i has an industrial structure identical to the rest of the EU, and takes maximum value two if it has no industries in common with the rest of the EU.

Values of these indices for each country are given in Table 5.1. They are calculated for four-year averages[3] at the dates indicated, with bold indicating the minimum value attained by each country. The table reports them for each country and, in the bottom two rows, the average (simple, and weighted by country size).

Looking first at the averages, we see a fall between 1970/73 and 1980/83, indicating that locations became more similar. But from 1980/83 onwards there has been a more or less steady increase, indicating divergence. Turning to individual countries, we see that from 1970/73 to 1980/83 ten out of fourteen countries became less specialised, while between 1980/83 and 1994/97, all countries except the Netherlands experienced an increase in specialisation. That is, they became increasingly different from the rest of the EU.[4]

The magnitude of the size of the changes is also informative. For example, given production in the rest of the EU, Ireland's coefficient of K-spec in 1994/97 took a value of 0.779, indicating that 39 per cent of total production would have to change industry to get in line with the rest of the EU (that is 0.779 per cent divided by 2, because the measure counts positive and negative deviations for all sectors). Thus, from 1980/83 to 1994/97 (the changes given in column 5), 7.8 per cent of Ireland's production changed to industries out of line with the rest of Europe.

Table 5.1   Krugman specialisation index (production data, 4-year averages)

	70/73	80/83	88/91	94/97	94/97– 80/83	94/97 Computed
Austria	0.314	**0.275**	0.281	0.348	0.073	0.057
Belgium	**0.327**	0.353	0.380	0.451	0.099	0.088
Denmark	0.562	**0.553**	0.585	0.586	0.033	0.026
Spain	0.441	**0.289**	0.333	0.338	0.049	0.043
Finland	0.598	**0.510**	0.528	0.592	0.083	0.034
France	0.204	**0.188**	0.207	0.201	0.013	0.019
UK	0.231	**0.190**	0.221	0.206	0.017	0.016
Germany	0.319	**0.309**	0.354	0.370	0.061	0.055
Greece	**0.531**	0.580	0.661	0.703	0.123	0.105
Ireland	0.701	**0.623**	0.659	0.779	0.156	0.197
Italy	**0.351**	0.353	0.357	0.442	0.089	0.119
Netherlands	**0.508**	0.567	0.547	0.517	−0.050	−0.046
Portugal	0.536	**0.478**	0.588	0.566	0.088	0.088
Sweden	0.424	**0.393**	0.402	0.497	0.103	0.110
Average	0.432	**0.404**	0.436	0.471		
Weighted average	0.326	**0.302**	0.330	0.354		

This growing divergence of production structures could be due either to initial differences being magnified by industries having different EU-wide growth rates (so a country with a high initial share in a fast growing industry will become more different), or to countries moving in and out of industries (which we call 'differential change'). The final column in Table 5.1 captures this differential change. It gives the difference between the actual 1994/97 specialisation index, and what it would have been had production in each industry in each country grown at the EU-wide rate for that industry (obtained by projecting the 1980/83 values for each industry forward at the EU average growth rate for that industry). We see that more than 80 per cent of the actual change is 'differential change', while the remainder is due to amplification of initial differences.

Table 5.1 reports outcomes for selected time points, based on a four-year moving average. A figure plotting the time series for all countries and each year is confusing, but it is insightful to plot a two-year moving average for countries grouped by their EU accession date. This is done in Figure 5.1. The different heights of the curves essentially reflect different country sizes (thus EC1 is relatively low because of the predominance of Germany, France and Italy). More interesting, are the different patterns of change.

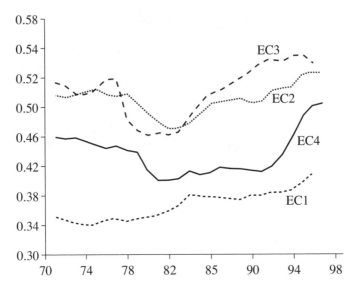

Note: EC1 comprises Belgium, France, Germany, Italy and the Netherlands. EC2 comprises Denmark, Ireland and the UK. EC3 comprises Greece, Spain and Portugal. Finally EC4 comprises Austria, Finland and Sweden.

Figure 5.1   Countries grouped by EC entry date (two-year moving average, unweighted)

For the initial entrants there is a more or less steady increase throughout the period. The 1973 and 1980s entrants (EC2 and EC3) exhibit an increase from the early 1980s. The last wave (EC4) show increasing K-spec measures from around 1992 onwards.

Our findings of a general increase in specialisation during the last decade are consistent with those of a recent study by WIFO (which only considers data for 1988 to 1998). With respect to individual countries, our results do not always coincide completely. This might be partly due to the fact that WIFO (1999) is based on analysis of value-added data, not gross production value data as employed here. As we suggested in Section 5.1, changes in value-added data may partly be driven by the large changes in the degree of outsourcing that we have witnessed in the last decades. Another possible reason for the discrepancies is the fact that we use four-year averaging to account for business cycle developments, while WIFO uses annual data. The WIFO report differs in one other important aspect – the degree of sectoral desegregation. Their use of the DAISIE data set allows a greater degree of desegregation than our data set. Midelfart et al. (2000a) provide a further comparison of the results and provide additional results at this more desegregate level. Two broad conclusions emerge. First, three-digit sectors tend to follow their two-digit counterparts suggesting that our aggregate measures are informative about movements at the more desegregate level. Second, the DAISIE data set, with its short time span, misses many of the larger changes in specialisation patterns that occurred pre-1988.

The Krugman specialisation index is just one measure of specialisation. However, other statistics paint the same broad picture. Here, we briefly consider results for alternative indices, beginning with the Gini coefficient. The Gini coefficient[5] is defined over the relative share measures, $r_i^k(t)$:

$$r_i^k(t) \equiv v_i^k(t) / \bar{v}_i^k(t) \tag{5.4}$$

We report the average Gini coefficient in Table 5.2. Just like the K-spec index, the Gini coefficient of specialisation indicates a general decline in specialisation from 1970/73 to 1980/83, that is followed by an increase in specialisation from 1980/83 to 1994/97. Other statistics can be computed, and they reveal further features of the shape of the distribution. Thus, we also look at the first to fourth moments of the distribution of $r_i^k(t)$, pooled across countries and industries. These summary statistics are also reported in Table 5.2. The most important points to note are that – from 1980/83 onwards – there has been a large increase in the variance of relative shares, once again indicating greater dispersion. The distribution has positive skew which increases over time, as would be expected if a process of clustering or extreme specialisation were taking place (with a few industries becoming particularly dominant in some locations). There is also some evidence of increasing kurtosis, indicating growing weight in the tails of the distribution.

Table 5.2 Summary measures of relative shares

	70/73	80/83	88/91	94/97
Gini	0.321	0.312	0.334	0.355
Mean	1.008	0.979	1.004	1.004
Variance	0.471	0.419	0.525	0.611
Skewness	2.357	2.34	2.38	2.56
Kurtosis	13.53	13.62	12.66	14.07

Finally, a simple experiment suggests that these reported changes may reflect an unravelling of specialisation patterns in the first decade, followed by a reinforcement of new patterns in the following two decades. Thus, if we regress 1980/83 log values of $r_i^k(t)$ on the 1970/73 values, we get a coefficient of 0.818 ($t = 39$). This suggests that, on average, a country which had a comparative advantage in any given industry in 1970, saw that comparative advantage weaken over the following decade. In contrast, a regression of the 1994/97 log values of $r_i^k(t)$ on the 1980/83 log values gives a coefficient significantly greater than unity (1.071, $t = 34$), indicating that there has been a 'deepening' of specialisation over the period. Industries that had a large share in a country tended to see this amplified.

How Similar are Countries' Industrial Structures?

The industry shares $v_i^k(t)$ for each country can be compared with the corresponding shares for the rest of the EU as a whole, as in Table 5.1, or with shares for other individual countries. Making this comparison yields a full matrix of bilateral differences between the industrial structures of pairs of countries. Tables 5.3a and 5.3b report these bilateral measures for 1980/83 and 1994/97 respectively. The tables are most easily read by selecting a country and reading across the row for that country; smaller numbers indicate similarity to the country in the column, and larger numbers indicate greater difference. We have highlighted the most different countries in bold and the most similar in bold italics.

The main point to note from these tables is that, of the 91 distinct pairs, 71 exhibit increasing difference between 1980/83 and 1994/97.

Element by element study of the matrices is laborious, but it is worth drawing attention to a few of the more important features. First, France, Britain and Germany are most like each other; between Britain and France the degree of similarity has increased, but Germany has become somewhat different. They are each fairly similar to Italy, although the degree of similarity has declined (Italy is most like Austria in both periods). France, Britain and Germany are most dissimilar to Greece and Ireland, and their dissimilarity is increasing.

Turning to the lower income countries, Greece and Portugal are most similar to each other, as well as to Spain, although becoming less so. Spain is, however, more similar to France and Great Britain than to Greece and Portugal. This observation is most likely explained by Spain being the most advanced country out of these three cohesion countries rather than a result of country size effects. The calculations presented below confirm that Spain has a very different industrial structure to the other two countries.

In 1994/97 Greece, Portugal and Spain shared the same most different economies – Finland, Sweden and Ireland. Finland and Sweden are most similar to each other. Ireland is most similar to Denmark, but very different from Finland and Sweden, and very (and increasingly) different from Greece and Portugal. The Netherlands – the only country that becomes more similar

Table 5.3a   Bilateral differences, 1980–83

	Austria	Belgium	Denmark	Spain	Finland	France	UK	Germany	Greece	Ireland	Italy	Netherlands	Portugal	Sweden
Austria	0.00	0.44	0.61	0.40	0.55	0.38	*0.32*	0.33	0.61	**0.67**	0.36	**0.67**	0.50	0.45
Belgium	0.44	0.00	0.59	0.34	0.59	*0.34*	0.42	0.43	0.59	**0.66**	0.51	0.42	0.49	0.63
Denmark	0.61	0.59	0.00	0.62	0.58	0.57	0.56	0.65	**0.74**	*0.42*	0.64	0.51	0.63	0.63
Spain	0.40	0.34	0.62	0.00	0.55	*0.26*	0.37	0.40	0.42	**0.67**	0.40	0.60	0.40	0.56
Finland	0.55	0.59	0.58	0.55	0.00	0.49	0.54	0.66	0.65	**0.82**	0.65	0.62	0.62	*0.41*
France	0.38	0.34	0.57	0.26	0.49	0.00	*0.22*	0.31	0.57	**0.63**	0.39	0.51	0.47	0.41
UK	0.32	0.42	0.56	0.37	0.54	*0.22*	0.00	0.25	0.61	**0.67**	0.40	0.53	0.55	0.39
Germany	0.33	0.43	0.65	0.40	0.66	0.31	*0.25*	0.00	0.73	**0.75**	0.43	0.64	0.64	0.42
Greece	0.61	0.59	0.74	0.42	0.65	0.57	0.61	0.73	0.00	**0.83**	0.62	0.64	*0.25*	0.80
Ireland	0.67	0.66	0.42	0.67	0.82	0.63	0.67	0.75	0.83	0.00	0.67	0.72	0.71	**0.85**
Italy	*0.36*	0.51	0.64	0.40	0.65	0.39	0.40	0.43	0.62	0.67	0.00	**0.78**	0.48	0.52
Netherlands	0.67	0.42	*0.51*	0.60	0.62	0.51	0.53	0.64	0.64	**0.72**	**0.78**	0.00	0.55	0.66
Portugal	0.50	0.49	0.63	0.40	0.62	0.47	0.55	0.64	0.25	**0.71**	0.48	0.55	0.00	**0.71**
Sweden	0.45	0.63	0.63	0.56	0.41	0.41	*0.39*	0.42	0.80	**0.85**	0.52	0.66	0.71	0.00

123

Table 5.3b Bilateral differences, 1994–97

	Austria	Belgium	Denmark	Spain	Finland	France	UK	Germany	Greece	Ireland	Italy	Netherlands	Portugal	Sweden
Austria	0.00	0.54	0.59	0.48	0.58	0.43	*0.39*	0.46	0.78	**0.81**	0.43	0.64	0.57	0.55
Belgium	0.54	0.00	0.54	0.47	**0.76**	0.44	0.48	0.61	0.63	0.69	0.57	*0.42*	0.64	**0.76**
Denmark	0.59	0.54	0.00	0.61	0.69	0.57	0.58	**0.72**	0.70	0.63	0.61	*0.51*	0.68	0.66
Spain	0.48	0.47	0.61	0.00	0.78	*0.33*	0.38	0.43	0.57	**0.85**	0.53	0.58	0.50	0.63
Finland	0.58	0.76	0.69	0.78	0.00	0.62	0.58	0.66	**0.97**	0.87	0.66	0.71	0.86	*0.42*
France	0.43	0.44	0.57	*0.33*	0.62	0.00	*0.19*	0.35	0.69	**0.78**	0.51	0.46	0.55	0.51
UK	*0.39*	0.48	0.58	0.38	0.58	*0.19*	0.00	0.36	0.72	**0.77**	0.47	0.46	0.59	0.51
Germany	0.46	0.61	0.72	0.43	0.66	0.35	0.36	0.00	**0.86**	0.82	0.49	0.61	0.74	0.49
Greece	0.78	0.63	0.70	0.57	0.97	0.69	0.72	**0.86**	0.00	0.91	0.76	0.62	*0.49*	**1.03**
Ireland	**0.81**	0.69	*0.63*	0.85	0.87	0.78	0.77	0.82	0.91	0.00	0.82	0.68	**0.99**	0.88
Italy	*0.43*	0.57	0.61	0.53	0.66	0.51	0.47	0.49	**0.82**	**0.82**	0.00	0.77	0.56	0.60
Netherlands	0.64	*0.42*	0.51	0.58	0.71	0.46	0.46	0.61	0.62	0.68	**0.77**	0.00	0.64	0.69
Portugal	0.57	0.64	0.68	0.50	0.86	0.55	0.59	0.74	*0.49*	**0.99**	0.56	0.64	0.00	0.84
Sweden	0.55	0.76	0.66	0.63	*0.42*	0.51	0.51	0.49	**1.03**	0.88	0.60	0.69	0.84	0.00

to the rest of the EU – also becomes more similar to all countries except Finland, Portugal and Sweden.

Evidently, many more comparisons can be made. The main point is that the vast majority of countries experienced a growing difference between their industrial structure and that of their EU partners.

Evidence from the Trade Data

Trade data offers a view of the process at a more sectorally desegregate level. With the data available it is possible to go to a very fine commodity desegregation, and here we present results for 104 industrial sectors. However, care needs to be taken in interpreting these results, as trade flows are only an indirect measure of the underlying production changes that we are interested in. Rapid growth of trade flows (both inter- and intra-industry) make it difficult to infer the underlying changes in production patterns from changes in the trade data alone.

Tables 5.4a and 5.4b are analogous to Table 5.1, but are based on export and import data respectively. Looking first at the export data, we see a dramatic decline in the difference between countries' export vectors between 1970/73 and 1980/83, this flattening out in the later periods. Like the production data, this suggests a qualitative change in the early 1980s, although the growing dissimilarity of later years is largely absent in the export data. One reason for this may be that rapid growth in trade – particularly intra-industry trade – has tended to make trade vectors more similar. To control for this we separate out the change due to growth of trade in each industry from each country's 'differential change'. The final column of Table 5.4a gives the actual 1993/96 measure minus the measure if all countries had experienced the same sectoral export growth rates. We see that this differential change measure reports growing dissimilarity for eight of the fourteen countries. In addition, the averages show increasing dissimilarity.

On the import side, the picture is similar, except that the growing similarity seems to last through to the late 1980s, only being arrested (and possibly reversed) in the period 1988/91–1993/96, in which seven of the fourteen countries experienced growing dissimilarity, and the means of the measures started to increase.

What do these changes in trade patterns really tell us about the underlying changes in production patterns? First, it appears that we have a fairly robust finding of decreasing specialisation in the 1970s. Further, the results for exports and imports suggest that our results for production data would most likely carry over to a more desegregated classification. From 1980 on, the data present a more mixed picture, with growing specialisation in production

Table 5.4a   Krugman specialisation index: exports (4-year averages)

	70/73	80/83	88/91	93/96	93/96 – 80/83	93/96 Computed
Austria	0.557	0.503	0.514	0.496	–0.007	–0.004
Belgium	0.618	0.62	0.639	0.605	–0.015	0.019
Denmark	0.710	0.648	0.675	0.694	0.046	0.065
Spain	0.771	0.568	0.529	0.556	–0.012	0.010
Finland	0.294	0.259	0.276	0.267	0.008	0.019
France	1.140	0.984	0.932	0.951	–0.033	–0.048
UK	0.294	0.259	0.276	0.267	0.008	0.019
Germany	0.403	0.347	0.339	0.345	–0.002	0.014
Greece	1.270	1.220	1.310	1.150	–0.063	–0.043
Ireland	0.828	0.797	0.948	1.080	0.280	0.280
Italy	0.466	0.590	0.619	0.642	0.052	0.076
Netherlands	0.594	0.576	0.490	0.523	–0.052	–0.014
Portugal	1.080	0.992	0.986	0.920	–0.072	–0.028
Sweden	0.304	0.334	0.286	0.305	–0.029	–0.020
Average	0.666	0.621	0.63	0.629	0.008	0.024
Weighted average	0.561	0.522	0.514	0.521	0.000	0.014

Table 5.4b   Krugman specialisation index: imports (4-year averages)

	70/73	80/83	88/91	93/96	93/96 – 80/83	93/96 Computed
Austria	0.386	0.33	0.255	0.29	–0.040	–0.008
Belgium	0.363	0.39	0.346	0.357	–0.032	–0.012
Denmark	0.291	0.369	0.318	0.297	–0.072	–0.036
Spain	0.565	0.448	0.255	0.259	–0.190	–0.170
Finland	0.249	0.190	0.121	0.117	–0.073	–0.046
France	0.405	0.334	0.238	0.316	–0.018	0.026
UK	0.249	0.190	0.121	0.117	–0.073	–0.046
Germany	0.304	0.270	0.212	0.201	–0.069	–0.048
Greece	0.614	0.609	0.436	0.398	–0.210	–0.130
Ireland	0.379	0.389	0.376	0.504	0.120	0.130
Italy	0.347	0.352	0.325	0.296	–0.056	–0.035
Netherlands	0.297	0.269	0.246	0.258	–0.011	0.019
Portugal	0.454	0.487	0.419	0.342	–0.140	–0.140
Sweden	0.296	0.289	0.242	0.267	–0.022	0.013
Average	0.371	0.351	0.279	0.287	–0.064	–0.034
Weighted average	0.334	0.301	0.238	0.249	–0.053	–0.024

patterns not reflected in changing patterns of trade. Although it is possible that the desegregate production structure is becoming more similar even while the aggregate production structure diverges, it is more likely that the trade results do not accurately reflect underlying changing production patterns. The main reason for this is the growing volume of intra-industry trade (widely documented, for example, CEP II, 1997), which will tend to make countries' trade vectors more similar. European integration, and the corresponding trade liberalisation, has – as trade theory would predict – vastly increased trade flows between European economies. To the extent that this is growth of intra-industry trade, it could have occurred without any changes in production patterns. Increasing integration also allows countries to specialise along (say) comparative advantage lines, changing production patterns as well as increasing trade volumes. If the former effect dominates, trade vectors will become more similar, even if production structures are unchanged or diverging. It seems likely therefore that changes in trade flows are not an accurate way of measuring changes in production patterns. Since we are primarily interested in the latter, trade data are at best an imperfect, and perhaps a misleading source of information.

What is the Industrial Specialisation of Countries?

In the previous two sections we have compared the industrial structures of countries, and considered whether or not countries are becoming more or less different, and more or less specialised. We would also like to know in what sort of industries countries are specialising. We address this, not by listing the industries that have moved to and from different countries, but instead by identifying key characteristics of industries and seeing how the characteristics embodied in each country's industrial structure have changed. This allows us to consider whether, say, France has come to have more industries that are, on average, highly capital intensive.

Formally, we have a set of industry characteristics, $\{z^k\}$, which are listed in Box 5.1. These are unchanging over time, and details of these characteristics are given in Appendix 5.B. We compute, for each country, the average score on each characteristic, where each industry characteristic is weighted by the share of that industry in the country's production. Thus, for each characteristic, we define the industry characteristic bias (ICB) of country i as

$$ICB_i(t) \equiv \Sigma_k v_i^k(t) z^k \qquad (5.5)$$

Figures 5.2–5.4 report these ICBs for selected characteristics, and illustrate how they have evolved over time. Each figure has a panel for each country

BOX 5.1   INDUSTRY CHARACTERISTICS

Economies of scale	Measures of minimum efficient scale (MES)
Technology level	High, Medium, Low (OECD classification)
R&D intensity	R&D expenditures as share of value added
Capital intensity	Capital stock per employee (K/L)
Share of labour	Share of labour compensation in value added
Skill intensity	Share of non-manual workers in workforce (S/L)
Higher skills intensity	Share of higher educated workers in workforce
Agricultural input intensity	Use of primary inputs as share of value of production
Intermediates intensity	Total use of intermediates as share of value of production
Intra-industry linkages	Use of intermediates from own sector as share of value of production
Inter-industry linkages	Use of intermediates from other sectors as share of value of production.
Final demand bias	Percentage of sales to domestic consumers and exports
Sales to industry	Percentage of sales to domestic industry as intermediates and capital goods
Industrial growth	Growth in value of production between 1970 and 1994

(all drawn to the same scale), and the right- and left-hand edges of each panel give the 1980/83 and 1994/97 values respectively.

The first figure, Figure 5.2, gives each country's ICB for technology levels and increasing returns to scale. As is apparent, the lines tend to move together, and we see some countries experiencing dramatic change, and others not. France, Britain and Germany are all countries with, on average, high-technology and high returns to scale industry, but a slight decline in scores (in contrast to Sweden). Finland and Ireland are the two countries for which the composition of industry has changed the most in favour of high-technology and increasing returns to scale industries. In contrast, Greece and Portugal started low and have declined somewhat.

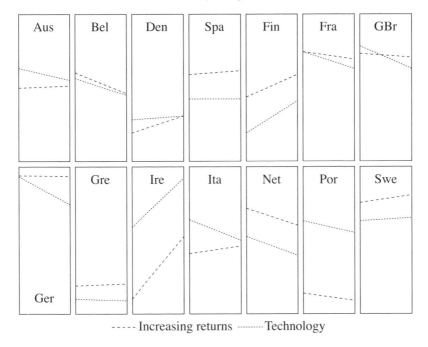

Figure 5.2   Industry characteristic bias of countries (economies of scale, technology)

Figure 5.3 reports the ICBs for factor intensities. Looking first at capital–labour ratios, we see high (and continuing high) levels in Finland and the Netherlands, and moderate levels increasing significantly in Greece and Portugal. Declines occurred in Ireland, Denmark and Germany – the last of these, curiously, from a low initial level. The industrial composition of the Netherlands, France and Britain, and then Austria, Germany and Sweden supports a high share of non-manual employees, while this is lowest in Portugal and Greece. For employees with higher education, the Netherlands is top, followed by France, Britain and Germany, with Portugal and Greece again the lowest. The dramatic change in Ireland is of course the most outstanding feature.

The characteristics reported in Figure 5.4 are intermediate goods usage and functional destination of industry output. Final demand bias (measuring the final consumer orientation of the industry) is highest in Greece and Portugal, and originally high but falling fast in Ireland and Denmark. Spain and Belgium (and increasingly Greece) have industries with a high intermediate goods input, while Finland and Italy have industries with a high share of intermediates from their own sector.

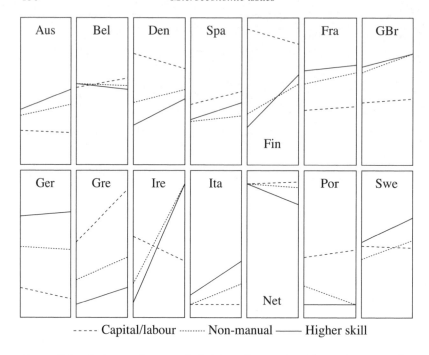

Figure 5.3   Industry characteristic bias of countries (factor intensities)

In Table 5.5 the industry characteristic biases of the EU countries are summarised for 1994/97. The selected characteristics are the same as those used in Figures 5.2–5.4: final demand bias, total use of intermediates, use of intermediates from own sector, economies of scale, technology level, share of non-manual workers in workforce, capital–labour ratio, share of higher educated in workforce. H (high) indicates that a country ranks among the five countries with highest ICB scores, M (medium) indicates a rank among the four countries with medium ICB scores, while L (low) denotes a rank among the five countries with lowest scores.

We see that the industrial structures of France, Germany and Great Britain are characterised by high returns to scale, high technology, and a relatively highly educated workforce. This is distinctly different from Greece and Portugal, which are biased towards industries with low returns to scale, low technology and a workforce with relatively little education, that have a high final demand bias and a low share of non-manual workers.

A comparison of the ICBs for Spain, Portugal and Greece reveals that Portugal's and Greece's industrial compositions are significantly more similar to each other than they are to that of Spain. This is in line with

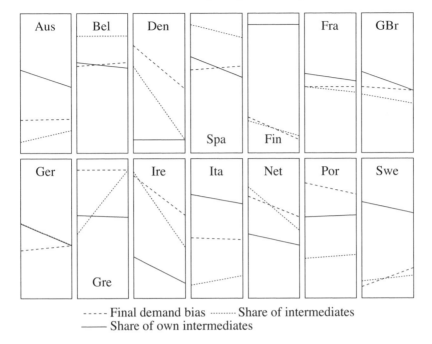

----- Final demand bias ········ Share of intermediates
——— Share of own intermediates

Figure 5.4   Industry characteristic bias of countries (intermediate goods
usage and functional destination of output

the findings on greater bilateral similarity between Greece and Portugal
than between Spain and each of these countries: on average, Spain has
industry with higher returns to scale and higher technology than Portugal
and Greece.

Country Analysis: Conclusions

The evidence presented in this section supports the idea that a quantitative
change in the behaviour of EU countries' relative industrial structures
occurred around 1980. A process of growing similarity was replaced by
slowly increasing dissimilarity and industrial specialisation. The process
affected almost all countries, relative to the rest of the EU as a whole and
relative to other countries individually.

Inspection of the industry characteristics of each country indicates
significant cross-country differences, broadly along the lines that would
be expected. Some dramatic changes stand out (notably for Ireland and
Finland), while for other countries (France, the UK and Germany) the
changes are much less significant. In Section 5.4 we undertake a formal

Table 5.5   Industry characteristic bias 1994/97

	FIN	INT	ITA	IRS	TEC	S/L	K/L	HS
Austria	L	L	M	M	M	L	L	M
Belgium	H	H	H	L	M	H	H	M
Denmark	M	L	L	L	L	M	H	L
Spain	H	H	M	H	M	L	M	L
Finland	L	L	H	M	L	M	H	M
France	M	H	M	H	H	H	L	H
UK	M	M	L	H	H	H	M	H
Germany	L	M	L	H	H	M	L	H
Greece	H	H	M	L	L	L	H	L
Ireland	H	M	L	M	H	H	L	H
Italy	L	L	H	L	M	L	L	L
Netherlands	M	H	L	M	L	H	H	H
Portugal	H	M	H	L	L	L	M	L
Sweden	L	L	H	H	H	M	M	M

Note: The characteristics are: final demand bias (FIN), total use of intermediates (INT), use of intermediates from own sector (ITA), economies of scale (IRS), technology level (TEC), share of non-manual workers in workforce (S/L), capital–labour ratio (K/L), share of higher educated in workforce (HS).

econometric analysis linking the characteristics of industries to the characteristics of countries in order to understand better the forces driving these changes.

5.3   THE LOCATION AND CONCENTRATION OF INDUSTRIES

In the previous section we looked at patterns of national specialisation in Europe, outlining the changes in individual country's industrial structures and the extent to which these structures are diverging. We now switch the focus from countries to industries and ask: How is the location of different industries evolving? Which industries are becoming more or less spatially concentrated?

How Concentrated are Manufacturing Industries?

Table 5.6 shows the structure of the European manufacturing sector as a whole. In the beginning of the 1970s, 63 per cent of all EU manufacturing was located in the UK, France and Germany (countries accounting for around 52 per cent of Europe's population). Over the last three decades, this share has fallen, reaching 58.7 per cent in 1994/97. Southern European countries (Italy, Greece, Portugal and Spain) raised their share gradually, from 19.9 per cent in the early 1970s to 24.6 per cent in 1994/97 (compared to a population share of 32 per cent). The smaller countries – Austria, Finland and Ireland – have also seen a steady increase in their share of European manufacturing, from 3.8 per cent in the early 1970s to 5.3 per cent in 1994/97.

Table 5.6   Regional structure of European manufacturing

$(s_i^k(t), k = \text{all manufacturing})$

	70/73 (%)	82/85 (%)	88/91 (%)	94/97 (%)
Austria	2.1	2.4	2.5	2.4
Belgium	3.9	3.3	3.4	3.8
Denmark	1.4	1.4	1.3	1.6
Spain	5.8	6.3	6.3	6.5
Finland	1.3	1.8	1.8	1.7
France	16.9	16.4	15.6	15.1
UK	16.9	15.5	14.3	13.9
Germany	29.4	27.7	28.8	30.0
Greece	0.7	1.0	0.7	0.7
Ireland	0.4	0.7	0.7	1.2
Italy	12.5	14.5	16.4	14.5
Netherlands	4.3	4.3	3.9	4.3
Portugal	0.9	1.2	1.2	1.4
Sweden	3.6	3.3	3.2	3.1
	100.0	100.0	100.0	100.0
UK + Germany + France	63.2	59.6	58.7	59.0
Spain + Italy + Greece + Portugal	19.9	23.0	24.6	23.1
Gini coefficient	0.576	0.549	0.56	0.549

Has the concentration of manufacturing as a whole increased or decreased? To measure the degree of concentration, we report the Gini coefficient of concentration in the bottom row of the table (the Gini coefficient of the variable $s_i^k(t)$ for k = all manufacturing).[6] If all countries have the same amount of manufacturing this measure is zero; if all manufacturing is in a single economy it would take value 1.[7] We see that according to this measure there has been a small decrease in concentration of the overall manufacturing sector.

What about individual industries? Midelfart et al. (2000a) report the Gini coefficient of concentration by industry for selected time periods. The pattern of change is summarised in Table 5.7. We see a majority of industries experiencing decreasing concentration during the 1970s and early 1980s followed by a majority showing increasing concentration in the later 1980s. During the 1990s the performance is more evenly balanced, although a majority became slightly less concentrated.

Table 5.7　Change in sectoral Gini coefficients of concentration

| Period | Number of industries (average change) | |
	Gini increase	Gini decrease
1970/73–82/85	11 (5.6%)	25 (–5.0%)
1982/85–88/91	23 (2.5%)	13 (–3.0%)
1988/91–94/97	15 (2.9%)	21 (–3.4%)

Is there any clear evidence here of increasing or decreasing average concentration? A number of authors have found increasing average concentration of EU manufacturing in the 1980s (Brülhart, 1998; WIFO, 1999). We find that the (un-weighted) average of the industry Gini coefficients decreases slightly from 1970/73 to 1982/85, followed by a slight increase in concentration through to the early 1990s and a decrease thereafter (see the 'average' line on Figure 5.5). However, these changes in the average are minuscule, and little weight should be attached to them.

How do we reconcile this with the changes in national specialisation observed in Section 5.2? First, as emphasised by WIFO (1999), the combination of both increased specialisation and constant or declining concentration is not necessarily a paradox; the two trends can indeed be reconciled as the EU Member States are not equal sized, nor are the industries.[8] Second, the experience of industries is much more heterogeneous than the experience of countries. Increasing average specialisation from the early 1980s (Table 5.1) reflects the experience of (almost) all countries. But, as is clear from Table 5.7, the experience of industries is much more mixed, and attempts to produce an average measure of concentration correspondingly less useful.

Since some industries are clearly concentrating and others dispersing, we look industry by industry, and ask which industries have become more or less concentrated. To answer this we divide the 36 manufacturing sectors into five groups according to the following criteria: first we took the 12 most concentrated industries in 1970/73; then we divided this group between those that were still among the 12 most concentrated in 1994/97, and those that had left the top 12. Similarly, we took the 12 least concentrated industries in 1970/73 and divided them into those which remained among the 12 least concentrated in 1994/97, and those which had left this group. Industries that meet none of these criteria form a residual group. Table 5.8 lists the industries that form each group, and Figure 5.5 plots the Gini coefficients for the first four of these groups, together with the average over all 36 industries. The differences in the behaviour of the selected groups is clear, and we now look at each of them in detail.

Table 5.8   *Industries grouped by levels and changes in concentration*

Concentrated industries that have remained concentrated over time (CC)	*Concentrated industries that have become less concentrated (CD)*
Motor vehicles	Beverages
Motor cycles	Tobacco
Aircraft	Office & computing machinery
Electrical apparatus	Machinery & equipment
Chemical products n.e.c.	Radio, TV & communication
Petroleum & coal products	Professional instruments
Dispersed industries that have become more concentrated over time (DC)	*Dispersed industries that have stayed dispersed (DD)*
Textiles	Food
Wearing apparel	Wood products
Leather & products	Paper & products
Furniture	Printing & publishing
Transport equipment n.e.c.	Metal products
	Non-metallic minerals n.e.c.
	Shipbuilding
Residual group (R)	
Footwear	Pottery & china
Industrial chemicals	Glass & products
Drugs & medicines	Iron & steel
Petroleum refineries	Non-ferrous metals
Rubber products	Railroad equipment
Plastic products	Other manufacturing

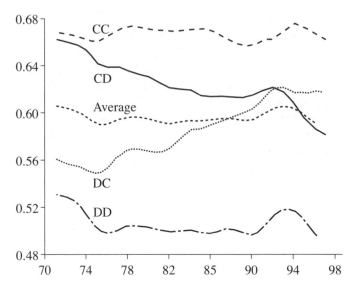

*Figure 5.5   Industry Gini coefficients: industries grouped by performance
(two-year moving average)*

(CC) Concentrated industries
The six industries in this group, motor vehicles, motorcycles, aircraft, electrical apparatus, chemicals n.e.c. and petroleum and coal products were among the most concentrated industries in 1970/73 and have remained so through to 1994/97. There are, however, some differences within the group. Thus, while motor vehicles, motorcycles and petroleum and coal products experienced a slight increase in concentration after 1991, aircraft, electrical apparatus and chemicals have recently become slightly more dispersed.

The increased concentration observed in the motor vehicles and motorcycles sectors reflects the fact that Germany has reinforced its position in both industries at the expense of both France and the UK. Although the overall pattern for the industry is dominated by this increased concentration in Germany, this is slightly offset by the increases in shares of production occurring in Portugal, Austria and Spain. For aircraft, Germany, the UK and France remain the dominant countries with a 78 per cent share of EU aircraft production in 1997. The UK and Sweden experienced tiny decreases in their share, while Belgium, France and Spain reported small increases.

Austria and Italy increased their share in electrical apparatus, but apart from this there was little relocation. Looking at the petroleum and coal industry, the most noticeable fact is that the UK's position has declined strongly, although not enough to make a significant impact on the figures for geographical concentration. In chemicals n.e.c., the UK, Germany and

France remain dominant despite Spain and Ireland capturing around 6 per cent of the industry.

(CD) Concentrated and dispersing industries

There is also a group of industries that were initially very concentrated, but which have become more dispersed over time. This group comprises office & computing machinery, machinery & equipment, radio, TV and communication equipment, professional instruments, beverages and tobacco.

In office & computing and in radio-TV and communication equipment the major decline in geographical concentration is observed between 1991 and 1997. The increased geographical dispersion is primarily driven by decreasing German dominance and reinforced by shrinking shares in the UK and France. In office and computing, machinery & equipment, radio, and TV and communication equipment and in professional instruments, between 7 per cent and 17 per cent of the EU production left Germany, France and the UK. Countries that strengthened their positions in some, or all, of these industries, were small countries such as Austria, Finland, Ireland and Sweden; and also the southern European countries Italy, Portugal and Spain. Most astonishing is perhaps the Irish performance: Ireland increased its share of EU production in all four industries. Also noteworthy is Finland, which increased its share in all except professional instruments.

For beverages and tobacco the patterns of relocation we observe are similar to those above, but relocation takes place between a slightly different set of countries. Germany and the UK lose, while Spain, Austria and the Netherlands gain.

(DC) Dispersed and concentrating industries

Textiles, wearing apparel, leather & products, furniture and transport equipment form the third group of industries. In 1970/73 they were all among the most dispersed industries in Europe, but became increasingly geographically concentrated up to 1994/97. Most of the increase took place prior to 1991. The first three industries are those where European integration appears to have allowed the southern European countries to exploit their comparative advantage.

France, Germany and the UK experienced reduced shares in textiles, wearing apparel and leather and products, while the southern European countries showed growing shares. The same patterns of relocation applied to furniture, but the extent of the shift was much smaller. The southern performance was however, surprisingly non-uniform. Italy reinforced its position in each of the four industries; particularly in leather and products, where it increased its share of EU production from 22 per cent to 48 per cent. This is also the industry that exhibits the largest rise in concentration. Spain got a slightly higher share of EU production in textiles and wearing apparel, although it experienced a decline in its share of leather and products. Portugal increased its shares in all four industries. Greece also obtained a slightly higher share of EU textiles production, but decreased its shares in wearing apparel and leather and products.

Transport equipment n.e.c. exhibits a clear increase in geographical concentration over time. But, in contrast to the other DC sectors, this did not reflect north–south movements. Instead, we see that Germany increased its share by 10 per cent while the UK and Spain experienced a combined decrease of 7 per cent.

(DD) Dispersed industries

Food products, wood products, paper and products, printing and publishing, non-metallic minerals n.e.c., metal products, and shipbuilding were initially among the 12 least concentrated EU manufacturing industries, and have remained so throughout the 1980s and 1990s. These are industries with production spread out in the north, as well as the south, of the EU. One possible explanation for the continued dispersion of such activities is national differences in tastes (food), culture, non-tariff barriers (food), as well as national industrial policies (shipbuilding).

(R) The residual

The residual group contains the industries that were the 12 medium concentrated industries in 1970. A number of these industries, like railroad equipment, glass and products, iron and steel and plastic products have remained in this medium concentrated group up till 1997. However, there are also industries that have experienced rather significant changes in the degree of geographical concentration. Drugs and medicines and industrial chemicals are industries that had around average concentration in 1970/73, but had moved down to the group of the 12 least concentrated industries in 1994/97. While drugs and medicines experienced the most significant decline in concentration before 1990, in industrial chemicals the main decline happened after 1990. Twelve per cent of drugs and medicines production moved out of Germany and Italy and this production was primarily absorbed by Denmark, the UK, Ireland and Sweden. Ten per cent of industrial chemicals left France, Germany and the UK – while Belgium, Ireland and Italy gained shares in the industry.

Footwear is an interesting example of a medium concentrated industry showing the opposite trend, where relocation has led to a large increase in concentration. In this sector, the three major manufacturing economies showed declining shares, while Italy reinforced its position from 29 per cent to 46 per cent, and Portugal also gained a considerably larger share.

Characteristics of Concentrated and Dispersed Industries

We would like to identify the characteristics of industries associated with the different concentration patterns that we have discussed in detail above. To do this, we show, in Table 5.9, how the five groups of industries differ in some of the industry characteristics listed in Box 5.1. For each industry characteristic, H (high) indicates an industry ranked among the top 12, M (medium) indicates an industry ranked among the middle 12, and L (low) indicates an industry ranked among the bottom 12.

Table 5.9 shows that geographically concentrated (CC) industries are typically high increasing returns, high/medium tech and have a high/medium final demand bias. Half the industries in the group use a high share of intermediates from their own sector, while most use little agricultural inputs. Most of the industries are capital intensive, and also relatively skill intensive.

What distinguishes the initially concentrated industries that have grown less concentrated over time (CD) from the former group? These CD industries tend to have lower increasing returns to scale, are less reliant on intra-industry linkages, but slightly more reliant on inter-industry linkages, have higher skill intensity, and less significant final demand bias. On average, the CD industries are also the industries that have shown the most rapid growth over the last three decades.

Turning to the initially dispersed industries that have concentrated over time (DC), we see that these are industries that are clearly different from those in the two previous groups. They are characterised by low increasing returns to scale, low tech, a high share of agricultural inputs, and low skill intensity. They are also industries that have grown relatively slowly.

The fourth group, the dispersed industries (DD), are more diverse. However, all seven industries in the group appear to be low tech and six use agricultural inputs intensively.

We can summarise the effect of these characteristics on industrial concentration by running some simple univariate regressions. The bottom two rows of Table 5.9 report the results from regressions of the Gini coefficients of concentration from 1970/73 and 1994/97 on each of the characteristics in turn. The fit is generally poor, and many of the industry characteristics are not significant in determining the extent of concentration. Studies that try to evaluate the forces driving location using summary indices as dependent variables, and industry characteristics as independent variables have encountered similar problems.[9] Mostly, these problems arise from two

Table 5.9   Industry characteristics

		IRS	TEC	ITA	ITE	K/L	S/L	GRT	FIN	AGR
CC	Motor vehicles	H	M	H	M	M	L	L	H	L
CC	Motorcycles	H	M	L	H	M	L	L	L	L
CC	Aircraft	H	H	H	L	M	H	M	H	L
CC	Chemicals n.e.c.	H	M	H	L	H	H	H	M	M
CC	Electric apparatus	M	H	M	M	L	M	H	M	M
CC	Petroleum & coal products	H	L	L	H	H	H	M	H	L
CD	Beverages	L	L	M	H	H	H	M	H	H
CD	Tobacco	L	L	M	H	H	M	L	H	H
CD	Office & computing	M	H	M	H	L	H	H	L	L
CD	Machinery & equipment	M	M	M	M	M	H	M	L	M
CD	Radio,TV and communication	M	H	M	L	L	H	H	M	L
CD	Professional instruments	M	H	L	M	L	H	H	M	M
DC	Textiles	L	L	H	L	M	L	L	H	H
DC	Wearing apparel	L	L	H	L	M	L	L	H	H
DC	Leather & products	L	L	H	L	M	L	L	H	H
DC	Furniture	L	L	M	M	L	L	M	M	H
DC	Transport equipment	H	M	L	H	M	M	L	L	L
DD	Food	L	L	M	H	H	M	M	H	H
DD	Wood products	L	L	M	M	L	L	M	M	H
DD	Paper & products	M	L	H	L	H	M	M	L	M
DD	Printing & publishing	M	L	H	L	H	H	H	L	H
DD	Non-metallic minerals	M	L	M	M	L	M	M	L	M
DD	Metal products	M	L	M	M	M	L	H	L	L
DD	Shipbuilding	H	L	L	H	M	L	L	M	M
R	Footwear	L	L	H	L	M	L	L	H	H
R	Industrial chemicals	H	M	H	L	H	H	M	M	M
R	Drugs & medicines	H	H	L	H	H	H	H	H	M
R	Petroleum refineries	H	L	L	M	H	H	H	H	L
R	Rubber products	L	M	L	H	L	M	L	M	H
R	Plastic products	L	M	L	H	L	M	H	M	H
R	Pottery	M	L	L	M	L	M	M	L	M
R	Glass & products	M	L	M	M	L	L	H	L	M
R	Iron & steel	M	L	H	L	H	M	L	L	L
R	Non-ferrous metals	H	M	H	L	H	M	M	M	L
R	Railroad equipment	H	M	L	H	M	M	L	L	L
R	Other manufacturing	L	M	L	M	L	L	H	M	M
Beta coefficient Gini70/73		.004*	.039*	–.080	.102	.000	.161*	.048	–.020	–.050
Beta coefficient Gini94/97		.000	.019	.030	–.060	.000	–.030	–.040	.000	–.256

Note: * = significant at 5% level. The following industry characteristics are included in the table: economies of scale (IRS), technology level (TEC), intra-industry linkages (ITA), inter-industry linkages (ITE), capital intensity (K/L), skill intensity (S/L), industrial growth (GRT), final demand bias (FIN) and use of agricultural inputs (AGR).

sources: first, the small number of data points (there are 36 observations; one for each industry); and second, the fact that theory is virtually silent on how different industry characteristics should affect summary measures of industrial concentration. Still, there are a few things that are worth noting. In the early 1970s, industry Gini coefficients are significantly correlated with industry increasing returns, technology level and skill intensity. By the mid-1990s, these factors appear to have become insignificant. This suggests that high IRS, high-tech and skill-intensive industries are, on average, not as concentrated as they once were, although this is obviously not the case for the most concentrated industries.

The main drawback of these types of econometric exercise is that they take as dependent variables summary measures of concentration, when in fact we have data on the complete distribution. In contrast, the econometric specification that we present in Section 5.4 uses information on the entire distribution.

Spatial Separation

The concentration index employed so far provides information about the extent to which each industry is concentrated in a few countries, but does not tell us whether these countries are close together or far apart. Using this measure, two industries may appear equally geographically concentrated, while one is predominantly located in two neighbouring countries, and the other split between Finland and Portugal. Distinguishing such patterns will provide additional insights on the geography of individual industries, about cross-industry differences and about the driving forces of economic geography.

Hence, as a complement to the traditional concentration indices, we propose an index of spatial separation, that can be thought of as a supranational index of geographical location. We define the spatial separation of industry k, (SP^k) as follows:

$$SP^k \equiv (C) \, \Sigma_i \Sigma_j (s_i^k s_j^k \delta_{ij}) \tag{5.6}$$

where δ_{ij} is a measure of the distance between i and j, s_i^k is the share of industry k in location i, and C is a constant. For a given location i, $\Sigma_j (s_i^k \delta_{ij})$ is the average distance to other production in industry k. The first summation adds this over all locations i, weighted by their share in the industry, s_i^k. The interpretation of $\Sigma_i \Sigma_j (s_i^k s_j^k \delta_{ij})$ is therefore a production weighted sum of all the bilateral distances between locations. The measure is zero if all production occurs in a single place, and it *increases* the more spatially separated is production.

Midelfart et al. (2000a) provide a complete table of spatial separation indices for all industries in the four periods 1970/73, 1982/85, 1988/91 and 1994/97. Here, we just provide a summary of those results. Figure 5.6 reports the time series for manufacturing as a whole and for selected industry groups (high-technology industries, high returns to scale industries, and industries with high capital–labour ratios).

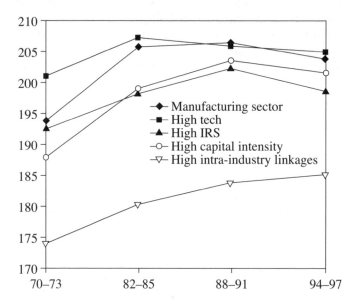

Figure 5.6   Spatial separation of manufacturing industries

For manufacturing activity as a whole, we find an inverse-U shape. There was a substantial increase in spatial separation between 1970/73 and 1982/85. The increase in separation then slowed down in the mid-1980s before reversing in the 1990s.

There are two things to note about the spatial separation of overall manufacturing. First, the geographical separation in activity that took place during the 1970s was of far greater magnitude than the clustering that took place in the 1990s. Second, the reported changes in the spatial distribution of European manufacturing appear to be largely driven by developments in southern Europe (and possibly Ireland). Comparing the changes of the southern European countries' total share of EU manufacturing (see Table 5.6) with the changes in spatial separation of manufacturing, we see that EU manufacturing dispersed as southern Europe experienced a significant increase in its manufacturing share (1970/73–1982/85). In the mid-1980s further increases in southern European manufacturing appear to be reflected in continued increasing spatial separation of EU manufacturing. However, in the 1990s, this trend was reversed, as southern Europe's share in EU manufacturing declined slightly, which again increases the extent of spatial clustering.

Figure 5.6 also shows that high-technology industries are the least separated throughout the entire time period and on average exhibited increasing separation. Individual results shows that drugs and medicines, office and computing, radio, TV and communication, electrical apparatus n.e.c. and professional instruments became increasingly spatially dispersed. Aircraft is the exception, becoming slightly less separated. The five high-tech industries that became increasingly spatially dispersed, are also industries that became less geographically concentrated (see Midelfart et al., 2000a). The evidence on spatial separation of these sectors tells us that the decline in geographical concentration reported on the basis of Gini coefficients is not only a story about the major EU countries trading shares, but about real geographical dispersion of economic activity.

High returns to scale and high capital intensity industries are initially more spatially separated than high-tech industries, and exhibit a similar pattern to manufacturing as a whole – increasing separation in the 1970s and 1980s followed by increasing clustering in the last period. Thus, different groups of industries also show increasing dispersion of economic activity in Europe between 1970 and 1990 in line with the increasing spatial dispersion of aggregate manufacturing.

There is significant cross-industry, and within-group variation in spatial separation. Overall, between 1970/73 and 1994/97, the general trend towards spatial dispersion is reflected in 29 out of 36 industries. In contrast, over the same period only 23 out of the 36 industries report declining Gini coefficients of concentration. Hence, moving beyond traditional measures of industrial concentration to an index that takes the relative location of countries into account strengthens the impression of a spreading out of European manufacturing activity.

Finally, one may note that most industries for which we report declining Gini coefficients are also found to be spatially separating, and vice versa. However, a number of industries clearly illustrate that this need not necessarily always be the case. Textiles, wearing apparel, rubber products, motor vehicles, motorcycles and bicycles all became more concentrated between 1970/73 and 1994/97. But, during the same period, they also became more spatially separated. This suggests that these industries are witnessing a pattern of increasing concentration in a smaller number of countries at the same time as they see a break-up of transnational clusters in central Europe.

Industry Analysis: Conclusions

Taking the economic geography of the EU as a whole, the above analysis shows that, on average, industries became somewhat more dispersed until the late 1980s, although there is now some evidence of a reversal of this trend. The aggregate picture masks substantial changes in the location of individual industries. Dividing industries into groups according to their concentration, we see that of those industries that were initially concentrated, one group – largely consisting of high returns to scale industries – has remained concentrated; others, including some relatively high-tech, high-skill, fast-growing industries, have become more dispersed. Of those industries that were initially dispersed, the slower growing and less skilled-labour-intensive ones have become concentrated in low-wage and low-skill-abundant economies.

5.4   ECONOMETRIC ANALYSIS

Hypotheses and Econometric Specification

In Sections 5.2 and 5.3 we drew out the broad trends of country specialisation and industry concentration, and offered descriptive material on the changing industrial characteristics of countries. This descriptive material considered just one country/industry characteristic at a time. In reality, location and specialisation patterns are driven by multivariate interactions between industry and country characteristics. Countries differ across a number of dimensions. Some are relatively abundant in physical capital, some relatively abundant in human capital; some are larger, some smaller; some are core locations – with easy access to many markets – others are peripheral. Industries also differ across a whole host of dimensions. They differ in their factor intensities; in the proportion of their output that is sold to final consumers as opposed to other producers; in their reliance on inputs from other producers; in the extent of their returns to scale. All of these different country and industry characteristics should interact to determine the pattern of location across the EU. In this section we evaluate which of these interactions are most important in driving the observed location patterns.

Hypotheses about the location of production all take the form of interaction between an industry characteristic and a country characteristic. To see why it is the interaction of these characteristics that is important, it is simplest to take a specific example. Thus, for example, if countries vary in their endowment of scientists, all industries might want to locate where scientists are more plentiful. However, in equilibrium, all industries cannot be in the same place, so it is industries that most value scientists that will produce where scientists are most plentiful, while industries in which scientists are less valued will be under-represented in such locations. This will be true more generally. Industries that are particularly intensive in any given factor will be drawn to countries that are relatively abundant in that factor. This means that, if we want to understand the forces driving industrial location patterns, we must consider the interaction of industry characteristics (listed in Box 5.1) with the appropriate country characteristics when seeking to explain those patterns.

Theory tells us which country characteristics should be interacted with which industry characteristics. Our initial econometric specifications included a large number of interaction variables. However, for the results we present here, we focus on just four country characteristics and six industry characteristics, giving the six interactions listed in Table 5.10. Two factors drive our choice of these particular interactions. First, they are emphasised by theory. Second, they all have a significant effect at some point in the time period that we are considering. Other variables were tried, including some policy variables, but the results were inconclusive. We return to these issues in our discussion of results.

Table 5.10   Interaction variables

	Country characteristic	Industry characteristic
$j = 1$	General market access	Sales to industry, % of output
$j = 2$	Market access to suppliers	Intermediate goods, % of total costs
$j = 3$	General market access	Economies of scale
$j = 4$	Agricultural production, % GDP	Agricultural input, % of total costs
$j = 5$	Secondary and higher education, % pop	Use of skilled labour, % of total costs
$j = 6$	Researchers and scientists, % labour force	R&D, % of total costs

We first briefly consider the interaction variables. The last three pairs of variables are factor abundance and factor intensity measures. Theory dictates the obvious pairing of each quantity measure of factor abundance with a measure of the share of that factor in each industry. Since we are focusing only on the structure of manufacturing, we take agricultural production as an exogenous measure of 'agriculture abundance' (rather than going back to an underlying endowment such as land). The education variable (characteristic $j = 5$) is interacted with the share of non-manual workers in the workforce, times the labour-share in the sector; this captures the skilled-labour intensity of the sector. We do not have a separate interaction for capital endowments and intensities, because of the high degree of capital mobility within the EU.

The first three pairs of variables are interactions suggested by the work on new economic geography. General market access uses a market potential measure to capture the centrality of each location. Market access to suppliers captures the centrality of each location with respect to intermediate good suppliers.[10] The three corresponding industry characteristics capture the following arguments. In reverse order, interaction between market potential and economies of scale ($j = 3$) captures the idea that industries with higher economies of scale (and perhaps also, therefore, less intense competition) may tend to concentrate in relatively central locations. Interaction between supplier access and the share of intermediates in costs ($j = 2$) captures a forwards linkage; we hypothesise that firms which are highly dependent on intermediate goods will tend to locate close to other producers, that is, in regions of high supplier access. Finally ($j = 1$) the interaction between market potential and the share of sales going to industrial users captures a backwards linkage; firms will want to be near their customers to minimise transport costs on final sales. We focus on industrial customers by taking the share of output going to industrial users although, a priori, the sign of this interaction is not clear; it depends on the importance of proximity to industrial customers relative to proximity to final consumers.

While this gives the forces that we believe are important in determining industrial location, the specific form of an estimating equation remains to be resolved. The first point is that our data require that we estimate a single relationship over all industries and countries. Estimating industry by industry is ruled out, since there are only 14 country observations; we cannot increase the number of observations by pooling across time, because we believe that increasing EU integration has changed the importance of different country characteristics over time (a belief that is confirmed by our empirical results). The second point is that, when it comes to estimating such a relationship for a general trade model (as opposed to one that tests a particular theory, such as Heckscher–Ohlin), the literature gives essentially no guidance on how to proceed. Unfortunately, it is just such a general trade model, incorporating both comparative advantage and new economic geography effects, that we believe is driving location patterns across the European Union.[11]

To resolve this specification issue, we constructed a very general simulation model which nests within it both factor abundance and new economic geography models, and simulated the way in which interactions between the variables listed in Table 5.10 determined the pattern of industrial location. We then used the simulation output to inform our choice of functional form for estimation, and settled on the following specification:

$$\ln(s_i^k) = \alpha\ln(pop_i) + \beta\ln(man_i) + \Sigma_j\beta[j] \, (y[j]_i - \gamma[j])(z[j]^k - \kappa[j]) \quad (5.7)$$

where s_i^k is the share of industry k in country i (as defined in Section 5.1); pop_i is the share of EU population living in country i; man_i is the share of total EU manufacturing located in country i; $y[j]_i$ is the level of the jth country characteristic in country i; $z[j]^k$ is the industry k value of the industry characteristic paired with country characteristic j (see Table 5.10). Finally, α, β, $\beta[j]$, $\gamma[j]$ and $\kappa[j]$, are coefficients.

Before presenting the results we give the intuition behind this particular functional form. The first two variables capture country size effects; all else equal, we would expect larger countries to have a larger industrial share in any given industry. The remaining terms in the summation capture the interaction of country and industry characteristics. To understand the specification, it is easiest to think about one particular characteristic, say j = R&D, so $z[R\&D]^k$ is then the R&D intensity of industry k and $y[R\&D]_i$ is the R&D abundance of country i. The specification says:

(i)   There exists an industry with R&D intensity $\kappa[R\&D]$, the location of which is independent of the R&D abundance of countries.
(ii) There exists a level of R&D abundance, $\gamma[R\&D]$, such that the country's share of each industry is independent of the R&D intensity of the industry.
(iii) If $\beta[R\&D] > 0$, then industries with R&D intensity greater than $\kappa[R\&D]$ will be drawn into countries with R&D abundance greater than $\gamma[R\&D]$, and out of countries with R&D abundance less than $\gamma[R\&D]$.

When we estimate the equation, we derive estimates of the three key parameters for each interaction variable – that is, estimates of $\kappa[j]$, $\gamma[j]$ and $\beta[j]$. We also derive estimates for the impact of the two scale variables – that is, estimates of α and β. In the discussion of our results, we concentrate on the $\beta[j]$'s which measure the sensitivity of *all* industries to variations in the location characteristics. Returning to the example of R&D, if R&D abundance is an important determinant of location patterns, then we should see a high value of $\beta[R\&D]$. The estimate of $\kappa[R\&D]$ tells us the level of R&D intensity which separates industries into 'high' and 'low' R&D intensive industries. The estimate of $\gamma[R\&D]$ tells us the level of R&D abundance that separates countries into 'abundant' and 'scarce' R&D

countries. Industries which are highly intensive (relative to $\kappa[R\&D]$) will be attracted to countries that are relatively abundant (relative to $\gamma[R\&D]$). Likewise, industries that have low intensity (again, relative to $\kappa[R\&D]$) will be attracted to countries where R&D factors are scarce (again, relative to $\kappa[R\&D]$). To emphasise, this need to consider both high and low intensities and high and low abundance is a result of the general equilibrium nature of the system which makes estimating these relationships so complex. It is also the general equilibrium nature of the system that stops us from guessing at the cut-off points $\kappa[R\&D]$ and $\gamma[R\&D]$ that define intensity and abundance. For example, there is little reason to think that the mean or median are the correct cut-off points, however intuitive these values might be. Finally, after adjusting for industry intensity and country abundance we can directly compare the importance of different country characteristics by considering the relative sensitivity of all industries to those characteristics as captured through the estimates of $\beta[j]$.

Estimation

In this section, we deal with some important estimation issues. First we do not estimate our specification directly, but instead, expand the relationship to give the estimating equation:

$$\ln(s_i^k) = c + \alpha\ln(pop_i) + \beta\ln(man_i)$$
$$+ \Sigma_j(\beta[j]y[j]_i z[j]^k - \beta[j]\gamma[j]z[j]^k - \beta[j]\kappa[j]y[j]_i) \quad (5.8)$$

For each time period, this equation was estimated by OLS, pooling across industries. The left-hand side is a four-year average of the industrial share of country i in the total output of industry k. Population and manufacturing data are also calculated as four-year averages. Country characteristics come from a wide variety of sources. Characteristics are measured at the start of the period and time averaged where possible.[12] Getting data on industry characteristics is not simple, so we use information on intensities that is not time-varying.

We omit three sectors – petroleum refineries, petroleum and coal products, and manufacturing not elsewhere classified (essentially a residual component). This leaves us with around 455 observations – the exact number of observations for each year are reported in the table. There are potentially two important sources of heteroscedasticity – both across countries and across industries. Because we cannot be sure whether these are important, or which would dominate, we report White's heteroscedastic consistent standard errors. We use these consistent standard errors for all hypothesis testing.

Results

Results are given in Table 5.11. The first two rows give results for the two size variables – measures of population share (share in total EU population) and manufacturing share (share in total EU manufacturing). The next six rows (interactions) give the coefficients on the interaction variables. From the estimating equation, we see that this is an estimate of β[*j*] – the sensitivity of industry location to the various country characteristics. We do not report results for the levels terms and instead concentrate on these sensitivity estimates, which capture the changing importance of the various factors driving industrial location patterns.

Table 5.11   Estimation results of equation (5.8)

Variable	1970	1980	1985	1990	1997
CONSTANT	11.56	19.732	−0.592	−10.446	−20.556
	(12.387)	(15.306)	(15.444)	(17.51)	(19.073)
Size variables					
ln(*pop*)	0.095	0.172	−0.093	−0.005	0.146
	(0.236)	(0.347)	(0.273)	(0.200)	(0.233)
ln(*man*)	0.342	0.425	0.795^{***}	0.404^{**}	0.516^{**}
	(0.261)	(0.32)	(0.198)	(0.203)	(0.208)
Interactions					
Market access	0.305^{***}	0.244^{***}	0.252^{***}	0.227^{**}	0.162^{*}
• sales to industry	(0.073)	(0.078)	(0.085)	(0.092)	(0.100)
Supplier access	−0.12	0.003	0.100	0.283	0.893^{*}
• intermediates in % costs	(0.428)	(0.503)	(0.548)	(0.552)	(0.600)
Market access	0.175^{***}	0.185^{***}	0.144^{**}	0.130^{*}	0.084
• economies of scale	(0.073)	(0.077)	(0.088)	(0.098)	(0.098)
Agriculture in % GDP	−0.088	−0.117	−0.069	−0.001	0.184^{*}
• agriculturals in % costs	(0.1)	(0.109)	(0.108)	(0.110)	(0.134)
Education	0.251^{***}	0.279^{***}	0.283^{***}	0.304^{***}	0.224^{***}
• skill intensity	(0.083)	(0.072)	(0.073)	(0.089)	(0.083)
Researchers	0.024	0.065	0.105^{*}	0.182^{**}	0.214^{***}
• R&D in % costs	(0.087)	(0.079)	(0.084)	(0.108)	(0.084)
Diagnostics					
Adjusted R^2	0.83	0.82	0.8	0.77	0.75
Number of observations	456	456	456	456	456

Note: We report standardised Beta coefficients. Standard errors reported in brackets; *** = significant at 1% level; ** = significant at 5% level; * = significant at 10% level. We report the results of one-sided tests where appropriate. All regressions are overall significant according to the standard *F*-test.

In discussing results, we initially focus on years from 1980 onwards. The variables ln(*pop*) and ln(*man*) soak up country size differences, as expected. In particular, coefficients on ln(*man*) are close to unity. Country and industry characteristics (not reported) all have negative coefficients, as expected. But, given the general equilibrium nature of the economic system, these coefficients are of little direct interest. We concentrate on the coefficients β[*j*], which measure the effect of the interactions and capture the sensitivity of location patterns to the various country and industry characteristics.

1. *General market access and sales to industry*   The coefficient on this interaction is positive and significant. This says that backward linkages between industrial sectors are important determinants of location. Industries which sell a high share of output to industry are, other things being equal, likely to locate in countries with high market potential.
2. *Market access to suppliers and share of intermediates in costs*   This interaction is positive and becoming significant at the 10 per cent level. The interpretation is that forward linkages are becoming increasingly important. Industries which are heavily dependent on intermediate goods are coming to locate in central regions with good access to intermediate supplies.
3. *General market access and economies of scale*   The coefficient on this interaction is positive, but steadily declining and becoming insignificant in later years. Theory predicts that the forces pulling increasing returns to scale industries into central locations are strongest at 'intermediate' levels of transport costs. The fact that this force is weakening supports the view that trade barriers in Europe may now have declined beyond these intermediate values.
4. *Agricultural production and share of agriculture in costs*   This interaction has the correct sign and increases slightly in strength, although at very low levels of significance.
5. *Educational level of the population and use of skilled labour*   This interaction is positive, highly significant, and slightly increasing throughout the period. It suggests the enduring importance of a skilled labour force in attracting skilled-labour-intensive industries.
6. *Researchers in labour force and R&D intensity*   This interaction is positive, increasing in strength and becoming highly significant. It points to the increasing importance of the supply of researchers in determining the location of high-technology industries.

The discussion above focuses on results from 1980 onwards. As we have seen in earlier sections of the chapter, going back to 1970 gives a somewhat different picture, and suggests a turning point in behaviour around 1980.

For example, looking at the time series of the $\beta[j]$ coefficients, five of the six have a turning point in 1980.

Summarising then, the econometrics paints a fascinating (and seemingly robust) picture of the changing interaction between factor endowment and economic geography determinants of location. The results indicate an increasing importance of forward and backward linkages and of the availability of skilled labour and researchers in determining the location of industry from 1980 onwards. At the same time, high increasing returns industries became better able to serve markets from less central locations.

What do our regression results tell us with respect to policy interventions aimed at affecting the location of industry? For example, why has Ireland been more successful than Portugal at attracting high-tech investments (as suggested by our analysis in Section 5.2). Is it due to the fact that Ireland offered greater financial incentives, or did the Irish economy already have the inherent characteristics required for an expansion of the high-tech sector?

It is hard to use our results to talk about policy for individual sectors because we do not have data on policy measures by country *and* sector. Using country-level data on policy expenditures, the coefficient just tends to reflect the relationship between these expenditures and the share of manufacturing in each country. If these are negatively related we get a negative (insignificant) effect of policy expenditures, reflecting the fact that less industrial countries are recipients of greater amounts of EU regional aid.

Can we say anything positive about the role of policy in explaining the location of industry across the European Union? First, and most importantly, our results suggest that it doesn't seem to have done too much harm. At the EU-wide level, specialisation according to comparative advantage and the forces identified by new economic geography, are beneficial. That is, specialisation driven by these forces increases *aggregate* welfare. Our results suggest that comparative advantage and new economic geography forces are becoming increasingly significant in explaining location patterns of industries. Second, and related, individual policies do not seem to be generally distorting the location of industrial activity. If they were generally distorting the location of industry, then we would not find that country characteristics and industry intensities were growing in importance.

To summarise, our regression results suggest that economic fundamentals are generally driving location patterns. Industrial policies may distort this picture, but they are not distorting the overall picture too much. Thus, Ireland's high-tech policy may well bias high-tech firms towards locating in Ireland. But, relative to Portugal, Ireland has twice the number of 25–59 year olds with at least upper secondary education (see the table in Appendix

5.B). If the availability of the correctly skilled labour force is important
in determining location patterns (and our regression results suggest that
it is), then the difference between the Portuguese and Irish experiences is
likely as much explained by this last fact as it is by the existence of Ireland's
high-tech policy.

Finally, to emphasise, our results suggest that ongoing specialisation in
the European Union is driven by factors that will increase aggregate welfare.
Individual countries may gain from policies that distort these forces, but
theoretical reasoning suggests that the EU as a whole loses. We return to
some of these issues in the conclusions.

5.5   SERVICE INDUSTRIES IN THE EUROPEAN UNION

So far, we have concentrated purely on manufacturing industries. There
are several good reasons for so doing. First, in general, manufacturing
products are inherently more tradable than service sector products, so we
would expect to see the largest relocation effects of European integration in
manufacturing. Second, current data availability severely restricts our ability
to describe location patterns of services and to study the forces driving the
location of those services. For example, we only have employment data
for five very aggregate service sectors, and we cannot classify these service
industries according to the industry characteristics that we used in Section
5.2. However, as service industries account for around 60 per cent of EU
employment, the geography of those services must be increasingly important.

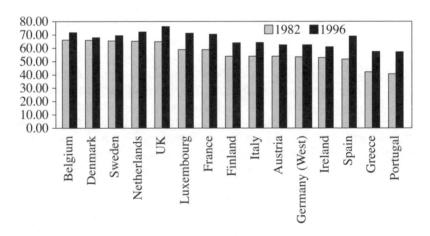

Figure 5.7   Share of employment in the service sector

In this section, we use the available data to discuss the distribution of service sectors. Our conclusions are that demand shifts can explain most of the changing scales of service sector activity, although we cannot rule out the possibility that trade and specialisation changes may be occurring at more disaggregate levels of service sector activity.

Aggregate Trends

EU countries differ substantially in the relative sizes of their service sectors (Figure 5.8).[13] In 1982, the share of service employment in total employment ranged from 40 per cent (Portugal) to 66 per cent (Belgium). By 1996 service employment shares had risen in all countries and ranged from a low of 57 per cent (Portugal) to a high of 76 per cent (UK). The full picture is given in Table 5.12, and we see that the increase was largest for the three countries with the smallest service sectors initially, namely Greece, Portugal and Spain, and correspondingly smallest for the three countries with the biggest sectors initially, Belgium, Denmark and Sweden.[14]

Table 5.12 *Country shares of the EU financial, insurance, real estate and business service sector (FIRE) (%)*

	1982	1995
Austria	2.62	2.55
Belgium	1.33	0.98
Denmark	2.09	1.82
Spain	3.21	4.84
Finland	1.50	1.26
France	18.78	17.84
UK	26.17	25.88
Germany	8.24	6.75
Greece	1.38	1.72
Ireland	0.80	0.82
Italy	25.13	25.10
Luxembourg	0.10	0.13
Netherlands	4.47	5.35
Portugal	1.14	2.01
Sweden	3.04	2.95
Total	100	100

Turning to individual service sectors, Figure 5.8 gives the time series of the Gini coefficient of concentration for five major sectors (financial services, insurance, real estate and business services (FIRE); wholesale and retailing; restaurants and hotels; transport; and communication).[15] Among these sectors, FIRE is the most concentrated and remains so from 1982 to 1996, even though its level of concentration decreases slightly. Transport services are least concentrated. The ranking of industries according to degree of concentration does not change over time, and all five service industries are less concentrated than manufacturing production as a whole.

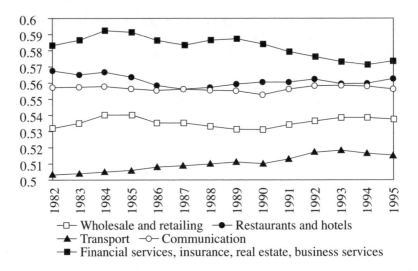

Figure 5.8   Gini coefficient of concentration, EU services

We briefly consider the relocation patterns that have caused the decrease in geographical concentration of the FIRE sector, by considering country shares, $s_i^k(t)$, for 1982 and 1995. From Table 5.12, we see that the UK and Italy more or less kept their dominant positions, while Germany experienced a slight decline in position. The countries that gained shares were Spain, Portugal and Greece and also the Netherlands. Hence, it seems that the decrease in concentration was indeed due to genuine geographical dispersion, and not just caused by relocation among the core countries in Europe.

The evidence presented above points to three broad trends in the service sectors:

*   Service activity is expanding across the EU as part of a general shift from manufacturing to services;
*   Poorer countries, with small initial services sectors, are catching up;

- Indices of concentration for services sectors confirm this general picture – services are in general more dispersed than the average manufacturing sector and, to the extent that we see any trends, we see increased dispersion over time.

The main reason for these changes lie in changing patterns of demand for services.

Changing Demand

Demand for services comes from final consumers and from use of services as intermediate goods, both of which have risen through time. A number of points can be made.

First, rising income levels across EU countries would lead us to predict an increasing share of services in consumption (because the income elasticity of demand with respect to services is known to be high). This, coupled with convergence of income levels goes a long way to explain the catch-up by countries with smaller initial service sectors.

Second, most manufacturing sectors have become more intensive users of services as intermediates in production. This may be a real shift, or may simply reflect the outsourcing of activities that were previously undertaken within manufacturing sector firms. The effects of this are quite large, as is clear from inspection of input-output tables. For the UK, the share of service inputs in the gross value of manufacturing output has risen from 12 per cent to 19 per cent over the last two decades. Focusing on specific sectors, the trend towards outsourcing becomes even more significant: office and computing, electrical apparatus, radio, TV and communication, motor vehicles and professional instruments all report increases in services inputs as a share of output of around 9–13 per cent. Input–output tables for other countries tell a similar story. For example, French manufacturing industries increased the share of service inputs in output from 13 per cent to 21 per cent.

Third, manufacturing industries vary in their service intensity, and highly service-intensive industries have been amongst the fastest growing. From input–output tables we rank industries according to their total use of services (exclusive of electricity, gas and water) as a share of gross output, and report the eight most intensive industries in Table 5.13; the service input shares in these industries range from 30 per cent to 21 per cent of the gross value of output.[16] Five of these eight industries are in the fastest growing third of EU industries and none in the slowest growing third (see Table 5.9).

These arguments indicate rising demand for intermediate usage of services across the EU as a whole. However, in addition, some of the most service-intensive industries are also those that have become increasingly dispersed. Seven out of the eight industries listed in Table 5.13 became more dispersed between 1970/73 and 1994/97. These sectors are especially intensive in the use of finance and insurance, real estate and business services, and communication. Changing location of manufacturing industries therefore goes some way to explain the increasing dispersion of service sector employment.

Table 5.13   Service-intensive industries

ISIC	Service intensive industries
3825	Office & computing
3610	Pottery
3620	Glass & products
3690	Non-metallic minerals
3832	Radio, TV & communication
3522	Drugs & medicines
3410	Paper & products
3420	Printing & publishing

Conclusion

Changes in demand – driven by increased income, increased outsourcing, and the changing sizes and locations of service intensive industries – probably explain most of the changing pattern of service sector employment. However, two other possibilities must be mentioned. The first is the possibility that there has been increasing international trade in services, and consequent relocation. For most service activities this is unlikely, because of the inherent non-tradability of the service. For other activities – notably FIRE – it is a greater possibility. Data limitations make it difficult to measure trade in this sector, but the employment data provides no indications that concentration is taking place. From Table 5.13 we see that the FIRE sector is the one that is *de*-concentrating most.

Finally, the five service sectors we work with are highly aggregated – they are each much larger than any of our manufacturing sectors. It is possible that more disaggregate data would reveal a different story of changing concentration and dispersion, and possibly of specialisation and agglomeration with their attendant efficiency gains. However, identifying such effects requires much more detailed data than are currently available.

5.6   AN EU–US COMPARISON

It has often been remarked that industries in the US are much more spatially concentrated than they are in Europe. Unfortunately, it is difficult to find a way in which this statement can be made precise. The US and Europe are different sizes and geographical shapes, and there is no correct way to aggregate US states to mirror the geography of countries in Europe. Nevertheless, in this section we perform three exercises to shed some light on the similarities and differences between the EU and the US. The first is simply to look at the time series of regional specialisation and industrial concentration in the two continents; this reveals quite different patterns of change, but makes no comparison of levels. The second is a comparison of the location patterns of the motor vehicle industry in the two continents. The third uses our spatial separation index (Section 5.3) to make a comparison on levels.

The Evolution of Specialisation and Concentration

US geography is different, and units of observation (states) smaller than the European counterpart. The likely effect of using smaller geographical units is to increase the value of measures both of specialisation and of concentration (because, for example, random variations in industry shares will show up more). This creates difficulties for direct comparison of levels of specialisation and concentration measures, although time trends of the series can be compared.

We have updated the work of Kim (1995) using employment data from US states. These data allow a comparison of the broad trends in the US with those in Europe. As EU and US data are collected at different levels of industry aggregation, the 36 EU industries are aggregated up to the 21 US industries before measures of specialisation and concentration are calculated and compared.

First, let us consider the specialisation of locations. Table 5.14 shows the Gini coefficients of specialisation for the EU and the same statistics for the US.[17] The obvious point is that there has been a steady decrease in the specialisation of US states, in contrast to the U-shaped performance of the European measures.

We now turn to the concentration of industries. Table 5.15 reports the (un-weighted) average Gini coefficients of concentration for the EU and the US (see Midelfart et al., 2000a, for a complete set of Gini coefficients over time and industries). We see that there has been a sharp decline in industrial concentration in the US between the early 1970s and the mid-1980s, consistent with the findings of Kim (1995). Our time series extend those of Kim for a further ten years, and we see that the trend of dispersion continues into the 1990s and up till 1994/97. Relative to the magnitude of the changes in concentration that have taken place in the US, neither the slightly 'wave'-shaped patterns of European industrial concentration, nor the decline in concentration between 70/73 and 94/97 in Europe industries, are very significant.

Table 5.14   Gini coefficients of specialisation: US and EU

	70/73	80/83	88/91	94/97
US average	0.450	0.413	0.391	0.372
EU average	0.248	0.234	0.249	0.261

Table 5.15   Gini coefficient of concentration: US and EU

	70/73	82/85	88/91	94/97
US average	0.675	0.648	0.636	0.618
EU average	0.591	0.574	0.584	0.577

What are the industries driving the dispersion taking place in the US? Only two out of 21 US manufacturing industries do not record a decrease in concentration between 70/73 and 94/97; they are tobacco products and textile mill products. The industries that dispersed the most are motor vehicles and equipment, miscellaneous manufacturing industries, electronics, industrial machinery and equipment, primary metal industries, instruments, and leather and products. In Europe 14 out of 21 industries show a decrease in concentration during the same interval, and the industries that dispersed the most were: industrial machinery and equipment, tobacco, instruments, chemicals, and electronics (office and computing, radio, TV and communication). Hence, electronics, machinery and instruments appear to be driving the industrial dispersion in the US as well as in Europe.

The Motor Vehicle Industry: A US–EU Comparison

Despite the difficulty in making cross-country comparisons, more detailed study of the motor vehicle industry is instructive. For three time periods we have selected the top two and the top four European countries in terms of the value of motor vehicles produced. The shares of these countries in vehicle production and in manufacturing as a whole are given in the top two rows of Table 5.16. We see the top two countries increasing their share of vehicle manufacturing (from 58 per cent to 62 per cent), with little change in their share of manufacturing as a whole. The share of the top four declines (from 86 per cent to 82 per cent), with a larger fall in their share of manufacturing as a whole.

Table 5.16   European and US motor vehicle production

		Share in 1970 (%)		Share in 1982 (%)		Share in 1996 (%)	
		Vehicle production	Manufacture as a whole	Vehicle production	Manufacture as a whole	Vehicle production	Manufacture as a whole
Top Europe	A	58	46	59	44	62	45
	B	86	76	84	74	82	65
Top US	A	56	13	61	25	63	33
	B	87	56	84	61	82	61

Notes:
For top Europe, A refers to top two countries and B to top four countries.
For top US in 1970, A refers to top two states and B to top ten states; in 1982, A refers to top four states and B to top twelve states; in 1996, A refers to top six states and B to top thirteen states.

We then select the top US states in terms of motor vehicle manufacture, choosing the number of states to be just sufficient to give a similar share of vehicle production as the top two and top four EU countries. Thus, in 1970, just two US states produced 56 per cent of vehicles (similar to the top two EU, producing 58 per cent) and the top ten states produced 87 per cent (similar to the top four EU countries, producing 86 per cent). The spread of the US industry is apparent, since we see that by 1996 it took six US states to produce the same share of output as did the top two EU countries, and thirteen states to match the share of the EU top four.

As the US industry has dispersed, so the states in which it is concentrated have become much less specialised. In 1970 the two top vehicle producers, responsible for 56 per cent of US vehicle production, only had 13 per cent of total manufacturing. The analogous number for the 1996 top six, responsible for 63 per cent of US vehicle production, was 33 per cent. However, notice that these states are still more specialised than the equivalent European countries. Thus, whereas these top six states account for 63 per cent of vehicle production and 33 per cent of total manufacturing, the four European countries account for 62 per cent of vehicle production and 45 per cent of the supply of total manufactures. However, this concentration of vehicles relative to manufacturing as a whole is much less marked at the next level: the top thirteen US states, producing 82 per cent of US vehicles, supply 61 per cent of manufactures as a whole, while the equivalent European countries, producing 82 per cent of EU vehicles, supply 65 per cent of manufactures.

Spatial Separation

The problem with direct comparison of the EU with the US is both that their geographies are inherently different, and that there are different size units of observation in the US. We can go some way to addressing these issues by using our index of spatial separation (Section 5.3). It simply gives a measure of distance between production units in each industry. We have computed this index for each of the 21 industries, for the EU and for the US (49 states, excluding Alaska and Hawaii). We find the spatial separation index generally larger for the US than for the EU.

This difference simply reflects the greater geographical size of the US. To control for this we want to condition each value on a measure of geographical size, and for this we use the index of spatial separation for manufacturing as a whole on each continent. We therefore define the *conditional spatial separation* index as the spatial separation index for each industry divided by that for manufacturing as a whole. Finally, we compared these conditional spatial separation indices, taking the ratio of the EU measure to the US measure for each industry.

Results are given in Table 5.17. Consider lumber and wood products from 82/85 onwards. The numbers say that, conditional on the relative sizes of the US and the EU, this industry is more spatially separated in the EU than in the US. Looking at motor vehicles we see much more marked EU spatial separation, although the margin is declining. On the other side, electronic equipment is less spatially separated in the EU than in the US, presumably reflecting the fact that the two US clusters of this industry are on opposite sides of the continent.

The conclusion is that, on average, the EU is more conditionally spatially separated than the US. This has not changed much over time. In 1982/85, 17 out of 21 industries were more spatially separated in the EU than in the US, a number which fell to 15 of the 21 industries by 1994/97. Thus, we see little evidence of convergence.

5.7   CONCLUSIONS

It seems clear from the analysis in this chapter that, from the early 1980s onwards, the industrial structures of EU economies have become more

*Table 5.17 EU conditional spatial separation/US conditional spatial
separation*

	Industry	70/73	82/85	88/91	94/97
413	Lumber and wood products	0.92	1.07	1.11	1.12
417	Furniture and fixtures	1.06	1.06	1.08	1.05
420	Stone, clay and glass products	1.03	1.09	1.09	1.07
423	Primary metal industries	1.26	1.23	1.2	1.22
426	Fabricated metal products	1.01	1.04	1.04	1.02
429	Industrial machinery and equipment	0.92	0.95	0.98	1.03
432	Electronic and other electric equipment	0.83	0.81	0.84	0.85
435	Motor vehicles and equipment	1.46	1.44	1.42	1.3
438	Other transportation equipment	0.86	0.81	0.76	0.80
441	Instruments and related products	0.99	0.87	0.83	0.89
444	Miscellaneous manufacturing industries	1.06	1.04	1.03	0.99
453	Food and kindred products	0.95	1.01	1.03	1.01
456	Tobacco products	1.63	2.08	2.27	2.19
459	Textile mill products	1.91	2.14	2.10	2.03
462	Apparel and other textile products	1.17	1.20	1.14	1.04
465	Paper and allied products	1.20	1.30	1.29	1.33
468	Printing and publishing	1.00	1.02	1.03	0.97
471	Chemicals and allied products	1.04	1.01	1.06	1.07
474	Petroleum and coal products	0.74	0.92	0.89	0.85
477	Rubber and misc. plastics products	1.07	1.03	1.07	1.05
480	Leather and leather products	1.46	1.35	1.29	1.24
Average		1.12	1.16	1.16	1.14

dissimilar. This is as would be predicted by trade theory (old and new)
during a period of economic integration. What are the main features of
this process of divergence?

First, it is slow. Over a fourteen-year period, most economies have only
seen a few per cent of their industrial production move out of line with that
of the rest of the EU. Of course, more activity might be expected to show up
in more disaggregate data, but nothing in our results suggest that the process
is particularly rapid. We see no marked effect on location and specialisation
patterns of the completion of the Single Market Programme.

Second, it is driven by a combination of forces. Some industries are
becoming more geographically concentrated, others more dispersed. This
fact alone tells us that there is no single process driving all industries in the
same direction. This is perhaps surprising, since trade theory (old and new)
generally predicts that falling trade barriers should make all, not just some,
industries become more geographically concentrated.

Our analysis sheds light on the mechanisms that are at work. Some of the forces encouraging medium and high increasing returns to scale industries to locate in central regions are diminishing. At the same time industrial linkages are encouraging some industries – for example those with high shares of intermediate goods in production – to move into central locations. And in addition, the supply of skilled workers and researchers is becoming increasingly important in moving some industries into countries well endowed with these types of workers.

Third, the process is in the opposite direction from the one we observe in the US. The US saw states becoming increasingly dissimilar from 1860 until around 1940, but a considerable amount of convergence has occurred since. Despite recent work in the area it is still not clear what forces drive these trends for the US.[18]

Is the process of growing dissimilarity in the EU likely to continue, or is it reaching some limit? We see no evidence that it is reaching a limit. In so far as any direct comparisons with the US are possible, it is likely that EU industry remains more dispersed than that of the US. The time series record for Europe indicates no evidence of a slowdown. And as we have seen, the process is slow; economies are nowhere near pressing against the limits of complete specialisation.

Finally, is the process to be welcomed? Our results suggest that the rate of structural change is sufficiently slow for it not to be associated with major adjustment costs. And if it is driven by a combination of comparative advantage and industrial linkages, then analysis suggests that it will lead to real income gains.

APPENDIX 5.A   DATA

1.   Manufacturing Production Data

The data set is based on production data from two sources: OECD STAN database and the UNIDO database.

OECD STAN (Structural Analysis) database

Data   National industrial data on value of output.

Period   1970–1997, annual data.

Countries 13 European countries: Austria, Belgium, Denmark, Finland, France, Germany, Greece, Italy, Netherlands, Portugal, Spain, Sweden, United Kingdom.

Sectors   36 industrial sectors specification.

UNIDO database

Data	National industrial data on value of output.
Period	1970–1997, annual data.
Countries	Ireland.
Sectors	27 industrial sectors; the specifications have been adjusted to be consistent with the classification employed in the STAN database, see notes on changes made to the data below.

NB: Some 3-digit data is missing in various years for various sectors. Where possible we break down 2-digit data using information on 3-digit shares from close time periods; if not possible, we break down 3-digit sectors by EU share. Approximately 7 per cent of the 3-digit data needs to be estimated in this way. Details are available on request.

2. Trade Data

UN Com Trade database

Data	Manufacturing trade data on total exports to the world.
Period	1970–1997, annual data.
Countries	EU-15: Austria, Belgium/Luxembourg, Denmark, Finland, France, Germany, Greece, Ireland, Italy, Netherlands, Portugal, Spain, Sweden, United Kingdom
Sectors	104 manufacturing sectors.

3. Service Data

Service data are based on OECD Services database.

OECD Services database

Data	Services employment and GDP data.
Period	1982–1995, annual data.
Countries	EU-15: Austria, Belgium/Luxembourg, Denmark, Finland, France, Germany, Greece, Ireland, Italy, Netherlands, Portugal, Spain, Sweden, United Kingdom.
Sectors	Total services; five individual service sectors.

4. US Data

US data are based on regional manufacturing employment data, provided by Gordon Hanson.

Data	Manufacturing employment data.
Period	1970–1997, annual data.
US states	51.
Sectors:	21 manufacturing sectors.

APPENDIX 5.B   INDUSTRY AND COUNTRY CHARACTERISTICS

(1) Industry Characteristics

- *Economies of scale*
  Indicators of economies of scale, source: Pratten (1988)
- *Technology level*
  High, medium, low, OECD classification, source: OECD (1994)
- *R&D intensity*
  R&D expenditures as share of gross value-added, source: ANBERD and STAN, OECD
- *Capital intensity*
  Capital stock per employee, source: COMPET, Eurostat
- *Share of labour*
  Share of labour compensation in value-added, source: STAN, OECD
- *Skill intensity*
  Share of non-manual workers in workforce, source: COMPET, Eurostat
- *Higher skills intensity*
  Share of employment with higher education, source: COMPET, Eurostat
- *Industrial growth*
  Growth in gross production value between 1970 and 1994, source: STAN, OECD
- *Agricultural inputs intensity*
  Use of primary inputs as share of value of production
- *Intermediates intensity*
  Total use of intermediates as a share of value of production
- *Intra-industry linkages*
  Use of intermediates from own sector as share of value of production
- *Inter-industry linkages*
  Use of intermediates (excluding inputs from own sector) as share of value of production
- *Final demand bias*
  Percentage of sales to domestic consumers and exports
- *Sales to industry*
  Percentage of sales to domestic industry as intermediates and capital goods

Agricultural inputs intensity, intermediates intensity, intra-industry linkages, inter-industry linkages, final demand bias, and sales to industry are all calculated using the OECD input–output tables database. EU average intensities are constructed on the basis of the input–output tables for Denmark, France, Germany and the UK in 1990.

(2) Country Characteristics

- *Market potential*
  Indicators of market potential based on GDP, source: European Commission, DGII
- *Supplier access*
  Indicators of supplier access based on GDP and sales to manufacturing, source: Midelfart et al. (2000b)
- *Labour force*
  Total labour force, source: Eurostat
- *Capital stock*, source: PennWorld Tables
- *Average manufacturing wage*
  For all countries except Ireland, annual labour compensation per employee in total manufacturing, source: STAN, OECD. For Ireland we use the labour cost survey by Eurostat (1996) and COMPET (CMPT3110), Eurostat. Due to lack of data on Ireland, we assumed that number of hours worked per week is the same in Ireland as in the UK
- *Relative wages*
  Wages for non-production/production workers, source: United Nations (1998). UNISD does not give data for Belgium, France, Netherlands and Portugal. For these countries we used Eurostat (1992), and COMPET (CMPT 3110), Eurostat, and assumed 4 weeks of work per month
- *Agricultural production*
  Agriculture share in GDP
- *Researcher and Scientists (RSE)*
  Researchers per 10 000 labour force, source: OECD
- *Education of population*
  Share of population aged 25–59 with at least secondary education, source: Eurostat
- *Regional aid*, source: European Commission (1995)
- *Total aid*, source: European Commission (1995)

The following table details the 1990 value of the four country characteristics that are used in the econometric specification that we report in Section 5.4.

(3) Country Characteristics (1990)

	Market potential	Supplier access	Agricultural production (% GDP)	Secondary and higher education (% population)	Researchers and Scientists (% labour force)
Austria	12 303.0	8.73	3.2	75.1	34
Belgium	13 263.8	8.90	1.9	60.6	53
Denmark	6 627.8	8.18	4.5	82.1	58
Spain	4 993.2	9.76	5.4	35.1	32
Finland	3 642.1	8.23	6.6	72.6	67
France	12 380.2	10.61	3.5	62.7	60
Germany	13 072.8	10.99	3.0	82.1	59
Greece	2 335.7	7.59	12.5	49.3	20
Ireland	3 791.5	7.46	9.6	51.3	58
Italy	8 715.1	10.57	4.1	41.4	32
Netherlands	12 839.9	9.01	4.0	65.9	46
Portugal	3 193.8	7.87	7.3	23.8	31
Sweden	5 810.5	8.90	3.4	76.7	78
UK	12 225.8	10.40	2.0	55.3	50

NOTES

*   The authors would like to thank staff at the Directorate-General for Economic and Financial Affairs for help and comments. In particular, Adriaan Dierx, Martin Hallet, Karel Havik and Fabienne Ilzkovitz have helped with data and provided specific comments that have substantially improved the study. Danny Quah, Victor Norman, Jan Haaland and Diego Puga have commented extensively on earlier drafts of this chapter and helped us resolve a number of important issues. Gordon Hanson kindly provided us with US data. Finally, Sandra Bulli, Monica Baumgarten de Bolle and Beatriu Canto and Dhush Puwanarajah have provided invaluable research assistance.
1. Our econometric approach is innovative. It is closest to that of Ellison and Glaeser (1999). Previous econometric studies of industrial location in Europe, such as Brülhart and Torstensson (1996), have looked at changes in summary measures of industrial location as a function of industry characteristics. Our approach uses the full measure of industry production by country, as determined by the interaction between country and industry characteristics.
2. Gross value of output measures are preferred if changes in outsourcing are primarily to other sectors, rather than own sectors. This appears to be the case from inspection of input–output matrices.
3. All the way through the chapter we shall use some sort of moving average to try to remove spurious fluctuations due to the differential timing of country and sector business cycles.
4. Despite the overall rise in specialisation in thirteen out of fourteen countries from 1980/83 to 1994/97, four countries – France, Great Britain, Portugal and the Netherlands – actually became marginally less specialised during the second half of this period (1988/91–1994/97). However, for France, Great Britain and Portugal these slight decreases in specialisation are not enough to undo the large increases that they saw during the 1980s. The overall picture is one of a general increase in specialisation over the last two decades.
5. The Gini coefficient of specialisation summarises the distribution of relative production shares, $r_i^k(t)$, across industries in a given country. The Lorenz curve associated with the

measure gives cumulated values of $v_i^k(t)$ on the vertical axis, against cumulated values of $\bar{v}_i^k(t)$ on the horizontal, and observations are ranked in descending order by the gradient, $r_i^k(t)$.

6. The Gini coefficient of concentration measures the dispersion of a distribution of absolute production shares, $s_i^k(t)$, across countries for a given industry. The Lorenz curve associated with the coefficient has cumulated $s_i^k(t)$ on the vertical (as before), cumulated number of locations on the horizontal (each interval with the same width, 1/N). Locations are ranked by $s_i^k(t)$ (the gradient of the Lorenz curve).

7. Traditionally researchers have tended to consider relative instead of absolute shares of industries when constructing summary measures of concentration, see for example, Brülhart and Torstensson (1996). Summary indices of concentration based on relative shares are less informative as they are beset with problems related to the different sizes of the units of observations (countries). An industry will be absolutely concentrated if particular countries – independent of the size of the countries – have very large shares of that particular industry. However, if we look at relative indices of concentration, the degree of concentration of an industry will depend on the size of the countries that have the largest shares of the industries. See Haaland et al. (1999) for further discussion of absolute versus relative indices.

8. Particularly since the smaller EU countries have grown more rapidly than the larger EU countries, and that the industries that have declined in concentration typically are industries where larger countries have tended to have the highest shares.

9. See, for example, Brülhart and Torstensson (1996), Amiti (1999) and Brülhart (1998), who regress these summary statistics on a number of industry characteristics.

10. It is constructed using information on gross value-added and individual industry sales to manufacturing. See Midelfart et al. (2000b) for details.

11. The standard references on testing trade theory are Leamer and Levinsohn (1995) and Helpman (1999). Davis and Weinstein (1998) test one hypothesis from economic geography, but fall short of developing a general specification.

12. Except for the1970/73 regression where contemporaneous endowment data is not available. Instead, we use the same endowment data as for the 1980/83 regression.

13. Gross production value is, to our knowledge, not available for the service sectors and time span employed in the present chapter; we therefore have to use another measure of activity in service industries – namely employment.

14. The OECD (1999) studies national and regional specialisation in Europe based on a sectoral output classification that covers both manufacturing and services (eight economic sectors), they report increased national specialisation over the period 1980 to 1996. However, moving to a more aggregated sectoral classification (three sectors: agriculture, manufacturing and services) while analysing regional (NUTS 1) instead of national specialisation, we see a fall in the average regional specialisation.

15. Note that data on all services apart from financial services, insurance, real estate and business services are missing for Ireland and Greece.

16. We use the average of the 1990 input–output value tables of Denmark, France, Germany and the UK.

17. Note that due to the fact that the EU sectors are aggregated up to the 21 US sectors before the indices are calculated, the indices reported in Table 5.14 are not identical to those in Table 5.3.

18. See Kim (1995) and Ellison and Glaeser (1999).

REFERENCES

Amiti, Mary (1999), 'Specialization patterns in Europe', *Weltwirtschaftliches Archiv*, **135**, 1–21.

Brülhart, Marius (1998), 'Evolving geographical specialisation of European manufacturing industries', *Weltwirtschaftliches Archiv*, **137** (2), 215–43.

CEP II (1997), 'Trade patterns inside the single market', *European Commission: The Single Market Review*, subseries IV: Impact on trade and investment.

Davis, D. and Weinstein, J. (1998), 'An account of global factor trade', NBER Working Paper, no. 6785.

Ellison, Glenn and Glaeser, Edward L. (1999), 'The geographic concentration of industry: does natural advantage explain agglomeration?', *American Economic Review*, 89, Papers and Proceedings, 311–16.

European Commission (1995), 'Fifth survey on state aid in the European Union in the manufacturing and certain other sectors'.

Eurostat (1996), 'Labour costs 1992', Luxembourg–Brussels.

Eurostat (1992), Earnings – industries and services 1990', Luxembourg–Brussels.

Haaland, Jan I., Kind, Hans J. and Midelfart, Karen Helene (1999), 'What determines the economic geography of Europe?', CEPR Discussion paper, no. 2072.

Helpman, E. (1999), 'The structure of foreign trade', *Journal of Economic Perspectives*, **13**(2), 121–44.

Kim, Sukkoo (1995), 'Expansion of markets and the geographic distribution of economic activities: the trends in U.S. regional manufacturing structure, 1860–1987', *Quarterly Journal of Economics*, 110, 881–908.

Krugman, Paul R. (1991), *Geography and Trade*, Cambridge, MA: MIT Press.

Leamer, E. and Levinsohn, J. (1995), 'International trade theory; the evidence', in G. Grossman and K. Rogoff (eds), *Handbook of International Economics*, vol. 3, Amsterdam: North-Holland.

Midelfart, Karen-Helene, Overman, Henry G., Redding, Stephen J. and Venables, Anthony J. (2000a), 'The location of European industry', DG Economic and Financial Affairs, Economic Paper, no. 142.

Midelfart, Karen-Helene, Overman, Henry G. and Venables, Anthony J. (2000b), 'Comparative advantage and economic geography: estimating the determinants of industrial location in the EU', CEPR Discussion paper, no. 2618.

OECD (1994), *Manufacturing Performance: A Scoreboard of Indicators*, Paris: OECD.

OECD (1999), *EMU: Facts, Challenges and Policies*, Paris: OECD.

Pratten, Cliff (1988), 'A survey of the economies of scale', in *Commission of the European Communities, Research on the 'Cost of non-Europe', vol. 2: Studies on the Economics of Integration*.

United Nations (1993), *Industrial Statistics Yearbook 1991*, vol. 1: General Industrial Statistics, UN, New York.

WIFO (1999), 'Specialisation and (geographic) concentration of European manufacturing', background paper for 'The competitiveness of European Industry; the 1999 report', EC Enterprise Directorate-General, working paper no. 1, Brussels.

PART II

Macroeconomic issues

6. Product market reforms and macroeconomic performance in the European Union

Adriaan Dierx, Karl Pichelmann and Werner Röger*

INTRODUCTION

Europe's key challenges of restoring full employment, creating a knowledge-based economy, preparing for population ageing and safeguarding social cohesion are closely interlinked and need to be addressed by a coherent and comprehensive economic policy strategy for the medium to long term. The overarching objective of the strategy adopted by the European Union is to enhance the capacity of its economy to generate high rates of non-inflationary growth over a prolonged period. Basically, this requires pressing ahead with deep, comprehensive reforms of product, capital and labour markets, backed up by a sound macroeconomic policy mix aiming at sustained rates of growth close to potential within an environment of price stability.

Against this background, this chapter looks at the structural reform efforts affecting EU product markets since the early 1990s and their impact on macroeconomic outcomes in terms of (un-)employment, real wages and growth. It also tries to take the interlinkages between reform areas into account, and to assess their impact on macroeconomic performance in a scenario analysis of different macroeconomic policy settings.

The chapter is organised as follows: Section 6.1 sets the stage for the analysis by providing some economic and political background considerations to the reform effort. The theoretical framework of the study is presented in Section 6.2, which describes the main transmission channels linking structural improvements in product markets with macroeconomic performance. Section 6.3 treats the interdependence between structural reforms in product and labour markets, and elaborates on the relation between structural reforms and the design of macroeconomic policy strategies. Section 6.4 briefly describes the main product market reforms carried out in the EU since the early 1990s. Section 6.5 models the impact of these reforms on macroeconomic performance using macro-model simulation analysis for different scenarios of macroeconomic policy settings. The intention of this section is to evaluate the impact of structural reforms on the speed limits to overall growth in the economy, to describe the adjustment towards a new equilibrium, and to illustrate how monetary and fiscal policy affects the adjustment process. Finally, Section 6.6 contains some concluding remarks.

6.1   SETTING THE STAGE

At their summit meeting in Lisbon in 2000, EU leaders set the ambitious goal for the EU to become the most competitive and dynamic knowledge-based economy in the world by 2010 and agreed on a comprehensive structural reform agenda to boost employment and liberalise markets, now known as the 'Lisbon strategy'. This renewed drive for economic reform was largely motivated by the observation of a persistent income gap with the US and a widespread perception of falling even further behind.

Indeed, at the turn of the century EU income levels – measured in terms of GDP per capita in purchasing power parities – stood, on average, at only some 70 per cent of the US level and the post-war process of catching up had come to a halt. Around 40 per cent of the income difference between the EU and the US may be attributed to a lower labour productivity per hour worked in the EU. The larger part of the difference in average levels of income, however, is explained by the fact that Europeans work less than their US counterparts, both in terms of employment rates and, if employed, in terms of average hours worked (see Figure 6.1).

Against this background, the four main planks of the comprehensive structural reform strategy to address the challenge to raise Europe's potential growth and to narrow the income gap aim at:

- Higher employment rates and lower structural unemployment;
- Improving competitive conditions;
- Fostering productivity and investment growth;
- Efficient, integrated financial markets.

Before providing a more detailed formal exposition of the main transmission channels from structural reforms to aggregate economic performance, we consider it useful to begin with a brief non-technical discussion of the basic relationships between labour and product market institutions and macroeconomic outcomes as identified in the economic literature.

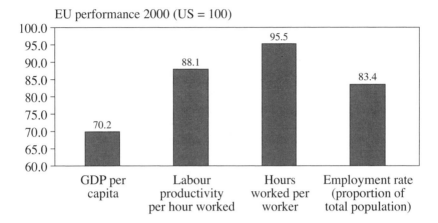

EU performance 2000 (US = 100)

Figure 6.1 EU performance relative to that of the US

Starting with labour market institutions, two different – though interconnected – perspectives on the macroeconomic impact of labour market reforms may be distinguished: (i) a productivity-enhancing channel, whereby better working labour markets allow for an efficient (re-)allocation of labour and provide improved framework conditions and incentives for human capital accumulation, thus raising growth and real incomes; and (ii) an employment-enhancing channel, whereby more employment-friendly institutional arrangements provide stronger incentives to participate in the labour market, crack down on insider–outsider barriers and reduce structural unemployment, basically by lowering the mark-up of wages over the reservation wage.

Productivity growth and equilibrium unemployment are jointly determined endogenous variables in the economy, and there are several theoretically plausible ways in which the fundamental determinants of equilibrium unemployment may affect productivity growth, and vice versa.[1] However, these relationships can go either way and there is little evidence that they are either important or robust, in particular over the medium to longer term; thus 'we should not expect to see any strong relationship between productivity growth and unemployment trends' (Krugman 1994, p. 32). As a consequence, this allows consideration of the impact of structural labour market reform policies on equilibrium unemployment and on long-run growth, treated separately.

Product market reform, broadly speaking, tries to increase competition and reduce monopoly rents in previously sheltered sectors, often in the form of removing entry barriers. A higher elasticity of product demand facing firms shifts the aggregate labour demand curve in a favourable way and implies, *ceteris paribus*, lower equilibrium unemployment; basically this mechanism works by driving away excess rents accruing to producers, labour, or both, which had caused output and employment to be lower than would have been the case under competitive conditions.

Moreover, the strengthening of competitive forces will reinforce economies' capacity to respond to adverse shocks. As prices and wages become more sensitive to market conditions, they should adjust faster than in the past, reducing cumulative losses in output and employment over the medium term which may be associated with the adjustment process.[2]

Product market liberalisation/deregulation may also have straightforward implications for efficiency. For example, new entrants may use more advanced technologies compared to incumbent producers. Similarly, previously sheltered sectors may be forced to reduce labour hoarding and excess capacity given higher competitive pressure. Moreover, more competition may well drive up the rate of technological and organisational innovation.[3] Indeed, there is increasing evidence against the view that firms enjoying significant market power plough back excess profits into higher rates of R&D and innovation. Rather it appears that lack of competition tends to provide little incentive for firms to pursue technological innovations, slows down its diffusion and impedes a higher variety and quality of goods and services delivered to consumers.[4]

6.2　MAIN TRANSMISSION CHANNELS

In synthesising empirical findings, the basic mechanisms sketched above suggest a distinction between two channels to analyse the effects of product market reforms on macroeconomic performance: (a) strengthening competitive conditions; and (b) increased productivity growth. Both channels are represented in the Quest II model developed by the European Commission (see Box 6.1).

BOX 6.1　BASIC CHARACTERISTICS OF THE QUEST II MODEL

This box sketches a small conventional growth model with imperfect competition in the labour and goods market. The model presents – though in a simplified manner – basic characteristics of the Commission's macroeconometric QUEST II model which are relevant for analysing effects of structural reforms. QUEST II

---

belongs to the class of 'modern' neoclassical–Keynesian synthesis models. This implies the model exhibits Keynesian features in the short run due to nominal wage and price rigidities, while the long-run properties are largely determined by the neoclassical growth model. Because of imperfections in goods and labour markets, the steady state generated by the model in terms of GDP and employment is below the long-term equilibrium values under perfect competition (for a general description of the QUEST II model see Roeger and in't Veld (1997).

The household sector maximises an intertemporal utility function over private consumption subject to a budget constraint. The optimality conditions imply the following decision rule for consumption:[a]

$$\frac{\dot{C}}{C} = \frac{(r-q)}{s}.$$
(1)

This consumption (savings) rule implies that next period consumption (C) (or current period savings) will be higher when the real interest rate (r) is above the rate of time preference (θ), and vice versa. This savings rule will be important for the subsequent analysis since it ties down the real interest rate to the rate of time preference in the long run. In other words, there is a unit elasticity of savings with respect to financial and human wealth. This property is basically due to the fact that consumption evolves proportional to (permanent) income and financial wealth in the long run.

The behavioural relations of the firm are derived from profit maximisation, subject to a constant returns to scale (Cobb–Douglas) technology

$$Y = AK^{1-a}L^a.$$
(2)

It is further assumed that firms' behaviour is monopolistically competitive with a perceived price elasticity of demand given by ε. The first order conditions yield an investment rule[b]

$$(1 - 1/\varepsilon)(1 - a)A(L/K)^a = r + \delta$$
(3)

and a labour demand condition

$$(1 - 1/\varepsilon)aA(K/L)^{(1-a)}$$
(4)

Under imperfect competition, firms require that (real) factor costs are equated to the marginal product of the corresponding factor adjusted for the price elasticity of demand. This adjustment is optimal for an imperfectly competitive firm, since it takes into account that an increase in output can only be sold at a lower price. It should be noted that ε is not a behavioural constant, but depends, in general, on the market structure, the number of competitors within a market, but also on macroeconomic conditions. To illustrate the macroeconomic link, assume that there is a wage reduction. If firms expect a demand expansion associated with this shock, say because of an expansionary monetary policy reaction, then the firm will have to reduce prices by less (or not at all) when expanding supply (and consequently ε will be small). However, if firms expect no expansion of aggregate demand or even a contraction, then increased supply can only be sold at a lower price and ε will be larger.

In the analysis we distinguish both short- and long-term effects. The short-term effects are those effects which emerge with a constant capital stock, while the long-run effects are those where the capital stock is allowed to fully adjust to its long-run equilibrium level.

Notes:
[a] In fact the savings equation in QUEST II is more complicated since finitely lived and partly liquidity constrained households are assumed.
[b] Because of adjustment and vacancy costs, the decision rules in QUEST II are more complicated.

6.2.1   Strengthening Competitive Conditions

In the QUEST II model, it is assumed that firms' actions are monopolistically competitive. Increased competition can thus be modelled as a downward shift in the aggregate price mark-up. Again, the shock is assumed to be permanent. The perceived price elasticity of demand of individual firms depends on factors such as market structures and the number of firms in the market. Therefore this shock could be interpreted as a partial removal of entry barriers, for example related to the EU's Internal Market Strategy.

Short-run adjustment
The immediate impulse of an increase in competition originates from the factor demand equations. Increasing competition lowers the perceived price elasticity of demand and leads to output and factor demand expansion. Obviously, in the short run the effect on ε is also influenced by the expectation of firms concerning the aggregate demand effects. The effect can especially

be mitigated by restrictive monetary policies which would force the output expansion to be accompanied by falling prices.

Long-run adjustment

For analysing the long-run effects of increased competition, it may again be useful to start from the investment and savings schedules (Box 6.1, equations (3) and (1)). Note that ε will be permanently lower. Therefore, provided the real interest rate returns approximately to baseline levels, a fall in the price mark-up shifts up the investment schedule and unambiguously increases the capital intensity of production and therefore labour productivity.[5] Note also that the investment and labour demand conditions (Box 6.1, equations (3) and (4)) do not by themselves determine the level of capital and employment in long-run equilibrium. However, since investment and labour demand is shifted upwards for given wages and real interest rates, the wage response is again crucial for the magnitude of the long-run employment expansion associated with increased competition. If wages respond strongly to increased demand, then the (long-run) employment and GDP expansion will be small.

For the wage rule used in the QUEST II model, there are essentially three channels through which wages respond to an increase in labour demand. First, wages increase with labour market tightness, second they can increase because an output expansion increases the reservation wage. This channel is ignored in the macro-econometric simulations in Section 3; the reservation wage is fixed to the baseline. However, a third mechanism, namely the presence of rent-sharing will exert downward pressure on wages with an increase in goods market competition. Therefore in the case of rent-sharing effects the employment and GDP multiplier should be largest.

6.2.2   Increasing Labour Productivity

Efficiency improvements arising from product market reform are captured by a positive and permanent increase in the level of total factor productivity (Box 6.1, *A* in equation (2)). An increase in the level instead of an increase in the growth rate was chosen for the macro-econometric simulations. The justification for this is the fact that previously protected and or state-owned firms may have produced with excess capacity, and increased competition forces firms to use available resources more efficiently.

However, it may also be argued that removal of entry barriers will allow for a more rapid inflow of competitors with more advanced technologies. Consequently, the growth rate of technical progress would increase. On the other hand, the loss of a secure market position could also have negative effects on R&D investments. Thus, while the level effect seems quite plausible, we are inclined to suggest that more empirical evidence needs to be gathered before one stipulates effects on the growth rate of technical progress.

Short-run adjustment
The way firms respond to an increase in efficiency depends crucially on the price response. If prices adjust only sluggishly, firms may face a temporary demand weakness, and in such a case the short-run employment effect of an increase in productivity is likely to be negative.

Long-run adjustment
Under the conditions for savings and investment, an efficiency improvement will increase the capital intensity in the long run. Therefore, similar to the case of increased competition, it will depend on the wage rule whether and by how much employment is going to expand. Note, however, that the employment effect of an efficiency improvement is likely to be smaller for two reasons: first, wages tend to be more strongly indexed to efficiency improvements, and second, the negative rent-sharing effect on wages is absent in the efficiency scenario.

6.3   POLICY INTERACTIONS

Structural reform policies need to be implemented in a coherent and coordinated manner, given that its elements are closely interlinked and mutually support each other. With a view to a smooth interaction of structural reforms in product and labour markets and a macroeconomic policy mix conducive to sustainable growth, two interconnected issues have to be borne in mind:

- *The need for a comprehensive reform design*   Interactions and complementarities between different structural reform policies make a strong case for a broad-based reform strategy, thus exploiting synergies arising from a comprehensive approach to improve the functioning of product, capital and labour markets. This argument is relevant both at the individual country level and for the EU as a whole.
- *The two-way interaction between structural reforms and macroeconomic policies*   Sound macroeconomic policies provide the best framework for reaping, as quickly as possible, the full benefits of structural reform policies. Stability-oriented fiscal and monetary policies can have a direct bearing on lowering structural unemployment, predominantly via the real interest rate channel. Simultaneously, successful structural reform policies affect potential output and raise the speed limits for growth, so that to allow aggregate demand expansion policy to operate without generating inflationary pressures.

6.3.1 The Need for a Comprehensive Reform Design

Obviously, the broad variety of institutional settings across countries requires a tailor-made structural reform design for improving the functioning of labour, product and capital markets, but both theoretical considerations and empirical evidence suggest a comprehensive strategy, given the various interactions and synergies between reforms in different areas.

The vigorous pursuit of economic reforms to improve product market competition can be expected to have a positive impact on labour market performance, essentially by shifting the labour demand curve resulting in higher employment over the medium term. The structure of product markets also has a bearing upon the composition of employment, in particular the level of self-employment. Lack of competition in product markets, on the other hand, is likely to curb the positive impacts of labour market reforms due to rent-seeking behaviour of workers and firms. Thus, more intense product market competition may by itself create additional pressures for more flexible labour market regulations and practices.

Thus, it should also be emphasised that product market reform, especially a reduction in price–cost margins has implications for wage setting. This is implied by standard trade union bargaining models of the labour market featuring rent-sharing behaviour between firms and workers. In such a framework, a reduction of the price–cost margins in the goods market inevitably also leads to a reduction of the mark-up of wages over the reservation wage. A similar type of argument has recently been put forward in a paper by Blanchard and Giavazzi (2001).[6] Broadly speaking, it is based on the notion that, if product market deregulation decreases total rents, the incentives for workers to appropriate a proportion of these rents may be decreased, making unions weaker, reducing insider power and leading to labour market deregulation.

Product market reforms alone, when not accompanied by efforts to improve the functioning of labour markets, run the risk of driving up short-term adjustment costs which, in turn, may reduce the willingness to implement structural reforms. Thus, obviously, the full benefits of increased product market competition will only materialise when the labour market structures in place allow for a smooth reallocation of labour.

6.3.2 The Two-way Interaction between Structural Reforms and Macro-policies

Sound macroeconomic policies have an important role to play in any integrated and comprehensive strategy to reduce high and persistent unemployment in Europe, not only in coping adequately with the external forces slowing down economic activity at the present conjuncture. When unemployment, which is initially cyclical, over time tends to be partially translated into structural, for example because of human capital deterioration when left idle, the avoidance of excessive cyclical fluctuations could, *ceteris paribus*, also contribute to containing trend increases in unemployment. The empirical evidence does indeed suggest that countries with a higher volatility in unemployment rates have also experienced a larger increase in trend unemployment; but clearly the degree to which initially cyclical unemployment tends to persist is closely related to the specific institutional settings in the markets for products, capital and labour.

A medium-term stability-oriented macroeconomic framework also better allows exploiting synergies with structural policies to improve labour market performance with the main channel, probably, operating via the impact on real interest rates. Thus, medium-term fiscal consolidation, for example, does not only restore room for budgetary manoeuvre in case of country-specific demand weaknesses, it may well also have a positive impact on trend unemployment.

From a reverse angle, structural reform policies obviously shape the appropriate design of macroeconomic policies, since more efficiently operating markets raise potential growth, thereby extending the boundaries within which macroeconomic policies can operate without generating inflationary pressures. Moreover, successful structural reforms will tend to be supported in due course by their impact on investment, providing further stimulus to productive capacities and growth of total factor productivity.

6.4 RECENT PRODUCT MARKET REFORMS IN THE EU

The structural reforms on European product markets since the early 1990s have covered a wide range of areas, including internal market and competition policies, regulatory and administrative reform, the liberalisation of network industries, and fostering the development of the knowledge economy. The aim of these various reforms is to improve European Union macroeconomic performance by strengthening competition and/or raising productivity growth. This section first provides a brief survey of the structural reforms targeted at raising the level of competition on product markets, to be followed by a presentation of the different policy measures more specifically targeted at improving productivity through investments in knowledge (for a more detailed survey, see Dierx et al. 2003; and European Commission, 2002c, chapter 2).

6.4.1   Improving Competitive Conditions

The objective of increasing the level of competition on European product markets has been pursued through a wide range of policy reforms, which can be split into three broad categories: first, policies aimed at furthering market integration; second, policies aimed at increasing market efficiency by removing market distortions and facilitating market entry; and third, policies specifically designed to open up the network industries (telecommunications, post, electricity, gas, railways and air transport) to competition.

Market integration
The focus of the Single Market Programme (SMP), which was at the centre of the reform effort in the first half of the 1990s, was to eliminate non-tariff barriers to trade and investment inside the European Union. The idea was to facilitate entry by competitors from other EU Member States into what were still largely national markets in the 1980s. This push towards the integration of European product markets was strengthened by the forces of globalisation.

In the second half of the 1990s, the SMP evolved into the more broadly-based Internal Market Strategy, which was aimed more at enhancing the efficiency of the increasingly integrated EU product and capital markets and at improving the business environment. Finally, at the end of the decade the SMP was complemented by the creation of Economic and Monetary Union (EMU), which, by eliminating exchange rate uncertainty, further lowered the risks associated with foreign trade or direct investment within the euro area. A second effect of the introduction of the euro is the increased transparency of price differences between the participating countries with possibly significant effect on the nature of competition in the euro area.

In order to be effective in furthering market integration, internal market rules need to be transposed into national legislation in all Member States and subsequently be enforced in a uniform way. However, substantial differences in the degree of market opening between countries and sectors remain (see Figure 6.2). In addition, technical barriers to cross-border trade continue to be a major obstacle for entrepreneurs wishing to enter markets in another EU Member State and public procurement markets are opening up only slowly.

Market efficiency
In Chapter 4, Veugelers shows that in concentrated industries progress with market integration (as measured by the decline in price dispersion) is slower and that competition is less fierce (as illustrated by higher price–cost margins). This illustrates the importance of a competition policy geared

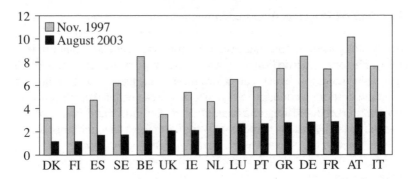

Figure 6.2   Percentage of Internal Market Directives not yet transposed into national legislation

towards preventing the creation and abuse of dominant positions in the market. The creation of a more integrated European market has therefore been complemented by the development of an EU-wide competition policy. By preventing restrictive practices (cartels, vertical and horizontal agreements and so on) and the creation (through mergers) and abuse of dominant positions in the market, the existence of strong and effectively independent competition authorities offers important benefits in terms of improving the competitive conditions in EU product markets. Similar benefits are derived from policies aimed at controlling state aids that distort competition on EU product markets.

More proactive measures to encourage market entry are essential as well. Blanchard and Giavazzi (2001) argue that with a given number of firms, product market deregulation resulting in increased demand elasticity has only a temporary effect on price–cost margins, whereas a decrease in entry costs leading to market entry has favourable consequences in the long term. This is one reason why the discussion on regulatory reform has focused on the time and costs required for setting up a new company. A recent study (CSES, 2002) shows substantial differences between EU Member States in this respect, with the typical time required for setting up a private limited company varying between 7 and 35 business days.

Using firm-level data, Scarpetta et al. (2002) report that strict regulations on entrepreneurial activity have a negative effect on both the entry of new firms and the rate of expansion of successful entrants in the initial years. Therefore, deregulation will not only contribute to a reduction in mark-ups because of increased competition, but will also have a direct positive effect on total factor productivity, as successful entrants tend to employ relatively new technologies in comparison with established firms that grow from within.

Liberalisation of the network industries

Amongst the different structural reforms undertaken within the European Union, much attention has been devoted to the evolution of the liberalisation process in the network industries. The key question here is whether liberalisation has led to increased competition amongst service providers resulting in lower prices and better quality for end users. Answering this question is complicated by the difficulty of separating competition effects from the effects of technological progress.

Liberalisation is most advanced in telecommunications. Community legislation imposed full competition in telecommunications by 1 January 1998, but some countries had derogations allowing them to postpone the introduction of full competition until 2002, at the latest. Other countries, however, had liberalised well before January 1998. In spite of the relative advancement of the liberalisation process in the telecommunication sector, the degree of market concentration remains high in many EU Member States, particularly in fixed telephony. Nevertheless, it is fair to say that the liberalisation process has started to pay off, as telecommunication services have become cheaper (see Figure 6.3). The European Central Bank (2001) reports a 23 per cent decline in telecom prices relative to the overall consumer price index over the period 1996–2000.

In the energy sector, the liberalisation process has been slower. The market share of the largest electricity generator, for example, remains quite high

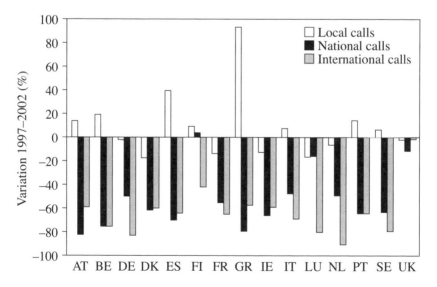

Figure 6.3   Evolution of prices in fixed telephony, 1997–2002

in many EU Member States. Moreover, interconnections between national energy networks are still largely insufficient to handle the increased cross-border demand. As a result of the relatively limited competition in most Member States, the benefits from liberalisation in energy have been smaller than in telecommunications.

In transport, the process of market opening has been slowed down by problems that new operators have experienced in receiving network access rights at competitive rates. In postal services, the liberalisation process is not very advanced as a large share of the market remains reserved for incumbents.

6.4.2   Fostering Investment in Knowledge, Increasing Productivity

Following the Lisbon summit, the European Union's transformation into a knowledge economy figures high on the policy agenda. This subsection reviews EU structural reforms aimed at raising the quantity and quality of Europe's human capital stock, stimulating innovation and R&D, and promoting the adoption of new information and communication technologies (ICT). These three types of investment in knowledge will be considered in turn.

Human capital formation
The development of human knowledge and skills remains central to equipping society with the tools required in a modern economy. By making the workforce more productive and by enabling greater flexibility in adapting to technological change, the formation of human capital is a crucial determinant of economic growth.

In terms of inputs, public education expenditure in the EU has declined slightly as a percentage of GDP but it remains around 5 per cent of GDP. However, the reading, mathematical and scientific literacy of 15-year-olds as measured by the OECD programme for international student assessment (PISA) appears to be only weakly correlated with education spending (European Commission, 2002a). This would seem to imply that Member States' efforts to increase the efficiency of their education systems are equally if not more important than spending increases.

Amongst the policy reforms introduced since the early 1990s, one should mention the introduction of national testing of pupils at key stages to improve standards in primary and secondary education; different measures to increase the quality and relevance of vocational and technical education; a lengthening of the duration of compulsory education; universal access to free secondary level education; and improved access to tertiary education. Moreover, Member States have started to develop and implement strategies to encourage lifelong learning. Nevertheless, the EU as a whole continues to lag behind the US and Japan in terms of the average years of education of the working population.

R&D and innovation

It is widely recognised that R&D-based innovation gives rise to important positive externalities. Knowledge generated by R&D activities in one firm or research organisation stimulates the development of new knowledge by others, or enhances their technological capabilities. Such cumulative external effects provide a theoretical basis for policy initiatives such as the Lisbon Strategy. Within the framework of this strategy, the European Council held in Barcelona in March 2002 agreed that EU investment in R&D should be increased with the aim of approaching 3 per cent of GDP by 2010. This is quite a tall order as EU R&D expenditure fluctuated around 1.9 per cent of GDP throughout the 1990s. Two-thirds of the additional investment is supposed to be financed by the private sector; this in light of the fact that the bulk of the R&D gap with the US (0.8 per cent of GDP in 2002), and most of its increase in recent years, is due to lower funding by EU industry.[7]

In response to the European Council's request, the Commission put forward an action plan aimed at stimulating investment in R&D. The action plan is wide-ranging but nevertheless focuses on providing better incentives for business to invest in R&D and making Europe a more attractive location to do research. This implies increasing the expected return on investment in R&D and innovation by improving the framework conditions in which businesses have to operate. The action plan also intends to make more effective use of public financing instruments thus increasing their leverage effect. The Member States as well have taken various measures to stimulate R&D and innovation, such as the provision of tax credits for R&D and innovation expenditures; measures aimed at improving cooperation between research and business; and support for university spin-offs. In addition, increased attention is paid to the diffusion of the knowledge gained.

Information and communication technologies (ICT)

The rapid growth of production in the ICT sector and the speedy adoption of new information and communication technologies by other sectors have been suggested as possible explanations for the spurt in US productivity growth in the second half of the 1990s. Estimates by Jorgenson and Stiroh (2000) and Oliner and Sichel (2000) of the growth contribution of ICT in the USA are around half a percentage point for the first half of the 1990s and around one percentage point for the second half. Estimates by van Ark et al. (2002), Daveri (2002) and the European Commission (2000) of the growth contribution of ICT in Europe are only half of the estimates produced for the United States.

Catching up with the United States in the ICT domain would imply on the one hand an increased specialisation in ICT-producing sectors and on the other, a more intensive use of information and communication technologies in other sectors. The former would imply increasing R&D expenditures in ICT to levels comparable to that in the United States, which would be an uphill task. Efforts to increase the use of ICT are likely to bear fruit within a shorter time frame.

ICT usage (including the use made of tools such as the internet) has continued to increase rapidly, both in the EU and the US. IT spending in the European Union remains well below that in the United States. Telecommunications spending as a percentage of GDP, on the other hand, is slightly above that in the United States, which is another illustration of the success of the reform effort in this sector.

6.5   ILLUSTRATIVE MACROECONOMIC SIMULATION SCENARIOS

6.5.1   Simulation Designs

The purpose of this section is to analyse the potential macroeconomic impacts of product market reforms on the EU economy in quantitative terms, using the European Commission's macro-econometric model QUEST II. Based on the empirical assessment and review of product market reforms in the EU provided in the previous section,[8] the econometric model is subjected to 'stylised reform shocks' designed to broadly represent the accomplishments of the past five years or so. It should be stressed at this point, however, that this section discusses only a limited number of interactions between structural reforms and macroeconomic policy responses; moreover, the structural reforms have typically been modelled as being implemented in a big bang approach, thus abstracting from timing and sequencing issues of gradually phased-in reforms. Thus, the following 'stylised reform shocks' will be analysed.

Scenario I: an improvement in competitive conditions
The numerous efforts undertaken in the second half of the 1990s to increase the level of competition on European product markets are probably best illustrated by the significant progress made in completing the Internal Market for goods and by the move towards liberalisation and deregulation of the network industries. The Internal Market has contributed to an increase

in intra-EU trade and investment flows. The effects of market entry by foreign firms were also reflected in a high level of turbulence in market leadership, even if industry concentration remained more or less constant. The liberalisation and deregulation in the network industries, notably in telecommunications and, to a somewhat lesser degree, in electricity, has paid off in terms of lower (relative) prices.

In addition, market integration and competition appear to have contributed to a permanent decline in price differences between EU Member States,[9] but the pressure put on mark-ups by the completion of the Single Market Programme may well have tended to recede somewhat over time (European Commission, 2002c, chapter 2).

There is some evidence, however, that structural reforms in the network industries have led to a more permanent decline in mark-ups. For example, simply summing up the estimated reduction in price mark-ups in the electricity and the telecommunication sector, weighted by their relative share in business sector output, results in a decline of the economy-wide mark-up of almost 0.5 basis points. Overall, roughly translated into aggregate figures to be used in the simulation assessment exercise, it is estimated that the sketched developments corresponded to a reduction in the average price mark-up of about half of a percentage point.

Recall from the theoretical discussion in Section 6.2 that product market reform, especially a reduction in price–cost margins, will most likely have repercussions on wage setting. As to the potential magnitude of such an effect, the trade union bargaining model presented in the Layard, Nickell and Jackman textbook (Layard et al. 1991), for example, suggests for a plausible configuration of parameters that a reduction of the price–cost mark-up by one half of a percentage point would reduce wages by about 2 per cent. The corresponding wage rule in QUEST II is somewhat less responsive, predicting a fall of wages in a magnitude of about 1 per cent in such a case.

Scenario II: increased productivity growth
As outlined in the previous section, structural reforms can also be expected to have a positive impact on both productive and dynamic efficiency in the economy. Typically, while firms produce at lowest cost under conditions of competition, they tend to operate inefficiently (through overstaffing, higher wages, lack of response to new opportunities, poor management) when competitive pressures are low. Thus, the process of restoring productive efficiency induced by structural reforms will be associated with a level increase of total factor productivity.

Arguably, there are also several channels through which structural reforms may have fostered dynamic efficiency, thus stimulating the growth rate of total factor productivity in a more permanent way. However, the empirical evidence is not at all supportive of a significant acceleration of total factor productivity (TFP) growth in the EU over the past couple of years. Against this background, we will therefore restrict ourselves in the simulation exercise to analyse a level shock to labour productivity; translated into QUEST II model terms, this is implemented as a once and for all level increase of TFP by 1 per cent, an order of magnitude that is similar to the one identified by Notaro (2002) in his analysis of the productivity impact of the SMP. It should be kept in mind, however, that this scenario is only intended to illustrate the dynamic response of GDP and employment to an increase in productive efficiency, but should not be interpreted as reflecting the stylised facts with respect to productivity developments in the past couple of years.

Macroeconomic policy responses
In the scenarios considered here it is assumed that both fiscal and monetary policy makers are strictly committed to simple rules, following either a restrictive or a neutral stance relative to potential output growth.

As regards monetary policy, a regime of fixed money supply (relative to the baseline scenario) is compared to an inflation targeting regime. Fixed money supply is interpreted here as a restrictive monetary policy rule, since it is assumed that the central bank continues to strictly target a pre-reform potential output path. Such a scenario may also be thought of as reflecting the situation of a single country acting alone, thus not being able to affect the European Central Bank (ECB) monetary policy.[10] In contrast, an inflation targeting regime is defined as an accommodating rule in which the central bank increases money supply as output expands in order to closely meet a baseline inflation target. Obviously, such a case may better reflect prevailing circumstances when countries act simultaneously to improve structural conditions, thereby revealing some of the benefits of coordinated structural reform.

In order to address both the stabilisation aspects and the distributional aspects of fiscal policy, two alternative fiscal responses are considered. The first fiscal rule stipulates that fiscal policy keeps expenditure (as a share of GDP) and tax rates constant, using all extra revenue (for example, from lower expenditure on unemployment benefits) to reduce the deficit. This rule implies a form of automatic stabilisation whereby the (potential) output expansion is accompanied by a negative fiscal impulse. In the second fiscal policy setting analysed here, fiscal policy remains neutral by keeping the deficit to GDP ratio constant. Of course, this rule can be implemented in several ways; here it is assumed that deficit stabilisation is achieved via reducing labour taxes, making it possible to address some of the distributional aspects as well.

Obviously, there are several other, more medium-term fiscal policy considerations to be addressed. Economic expansion creates room for reducing the tax burden which, in turn, could further enhance growth. In the simulations presented in this chapter, however, this aspect is not further examined. A more rigorous discussion would also require an analysis of capital tax reductions and a more elaborated analysis of the interaction between tax and social benefit reforms. The benefit rule entertained in the model, namely indexation of benefits to net wages, has been deliberately chosen in order to render labour taxes non-distortionary. Therefore, no additional employment effects can be expected from lowering labour taxes in this case, and the role of tax policy in the scenarios presented below is largely restricted to intertemporal labour income shifting.

6.5.2 Simulation Results

Scenario I: an improvement in competitive conditions
Basically, in the case of scenario I, the growth and employment effects relative to the baseline (see Figure 6.4) emerge because of outward shifts in the labour demand and investment schedules. In the scenario, product market reform is associated with wage moderation due to reduced possibilities for rent-sharing.

With a fall in the price mark-up and the resulting wage moderation, firms are expanding employment because they find it profitable to employ labour at a lower marginal product. Therefore, *ceteris paribus*, labour productivity initially declines; due to higher rates of investment, this process is reversed after some time. Moreover, with reduced possibilities for rent-sharing between workers and firms, product market deregulation implies that real wages fall below baseline in the short run. However, the positive effects of product market reform, by expanding labour demand and investment, eventually dominate and allow real wages to grow more strongly than labour productivity in the medium term.

The case without monetary policy accommodation is indicative of the potential effects of EMU countries pursuing structural reforms in isolation; with unchanged monetary policy, product market reforms could well be associated with a protracted period of prices falling well below baseline levels. This implies that for a given inflation objective monetary policy can respond in an expansionary fashion and may, thus, cushion the negative impact on real wages in the transition period, albeit to a fairly limited extent; and it will not be able to influence the growth process in the longer run. Without monetary policy accommodation, lower inflation is the key factor in crowding-in extra activity, via its effects on domestic demand as well as on foreign demand through improved competitiveness; with accommodation, the crowding-in effect relies more on domestic demand.

Fiscal policy could in principle support this process as well, by lowering labour taxes. Using the net revenue from output expansion and lower unemployment to reduce labour taxes could compensate workers for the initial income loss.[11] However, alternative fiscal options could also be considered. There would also be room for corporate tax reductions without violating distribution targets.

1. 'Unchanged' macroeconomic policies

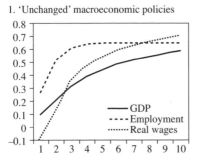

2. With fiscal and monetary policy response

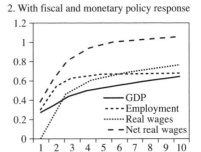

Figure 6.4   Scenario I – deviations from baseline

Scenario II: increased productivity growth

The second set of simulations investigates the effects of a positive shock to productivity (see Figure 6.5). Clearly, both an increase in productive efficiency – for example induced by restructuring and rationalisation of production and management processes – and/or an increase in dynamic efficiency related to product and process innovation will stimulate output and real wages. However, the simulation results also indicate that the interim adjustment period is likely to be associated with a significant fall of employment below baseline levels. Indeed, it may take up to four or five years before job losses abate and employment returns to its original level.

Fiscal and monetary policy can apparently do little to alleviate the short-run adjustment burden in that case. The lesson to be drawn is rather that coherence and comprehensiveness of reforms are essential. As becomes immediately evident when one considers the combined effects of the scenarios described above, for maximum effectiveness, comprehensive product market reforms need to be introduced, preferably jointly with labour market reforms. This would allow minimising the potentially negative short-run impacts on employment and real wages; moreover, monetary and fiscal

Figure 6.5 Scenario II – deviations from baseline

policies could support the adjustment process and limit the distributional implications in terms of consumption wages.

Nonetheless, the pay-off to structural reforms does not come instantaneously, requiring a firm and continued commitment to reform. However, as the above analysis suggests, the full benefits can indeed be quite substantial. Just taking the combined effects of the two scenarios together, the simulation results suggest a medium-term increase of GDP of about 2 per cent relative to its no-reform baseline level.

6.5.3 Discussion of Simulation Results

First, to put these results into perspective, we summarise available empirical evidence on the impact of structural reforms on macroeconomic outcomes. As already argued, it is inherently difficult to provide a quantitative macroeconomic assessment of the impact of structural reforms. Clearly, the design of market institutions is multifaceted and often of a highly qualitative nature, which is not easily captured in aggregated quantitative indicators. Moreover, significant gaps in data that are comparable across countries and over time pose serious obstacles to econometric analysis.

Basically, these difficulties can be tackled by either taking a simulation approach or relating simple indicators of the regulatory environment to macroeconomic outcomes. Typical examples of the simulation approach are the OECD (1997) study on regulatory reform and the Commission studies on the macroeconomic impact of the Single Market Programme. In the OECD study, using industry-specific estimates of efficiency gains in a plausible, medium-term programme of regulatory reform, combined with input–output aggregation and a dynamic simulation with the OECD's Interlink macro-econometric model, labour productivity and GDP gains were found to be positive for all eight countries examined. The long-run potential output gains (over a period of 15 to 20 years) varied from 5–6 per cent for Japan and Spain, almost 5 per cent for Germany and France, to less than 1 per cent for the US, reflecting the different state of existing regulations in different countries.

The European Commission's Directorate-General for Economic and Financial Affairs (1996) employed both a dynamic computable general equilibrium (CGE) model and its multi-country dynamic macro-model for an ex-post assessment of the Single Market Programme. Based on a scenario analysis focusing on the gains from the increase in competition/ efficiency and the rise in total factor productivity, the study found that the SMP had produced, by 1994, a gain in GDP in the range of 1.1–1.5 per cent. It should be noted that these numbers stand in some contrast with the ex-ante estimate provided in the so-called Cecchini report (1988). Using modified versions of the EC Hermes and OECD Interlink models, the Cecchini report estimated that the completion of the Internal Market had the potential, over the medium term, to raise the level of GDP by somewhere between 3.2 and 5.7 per cent above the level that would prevail in the absence of the SMP.

While these differences in estimates should not come as a big surprise given the somewhat different methodological approaches, the different time horizon and implementation deficiencies, they are also indicative that an unfavourable macroeconomic environment – as was present in the early 1990s – may, at least in the short run, have a restraining impact on the potential positive effects of structural reform efforts.

A more recent assessment of the macroeconomic effects of the Single Market Programme after 10 years, based on an estimated average decrease of price mark-ups by around 0.9 percentage points and an increase of productivity by around 0.5 per cent, suggests that real GDP would have been 1.4 per cent lower in 2002 without the single market programme; this translates roughly into 2.5 million additional jobs (European Commission, 2003a).

The overall finding in simulation studies of sizeable and positive long-run effects of structural reforms on output, employment and productivity is corroborated by a variety of studies relating simple indicators of the regulatory environment and the institutional design in product, labour and capital markets to macroeconomic outcomes. For example, Salgado (2002) finds in a recent IMF working paper using a panel analysis of 20 OECD countries that structural reforms implemented in the period 1985–95 have increased total factor productivity growth in the long run by 0.2 to 0.3 percentage points on average. Also, the 2003 IMF World Economic Outlook claims that more competition-friendly policies on euro area product markets would lead in the long run to a GDP increase of 4.3 per cent.

The latter approach is also typically employed to analyse the finance–growth nexus, linking financial development indicators to GDP per capita in cross-country growth regressions. A recent OECD study (Bassanini et al., 2001) for instance, suggests that a permanent increase of 1 per cent in the ratio of private bank loans to GDP would raise per capita GDP by 0.1 per cent and a corresponding increase in stock market capitalisation relative to GDP would raise per capita GDP by 0.3 per cent. In a sample of 14 OECD countries Carlin and Mayer (1999) found that, in particular, the growth of industries relying on R&D is strongly affected by financial variables, while the estimates are less robust in respect of fixed capital formation. Accordingly, they conclude that financial development stimulates growth in industrial countries more by promoting investment in R&D than by facilitating physical capital accumulation.

Turning now to our own results, the simulation exercise presented in this chapter has tried to illustrate the macroeconomic impact of structural reform efforts which are assumed to be broadly equivalent in scale to a reduction of the economy-wide price mark-up of about 0.5 of a percentage point and a 1 per cent level increase of TFP.

The price level response of the structural reform scenarios is in the order of magnitude the OECD has recently calculated from a simulation with the INTERLINK model, which evaluates the macroeconomic consequences of the fall of telecom and electricity prices as observed in the last two years. Taking into account all macroeconomic repercussions, in particular the wage response, the OECD arrives at a price level effect of –0.85 per cent after 10 years.

The employed scenario analysis allows explicitly for significant interactions between structural reforms in product and in labour markets, taking into account two main mechanisms through which product market reforms can affect labour markets. First, stepping up competition on the product market increases output and the demand for labour, and makes the latter more sensitive to wages. Second, competitive pressures in the product market dissipate economic rents, putting downward pressure on the associated wage premiums.

Allowing for such interaction effects, a stylised scenario combining a reduction in the price mark-up by 0.5 of a percentage point and a level increase of TFP by 1 percentage point has been analysed. The simulation results suggest a medium term increase in GDP of about 2 per cent; in terms of growth rates, this translates into an acceleration of output growth by about 0.25 of a percentage point annually over a period of seven to eight years. However, bearing in mind that the TFP effect is not well supported in the data for the second half of the 1990s, a more cautious assessment would shave off 1 percentage point of the overall GDP effect, and one tenth of a percentage point of the temporary acceleration of potential growth.

Typically, in simulation exercises of this type, structural reforms stimulate growth only temporarily; they raise output and employment levels, but they are not associated with a permanent increase of potential growth rates. Basically, the latter would require a permanently higher rate of growth of total factor productivity, with the main channels to raising equilibrium growth rates, as identified in the endogenous growth literature, being associated with institutions which raise savings, raise human or physical capital accumulation, increase technological and managerial innovation, and raise the start-up rate of new companies (see also chapter 2 in European Commission, 2003b).

The simulation exercises also offer some insights into the adjustment dynamics to structural reforms. Obviously, the impacts on employment and wages can be quite different in the short and the long run; for example, productivity improvements induced by increased competitive pressures may go hand in hand with labour shedding in the short run, while output expansion and entry of new firms will only gradually materialise to offset the short-run employment losses over the medium to long term. While the exact nature of such unpleasant trade-offs facing policy makers has not yet been fully explored, the simulation results suggest that short-run costs in terms of real wages and employment are minimised in comprehensive reform scenarios that take the interactions between the institutional design in labour and product markets into account.

6.6   CONCLUDING REMARKS

This chapter has explored the potential interactions between structural reforms and macroeconomic performance in terms of output growth, (un-)employment and real wages in the EU. Reviewing the broad patterns of structural reforms and improvements in the functioning of product markets in the past couple of years, we find in a backward-looking illustrative macro-econometric simulation exercise a medium-term increase in GDP relative to its baseline level of about 2 per cent. In terms of growth rates, this translates into an acceleration of output growth by almost 0.25 of a percentage point annually over a period of seven to eight years. Thus, structural reform efforts have indeed borne fruit and delivered significant benefits in terms of output and employment levels.

However, it has to be kept in mind that typical estimates of the euro area's potential output growth rate have been in the 2.25 to 2.5 per cent range; moreover, as our results indicate, the growth stimulus from past structural reforms tends to fade away over time. Indeed, if reform fatigue were to win the day, Europe would appear destined to suffer a setback to a medium-term growth path barely exceeding 2 per cent; in fact, in the absence of policy change, population ageing will push Europe's potential growth even below this level. Thus, to achieve an annual rate of growth of around 3 per cent for the EU as a whole over a prolonged period of time, as formulated at the Lisbon summit, the momentum and the breadth of structural reforms will certainly have to be maintained and increased. This is to be combined with growth supportive macroeconomic policy making, which – while maintaining price stability and a sound medium-term orientation of fiscal positions close to balance or in surplus – should aim at stabilising growth close to potential.

NOTES

*   We are indebted to Mandeep Bains, Bjoern Doehring, Fabienne Ilzkovitz, Mary McCarthy, Alberto Garralon, Peter Shanley and Jan Host Schmidt for helpful comments on an earlier version of this chapter. Of course, the usual disclaimer applies.
1. Imperfect matching between unemployment and vacancies in combination with an innovation externality, for example, may be associated with a too low productivity growth rate and drive up equilibrium unemployment. For an overview discussion of the relationship between labour market institutions and economic performance in terms of unemployment and growth, see Nickell and Layard (1999).
2. An analysis of structural impediments to quick and efficient adjustment to macroeconomic shocks, however, is outside the scope of this chapter.
3. These arguments have been developed extensively in the endogenous growth literature; for a survey, see for example Barro and Sala-i-Martin (1995).
4. For an overview on the relationship between competition and innovation see for example Ahn (2002), OECD (1997).
5. If one additionally considers financial services in the context of a comprehensive reform package, then a fall in real capital costs for firms is to be expected.
6. Very similar arguments have already been developed by, *inter alia*, S. Nickell (1999).
7. Differences between countries in terms of R&D spending and innovation performance can be associated with differences in industry structure. The United States, for example, is specialised in high-tech and research intensive sectors, which is one explanation why its expenditures on R&D are relatively high (2.8 per cent of GDP in 2002 as opposed to 2.0 per cent of GDP in the EU). On the other hand one could argue that the successful development of the ICT and other high-tech sectors in the US is the natural outcome of research efforts in previous years.
8. See European Commission (2002b and 2002c) for more detail.
9. In 1990 the coefficient of variation of private consumption deflators across the EU-15 was 21.4 per cent; this had fallen to 14.6 per cent in 1998, though it has since stabilised around that mark.
10. A different, perhaps somewhat less benign interpretation of such a scenario would be failure of the ECB to correctly identify an increase in potential growth resulting from structural reform.
11. Clearly, exercising such an option must not compromise overarching objectives to restore the room for manoeuvre for fiscal policies.

REFERENCES

Ahn, S. (2002), 'Competition, innovation and productivity growth: a review of theory and evidence', OECD Economics Department Working Papers No. 317.

Barro, R.J. and Sala-i-Martin, X. (1995), *Economic Growth*, New York: McGraw-Hill.

Bassanini, Andrea, Scarpetta, Stefano and Hemmings, Philip (2001), 'Economic growth: the role of policies and institutions. Panel data evidence from OECD countries', OECD Economics Department Working Paper No. 283.

Blanchard, O. and Giavazzi, F. (2001), 'Macroeconomic effects of regulation and deregulation in goods and labor markets', NBER Working Paper 8120.

Carlin, W. and Mayer, C. (1999), 'Finance, investment and growth', CEPR Discussion Paper No. 2233.

Cecchini, P., Catinat, M. and Jaquemin, A. (1988), *The European Challenge 1992: The Benefits of a Single Market*, Aldershot: Wildwood House.

CSES (2002), 'Benchmarking the administration of business start-ups', Report to the European Commission, DG Enterprise, January.

Daveri, F. (2002), 'The new economy in Europe: 1992–2001', *Oxford Review of Economic Policy*, **18**(3), 345–62.

Dierx, A., Ilzkovitz, F. and Sekkat, K. (2003), 'Structural reforms on European product markets: the Cardiff process', mimeo, Directorate General for Economic and Financial Affairs, European Commission, Brussels.

European Central Bank (2001), 'Price effects of regulatory reforms in selected network industries', March.

European Commission (1996), 'Economic evaluation of the Internal Market', *European Economy*, No. 4, Directorate-General for Economic and Financial Affairs.

European Commission (2000), 'The EU economy: 2000 review', chapter 2, *European Economy*, no. 71.

European Commission (2002a), 'The report on the implementation of the 2001 broad economic policy guidelines', *European Economy*, no. 1/2002.

European Commission (2002b), Commission Communication, 'Taking stock of five years of the European Employment Strategy' (COM (2002) 416).

European Commission (2002c), 'The EU economy: 2002 review', *European Economy*, no. 6, Directorate-General for Economic and Financial Affairs.

European Commission (2003a), 'The macroeconomic effects of the Single Market Programme after 10 years', http://europa.eu.int/internal_market/10years/background_en.htm.

European Commission (2003b), 'The EU economy: 2003 review', *European Economy*, no. 6, Directorate-General for Economic and Financial Affairs.

IMF (2003), 'Unemployment and labor market institutions: why reforms pay off', chapter 4 in 2003 World Economic Outlook.

Jorgenson, D. and Stiroh, K. (2000), 'Raising the speed limit: US economic growth in the information age', *Brookings Papers on Economic Activity*, no. 1.

Krugman, P. (1994), 'Past and prospective causes of high unemployment', in *Reducing Unemployment. Current Issues and Policy Options*, Jackson Hole Symposium, The Federal Reserve Bank of Kansas City, 49–80.

Layard, R., Nickell, S. and Jackman, R. (1991), *Unemployment*, Oxford: Oxford University Press.

Nickell, S. (1999), 'Product markets and labour markets', *Labour Economics*, **6**.

Nickell, S. and Layard, R. (1999), 'Labor market institutions and economic performance', in O.C. Ashenfelter and D. Card (eds), *Handbook of Labor Economics*, Vol. 3C, Amsterdam: Elsevier, 3029–84.

Notaro, G. (2002), 'European integration and productivity: exploring the gains of the Single Market', London Economics, Working Paper, May.

OECD (1997), *The OECD Report on Regulatory Reform*, Vol. II, 'Thematic studies', Paris: OECD.

OECD (2001), Special Issue no. 32 on 'Regulatory reform', OECD Economic Studies, Paris: OECD.

Oliner, S. and Sichel, D. (2000), 'The resurgence of growth in the late 1990s: is information technology the story?', *Journal of Economic Perspectives*, **14**(4), 3–22.

Roeger, W. and in't Veld, J. (1997), 'QUEST II. A multi-country business cycle and growth model', *Economic Papers*, no. 123, European Commission.

Salgado, R. (2002), 'Impact of structural reforms on productivity growth in industrial countries', IMF Working Paper, WP/02/10, January.

Scarpetta, S., Hemmings, P., Tressel, T. and Woo, J. (2002), 'The role of policy and institutions for productivity and firm dynamics: evidence from micro and industry data', OECD Economics Department Working Paper, no. 329.

Van Ark, Bart, Mulder, Nanno and McGuckin, Robert (2002), 'ICT investment and growth accounts for the European Union, 1980–2000', Study prepared for the European Commission, DG Economic and Financial Affairs.

7. The sensitivity of European sectors to exchange rate fluctuations*

Michel Fouquin and Khalid Sekkat

INTRODUCTION

The adoption of the euro in 1999 eliminated exchange rate variability between eleven[1] European currencies. This is beneficial to intra-European trade because the economic literature has shown that exchange rate variability reduces the volume of trade. The adoption of the euro will not, however, make the European economy immune to all types of exchange rate variability. Indeed, about one-third of European Union (EU) trade involves partners outside the euro area. Outside Europe the dollar is generally the main currency used for international trade. Hence, exchange rate variability, particularly euro/dollar variability, is still an important determinant of European trade performance.

The present chapter focuses on the likely impact of euro/dollar fluctuations on European Union manufacturing. Building on previous theoretical and empirical research which emphasises the difference in sensitivity to exchange rate fluctuations across sectors, we try to classify European sectors according to their sensitivity to dollar exchange rate fluctuations. Such sensitivity depends on the exposure to competition from the dollar zone and on the elasticity of sectors' trade to exchange rate fluctuations.

Exposure is measured by an original indicator which takes into account the fact that the dollar zone (that is, the zone of currencies which fluctuates more or less in conjunction with the dollar) is larger than just the United States. In particular, most Asian emerging countries belong to the dollar zone, as do countries in Latin America. The indicator of exposure to the dollar zone concerns competition not only on the export markets but also on the domestic market and on third country markets. The analysis shows that textile products, leather products, machinery and equipment, electrical optical equipment and transport equipment and, to a lesser extent, chemicals are the sectors facing the maximum of competition from the dollar zone. Competition concerns both European and foreign markets except for the machinery and equipment and the chemicals sectors where competition is more important in foreign markets.

With respect to the elasticity of sectors' trade to exchange rate fluctuations, two issues are addressed: is there a difference across sectors regarding the elasticity of trade? To what extent do market structure and goods characteristics determine such a difference? To estimate these elasticities, the regression related trade volumes to exchange rate variables, cost variables and market structure variables. The analysis focused on bilateral imports and exports of eleven countries from or to seventeen partner countries. Fourteen sectors were considered according to the NACE revision 1 nomenclature. Exchange rate variables include volatility, exchange rate changes and expectations of future exchange rate changes. Four market structure indicators are considered: concentration, segmentation, differentiation and scale economies. The estimation results show that the impact of exchange rate changes on trade varies across sectors. The variations are explained by industry concentration and dynamics. The sectors having the highest elasticity of trade to exchange rate fluctuations are energy, food, paper products, machinery, electrical products for imports and energy, machinery and transport equipment for exports.

Combining the exposure indicator and the elasticity estimates, a sector classification emerges where the three sectors which have the highest elasticity and are the most exposed are machinery and equipment, electrical and optical products and transport equipment. These sectors are important and represent together about one-third of European manufactured output. Textiles and leather (low elasticity–high exposure) are of little importance in the economy. Except for basic metals, the low elasticity–low exposed sectors (wood and wood products, rubber and plastic products, other non-metallic mineral products and basic metals and fabricated metal products) do not account for much total value-added in Europe. On the other hand, among the remaining sectors, energy, food and paper (high elasticity–low exposure) are important to the European economy.

A detailed assessment of the effect of a 10 per cent dollar depreciation on the market share of each sector was also conducted. On the imports side, the most affected sectors are energy and electrical products. The dollar zone market shares in the European market increase by 0.74 and 1.45 percentage points respectively. Regarding exports, the larger impacts concern machinery and transport equipment. For both sectors the European market share in the dollar zone decreases by 1 percentage point.

The rest of the chapter is organised as follows. Section 7.1 presents the conceptual framework. In Section 7.2 the exposure indicator is computed and analysed. Section 7.3 deals with the econometric estimation of the elasticity of trade. The results of Sections 7.2 and 7.3 are combined in

Section 7.4 to classify sectors according to their sensitivity to the euro/dollar fluctuations. Section 7.5 concludes.

7.1   THE CONCEPTUAL FRAMEWORK

Exposure

To measure industry exposure to foreign competition, a traditional measure compares domestic production and domestic sales to imports and to exports. On the import side, the penetration index relates imports to final domestic demand: $M/(Q + M - X)$ or M/D. On the export side, exports are linked to production: X/Q. This is the share of production sold on foreign markets. The OECD used another measure (see Coppel and Durand, 1999) which combines the two previous measures: $IOECD = X/Q + (1 - X/Q) \times M/D$.

Campa and Goldberg (1997) criticised the most popular indices of openness on the ground that these ratios do not take into account the imported inputs used by the industry. To correct for this they calculate two new indices: the index of imported inputs (MI/Q) and the net exposure to international competition ($X/Q - MI/Q$).

The idea behind this index is to carry out a cost/benefit analysis by industry of the impact of a given dollar fluctuation. In the case of a dollar appreciation, the impact on American manufacturing depends on the share of production exported (X/Q is a good measure). But in the case of imports, US industry benefits through the lower cost of its imported inputs measured by the index of imported inputs. The difference between the two indices is the Net External Orientation. The final index shows the potential impact on profits of a dollar fluctuation, other things being equal.

This indicator is, however, unsuitable to measure the impact of currency fluctuations for two reasons:

- focusing on the costs of imported inputs, it does not take into account the effect on the final demand for imports (consumer goods and capital equipment) which represent the major share of total imports;
- the index does not take into account the geographical breakdown of the origin of the products. It considers the external world as homogenous vis-à-vis the dollar which is certainly not the case.

To take into account the above shortcomings, we propose another indicator based on a multinational framework. First, we assume that the world is divided into three currency zones, and second we take into account competition between the different zones on a bilateral basis (for example, the direct confrontation of euro zone against the dollar zone). Subsequently, we take into account the confrontation of the two zones with third zones, which are neither included in the dollar zone nor in the euro zone. The exposure indicator is described in Box 7.1. For simplicity, we divided the world into three zones: the dollar zone, the euro zone and the 'rest of the world' zone. The indicator is the following:

$$S_k = \left(\frac{Q_{EU,k} - X_{EU,k}}{Q_{EU,k}} \times \frac{X_{\$,EU,k}}{D_{EU,k}} \right) + \left(\frac{X_{EU,\$,k}}{Q_{EU,k}} \times \frac{Q_{\$,k} - X_{\$,.,k}}{D_{\$,k}} \right) + \sum_j \left(\frac{X_{EU,j,k}}{Q_{EU,k}} \times \frac{X_{\$,j,k}}{D_{j,k}} \right)$$

(7.1)

with

$$\frac{Q_{EU,k} - X_{EU,k}}{Q_{EU,k}} + \frac{X_{EU,\$,k}}{Q_{EU,k}} + \sum_j \frac{X_{EU,j,k}}{Q_{EU,k}} = 1$$

Where Q: production; X: exports; D: domestic demand; EU: European Union; $\$$: dollar zone; j: rest of the world; k: sector; $X_{EU,k}$: total exports

---

BOX 7.1 EXPOSURE INDEX

Q stands for production or sales, M stands for imports, X stands for exports, D stands for the final demand, EU for European Union (depending on the test, EU refers to the euro zone made up of 11 countries or of the 15 members of the EU).

On the 'diagonal' (Table A), the value of the production sold in the domestic market is displayed. In the other cells of the matrix, the value of trade between the exporting zone (indicated in rows) to the importing zone (in columns) is shown. The row sum equals the production value and the column sum equals the demand value of the zone.

Table A   Production and trade matrix

	EU-15	$ zone	Rest of world	Total
EU-15	$Q_{EU}\text{-}X_{EU}$	$X_{EU,\$}$	$X_{EU,1/3}$	Q_{EU}
$ zone	$X_{\$,EU}$	$Q_{\$}\text{-}X_{\$}$	$X_{\$,1/3}$	$Q_{\$}$
Rest of world	$X_{1/3,EU}$	$X_{1/3,\$}$	$Q_{1/3}\text{-}X_{1/3}$	$Q_{1/3}$
Total	D_{EU}	$D_{\$}$	$D_{1/3}$	$Q_w = D_w$

Given the matrix above we can calculate two ratios. By rows, we find the shares of world sales or demand by region (the destination share point of view) as shown in Table B; By columns, the market share matrix can be computed as done in Table C.

Table B   Destination of production matrix

	EU-15	$ zone	Rest of world	Total
EU-15	$\dfrac{Q_{EU} - X_{EU}}{Q_{EU}}$	$\dfrac{X_{EU,\$}}{Q_{EU}}$	$\dfrac{X_{EU,1/3}}{Q_{EU}}$	1
$ zone	$\dfrac{X_{\$,EU}}{Q_\$}$	$\dfrac{Q_\$ - X_\$}{Q_\$}$	$\dfrac{X_{\$,1/3}}{Q_\$}$	1
Rest of world	$\dfrac{X_{1/3,EU}}{Q_{1/3}}$	$\dfrac{X_{1/3,\$}}{Q_{1/3}}$	$\dfrac{Q_{1/3} - X_{1/3}}{Q_{1/3}}$	1

Finally, with the two matrices we can calculate the exposure of the European industry to dollar zone competition, by multiplying the first line of Table B by the second line of Table C. That is to say, we calculate the weighted average of exposure of European producers in the different markets to the dollar zone.

Table C   Market share matrix

	EU-15	$ zone	Rest of world
EU-15	$\dfrac{Q_{EU} - X_{EU}}{D_{EU}}$	$\dfrac{X_{EU,\$}}{D_\$}$	$\dfrac{X_{EU,1/3}}{D_{1/3}}$
$ zone	$\dfrac{X_{\$,EU}}{D_{EU}}$	$\dfrac{Q_\$ - X_\$}{D_\$}$	$\dfrac{X_{\$,1/3}}{D_{1/3}}$
Rest of world	$\dfrac{X_{1/3,EU}}{D_{EU}}$	$\dfrac{X_{1/3,\$}}{D_\$}$	$\dfrac{Q_{1/3} - X_{1/3}}{D_{1/3}}$
Total	1	1	1

of *EU* in sector k; Q and D are different from 0. This indicator fluctuates between 0 and 50 per cent. Intra-zone trade was removed from EU trade.

To compute the indicator one should identify currency zones. To this end, one possibility is to refer to the currency used in international transactions. However, in this case one needs bilateral data on the use of currency. Except for a few countries (for example Japan, France, the US) such information is not available.

Another possibility is to use an empirical analysis to identify a country's pegging strategy. A country pegging its currency to, say, the US dollar is assumed to belong to the dollar zone. To identify the pegging strategies we used an indicator (Bénassy-Quéré, 1996) which measures the volatility of a currency vis-à-vis another currency. Here the reference currencies are the US dollar and the ECU, in order to define a dollar zone as well as a euro zone (the reference to ECU is due to the fact that the period of estimation was before the birth of the euro). The method is described in Box 7.2. It

---

BOX 7.2   RELATIVE VOLATILITY INDEX

A currency's relative volatility vis-à-vis the US dollar or the ECU, λ_{ij}, defines the link of a currency to a nominal monetary zone. The index compares the volatility of the currency with the US dollar (or the ECU) to the total volatility of the currency towards both the US dollar and the ECU. If the index is low, it means that the currency tends to vary in accordance to the reference currency, the US dollar (or the ECU). In this case, the currency belongs to the US dollar (or the ECU) zone.

$$\lambda_{ij} = \frac{\sigma_{ij}}{\left(\sigma_{i\$} + \sigma_{iEcu}\right)}$$

With i the country currency, j the US dollar or euro, and σ the deviation of the log of nominal quarterly exchange rates. Estimates are made alternatively vis-à-vis the US dollar and the ECU, for two periods: from the 1st quarter of 1978 to the 4th quarter of 1998, and for a sub-period from the 1st quarter of 1996 to the 4th quarter of 1998, to take into account the effect of the financial crisis of 1997–1998.

If the index is lower or equal to 0.45 when j = US dollar, then the currency of country i is linked to the dollar and the country is classified as belonging to the dollar zone; the same applies to the ECU when j = ECU. Otherwise, the country is classified as belonging to the 'rest of the world' zone.

was implemented on a sample of 54 currencies, of which we found that 25 currencies were linked to the US dollar.

For the euro zone, we could have chosen an extended set of currencies related to the ECU, although they are not members of the Monetary Union. Countries such as Norway, Switzerland, Morocco or Tunisia have de facto linked their currency to the euro over the long run. East European countries, such as Hungary, the Czech Republic or Poland are converging to a euro peg. The subject of this study being the analysis of EU industries' sensitivity to the dollar, an institutional approach of the euro-land was finally used. Two definitions of the euro zone are considered: the 15 member countries of the EU, although the United Kingdom has a diverging currency, and the 11 countries which chose to adopt the euro as their official currency.

The other countries are de facto classified in the 'rest of the world' zone, which is very heterogeneous.

Elasticity of Trade

A number of papers have shown that the elasticity of trade to exchange rate fluctuations differs across sectors and depends on market structure. The intuition behind the relationship between sector elasticity, exchange rate changes and market structure can be illustrated using the following simple model of exporter behaviour. Consider that the demand function perceived by the exporter i is:

$$P_i = f(Q_i) \qquad (7.2)$$

where P_i and Q_i denote the price (in the importing country's currency) and quantities respectively and $f' \le 0$. Consider also a constant marginal cost of production c. There is no production of a comparable good in the importing country. Basic microeconomic theory shows that the exporter decision should satisfy the following condition:

$$e(P_i + Q_i f') = c \qquad (7.3)$$

where e is the exchange rate (the units of the exporter's currency for one unit of importer's currency). An increase in e implies a depreciation of the exporter's currency.

In a perfectly competitive environment $f' = 0$ and (7.3) reduces to $eP_i = c$. Hence, any increase in e will be compensated by an equal decrease of P_i. A depreciation of the currencies of exporters with respect to, say, the Deutschemark (DM) implies that the German price of the exported good, to Germany, will decrease. Perfect competition between exporters (free entry, exit of producers and price competition) will drive profit to zero. Exports to Germany will increase.

In an imperfectly competitive environment $f' < 0$. Hence an increase in e will be matched by both a decrease in P_i and the induced increase in Q_i. The German price of the exported good will fall less than in the perfectly competitive case. Hence, Q_i will also grow more slowly. The fact is that f' < 0 gives the exporter more 'freedom' to adjust to a depreciation. He/she is able to keep price above marginal cost and not match a depreciation one for one without losing all of his sales. It follows that export volume will react less to an exchange rate change for imperfectly competitive sectors than for perfectly competitive sectors.

Dornbush (1987) went beyond the simple model above in order to examine the relationship between trade variables and exchange rate changes. He showed that with homogeneous products and Cournot competition, a depreciation of exporters' currencies with respect to the DM will reduce the German prices of exports to Germany less than with perfect competition. With differentiated products, the extent of the decline will depend on the degree of differentiation and on the number of home and foreign firms. The imperfect competition explanation for the difference in sector elasticity to exchange rate changes, although relevant, is incomplete because of its static nature. A permanent DM depreciation would have the same impact on exports to Germany as a depreciation followed by an appreciation. The behaviour of the US trade deficit in relation to the depreciation of the dollar after 1985 motivated an extension of the analysis to a dynamic framework.

The dynamic extension focuses on the cost of reversing changes in foreign market shares. Two types of dynamic imperfect competition models have been used to show that exchange rate changes may not be passed through into trade prices, due to concerns about market share. Supply-side models by Baldwin and Krugman (1989) and Dixit (1989) postulate that firms face non-recoverable fixed costs (sunk costs) of entry into foreign markets. An exporter of cars wishing to expand sales on the German market, following a DM appreciation, should enlarge the dealer network, launch an advertising campaign, and so on. In order for these non-recoverable expenses to be profitable, the appreciation of the DM should continue to hold in the future. Otherwise, the exporter would not incur such costs. Demand-side models, introduced by Froot and Klemperer (1989), assume that due to consumer switching costs (network externalities, learning effects and so on), firms' future demands depend on current market shares. In this context, a DM depreciation will not lead to an increase in export price unless it is perceived as permanent. The exporter may prefer holding its export price in foreign currency constant if depreciation is temporary, in order to preserve its market share.

The empirically testable hypothesis implied by the above theories is that the price of the exported good in the importer currency will react less to exchange rate changes the less perfectly competitive is the market and the less permanent are exchange rate changes. Export volumes will also react less in imperfectly competitive markets and in face of temporary exchange rate changes. Most papers testing these implications were on Germany, Japan and the USA.

A first test by Feinberg (1986) was conducted on the German data. He tried to identify the determinants of pass-through. The author found a pass-through of about 24 per cent in real terms, that is, an 8.4 per cent depreciation of the DM increases German producer prices by 2 per cent relative to the GNP deflator. Increased market concentration reduced pass-through.

Two other papers by Feinberg (1989, 1991) conducted similar analyses for the US. On average pass-through equalled 16 per cent in real terms. The pass-through was close to one in industries heavily reliant on imported inputs and producing highly substitutable goods. It was much lower for concentrated or protected (barriers to entry) industries. Mann (1989) examined the pass-through issue for seven US imported goods and nine US exported goods. She found exporters to the US squeezing profit margins in response to the dollar depreciation. She also identified an asymmetry in pass-through during depreciation and appreciation. Feenstra (1989) concentrated on three specific products (motor cars, compact trucks and heavy motorcycles) imported by the US from Japan. He found differences in pass-through but no asymmetry.

For Japan, Ohno (1989) analysed data for seven 2-digit industries and found a pass-through of around 80 per cent. Martson (1990) used actual export prices for 17 products and found evidence of incomplete and asymmetric pass-through. Athukorala and Menon (1995) also identified incomplete pass-through for Japanese exports.

Finally, the issue of dynamics was addressed empirically by Froot and Klemperer (1989) for the US and by Sapir and Sekkat (1995) for Europe. The study for the US found that appreciation regarded as temporary leads to a lower pass-through and hence that both present and expected future market shares affect the degree of pass-through. The study for Europe provided strong evidence in favour of the impact of the perception about exchange rate changes on pass-through.

Almost all empirical studies in the field only tested for the difference of price responses to exchange rate changes across sectors. The impact on trade volume has never been considered. Moreover, except for Feinberg (1986), the extent to which these differences are due to market structure was never explicitly examined. In Section 7.3 we will both identify differences in sector elasticity and test the extent to which market structure indicators account for these differences.

7.2 THE SECTOR EXPOSURE FOR EU-15 AND EU-11

The statistical analysis which follows starts with the measure of exposure of European industries to competition from the dollar zone. We choose to compare two definitions of EU: EU-15 which includes notably the UK and EU-11 which corresponds to the monetary union at the time of the study. As the integration of the United Kingdom is open to question, the alternative EU-15 and EU-11 will be considered, and the impact of competition on both zones will be compared.

The Market Share Distribution

As far as the sharing of the world economy in three monetary zones is concerned, differences between degrees of openness are rather small, and the weight of the different zones in the different markets relatively similar. The degree of openness lies between 9.5 per cent for the dollar zone, 10.3 per cent in Europe and 12.6 per cent for third countries (Table 7.1). Furthermore, the breakdown of each market across the different partners is rather balanced, in a bracket from 4.5 per cent (market share of third countries in the European market) to 6.7 per cent (market share of EU-15 in the third countries).

As for Europe, once intra-zone trade is removed, the degree of openness is a little more than 10 per cent of domestic demand for manufactured products. Yet, a very wide dispersion around the average degree of openness can be observed across sectors.

The most open sectors with respect to international competition, for which the penetration ratio is greater than 30 per cent, are computers, wearing apparel, leather and shoes, professional goods and industries n.e.s. Except for professional goods and computers, these sectors are dominated by exports from Asian countries, the Central and Eastern European countries (CEECs) and North Africa. In the computer industry, the emerging countries from Asia prevail with a market share of 17.8 per cent, followed by the United States (9.6 per cent), and Japan (5.6 per cent).

The most closed sectors to international competition are those with degrees of openness below 5 per cent: publishing and printing, tobacco, beverages, glass products, refined petroleum, food, steel and wood.

Table 7.1 Market shares in the European Union, the dollar zone and third countries, 1996

	Market share of EU-15	EU-15		$ zone			Third countries		
		Market share of $ zone	Market share of third zone	Market share of EU-15	Market share of $ zone	Market share of third zone	Market share of EU-15	Market share of $ zone	Market share of third zone
Manufacturing	**89.8**	**5.8**	**4.5**	**4.6**	**90.5**	**4.9**	**6.7**	**5.9**	**87.4**
Food products	96.0	2.5	1.5	1.2	98.0	0.8	2.6	7.3	90.2
Textiles	87.5	7.8	4.7	2.3	95.5	2.2	11.5	7.1	81.4
Wearing apparel	67.6	15.7	16.7	3.0	95.8	1.2	14.8	30.3	55.0
Leather and leather products	70.1	22.5	7.4	12.0	85.5	2.5	22.9	24.0	53.1
Wood and wood products	95.1	2.7	2.2	0.8	99.0	0.2	2.4	5.8	91.8
Furniture	92.9	2.5	4.6	3.9	95.5	0.6	9.8	6.7	83.5
Publishing and printing	98.7	0.8	0.4	0.9	98.9	0.2	2.0	0.6	97.4
Plastic products	92.0	4.4	3.6	3.7	92.6	3.7	8.8	3.8	87.4
Metal products	93.1	3.1	3.7	4.7	91.1	4.2	5.9	2.4	91.7
Machinery and equipment	89.2	5.0	5.8	11.3	79.2	9.5	9.8	3.7	86.5
Professional goods	73.7	14.4	11.9	8.6	78.3	13.1	17.9	19.1	62.9
Manufacturing n.e.c.	73.3	19.0	7.7	6.2	85.4	8.4	11.1	14.9	74.0
Chemicals except pharmaceuticals	90.6	4.8	4.6	5.3	90.3	4.4	10.1	6.2	83.7
Beverages	97.0	2.2	0.8	4.3	95.3	0.3	3.7	1.4	94.9
Tobacco	98.7	1.1	0.2	0.9	98.7	0.3	1.2	6.5	92.2
Paper products	93.7	3.8	2.5	2.5	96.3	1.2	6.6	3.7	89.7
Coke, refined petroleum products	96.1	1.6	2.3	1.2	96.7	2.1	3.0	5.2	91.7
Rubber products	90.8	4.5	4.7	2.6	93.2	4.2	5.3	2.7	92.0
Ceramic products	95.3	2.2	2.5	5.6	91.5	3.0	14.5	3.6	82.0
Glass and other non-metallic min. prod.	97.0	1.0	2.1	1.9	96.4	1.7	1.9	1.4	96.7
Iron and steel	95.1	1.3	3.5	3.9	89.1	7.0	4.2	2.7	93.1
Non-ferrous metals	83.7	6.2	10.2	2.8	91.1	6.1	5.0	7.6	87.4
Electrical machinery	80.5	11.9	7.6	6.0	84.2	9.8	6.0	7.7	86.3
Pharmaceuticals	92.2	3.3	4.5	5.7	92.5	1.9	8.7	2.1	89.2
Office machinery and computers	65.6	27.4	6.9	5.8	82.9	11.3	7.2	15.6	77.2
Transport equipment except cars	82.6	15.5	1.9	9.2	89.3	1.5	2.1	3.8	94.1
Automobiles	93.5	2.3	4.2	4.6	88.2	7.3	10.8	3.5	85.7

Sources: Authors' calculations from the CEPII CHELEM database for trade; UNIDO and national sources for production.

The Indicator of Exposure to Competition for EU-15

Figure 7.1 shows that the exposure to competition with the dollar zone is greater than the average of the manufacturing sector (measured by the length of the arrows) in both European and foreign markets for the following sectors: computers, leather, toys, transport, wearing apparel, professional goods and electrical machinery. Textiles and non-ferrous metals experience greater competition than the average in the European market alone, while machinery and equipment, chemicals and ceramics are open to greater competition than the average for both Europe and the dollar zone in the foreign markets only (see Table 7.2).

EU-15 Compared to EU-11

Table 7.3 encapsulates the exposure differences of the euro zone when it is enlarged, with respect to its relationship with the dollar zone. The results suggest two things: on the one hand, the degree of exposure gets stronger

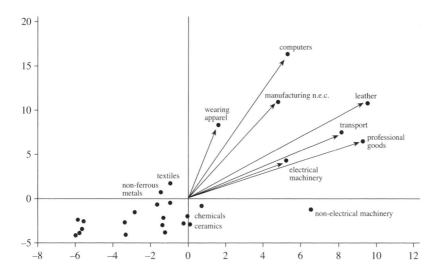

Note: On the X-axis, the degree of sectoral exposure to competition from the S zone on the foreign markets (dollar market and third markets) relative to the average of the manufacturing sector; on the Y-axis, the degree of sectoral exposure in the European market relative to the average of the manufacturing sector.

Sources: Authors' calculations from CEPII, CHELEM database and UNIDO.

Figure 7.1   The most exposed sectors to competition from the dollar zone in the EU-15 and foreign markets

Table 7.2   The sector exposure of EU-15 to the competition from the dollar zone, 1996

	EU-15			$ zone			Third zone indicator	Total	Relative total
	Share in EU-15 production	Market share of the $ zone	Indicator	Share in EU-15 production	Market share of the $ zone	Indicator			
Manufacturing	**86.7**	**5.8**	**5.0**	**7.9**	**90.5**	**7.1**	**0.3**	**12.4**	**0**
Office machinery and computers	77.6	27.4	21.3	12.7	82.9	10.6	2.1	33.9	22
Leather and shoes	69.7	22.5	15.7	17.0	85.5	14.5	2.4	32.5	20
Transport equipment except cars	80.3	15.5	12.4	16.5	89.3	14.8	0.7	27.9	16
Manufacturing n.e.c.	77.9	19.0	14.8	11.2	85.4	9.6	1.4	25.8	13
Professional goods	73.5	14.4	10.6	17.0	78.3	13.3	1.4	25.3	13
Electrical machinery	78.2	11.9	9.3	14.2	84.2	12.0	0.6	21.9	9
Wearing apparel	83.0	15.7	13.0	6.5	95.8	6.3	2.4	21.7	9
Machinery and equipment	75.1	5.0	3.7	17.0	79.2	13.5	0.5	17.7	5
Textiles	84.3	7.8	6.6	5.9	95.5	5.7	0.5	12.8	0
Chemicals except pharmaceuticals	85.5	4.8	4.1	8.6	90.3	7.8	0.3	12.2	0
Non-ferrous metals	89.5	6.2	5.5	6.0	91.1	5.4	0.2	11.2	−1
Pharmaceuticals	86.4	3.3	2.9	7.5	92.5	7.0	0.2	10.0	−2
Rubber products	89.7	4.5	4.1	5.6	93.2	5.2	0.2	9.4	−3
Plastics	87.8	4.4	3.9	5.6	92.6	5.1	0.3	9.3	−3
Ceramics	87.7	2.2	2.0	7.4	91.5	6.8	0.2	8.9	−3
Metallic products	88.7	3.1	2.8	6.4	91.1	5.9	0.1	8.8	−4
Automobiles	86.6	2.3	2.0	7.1	88.2	6.3	0.3	8.6	−4
Beverages	90.5	2.2	2.0	6.2	95.3	5.9	0.1	8.0	−4
Paper	90.8	3.8	3.5	4.5	96.3	4.4	0.1	7.9	−4
Iron and steel	89.6	1.3	1.2	6.8	89.1	6.0	0.1	7.3	−5
Furniture	90.8	2.5	2.2	3.9	95.5	3.8	0.1	6.1	−6
Glass and other non-metallic min. prod.	93.3	1.0	0.9	4.1	96.4	4.0	0.0	4.9	−7
Food	96.5	2.5	2.4	1.7	98.0	1.7	0.1	4.2	−8
Wood products except furniture	96.4	2.7	2.6	1.4	99.0	1.4	0.0	4.0	−8
Coke, refined petroleum products	96.8	1.6	1.5	1.7	96.7	1.6	0.0	3.2	−9
Tobacco	97.8	1.1	1.1	1.5	98.7	1.5	0.1	2.6	−10
Publishing and printing	97.0	0.8	0.8	1.4	98.9	1.3	0.0	2.2	−10

Sources: Authors' calculations from CEPII CHELEM database for trade; UNIDO and national sources for production.

with the EMU enlarging to the United Kingdom, Sweden and Denmark, but on the other hand, this increase in exposure is rather weak. The increase of the degree of exposure stems from three factors:

- when the euro zone gets larger, the external trade level of the EU is lessened since trade inside between the United Kingdom, Sweden and Denmark and the smaller euro zone is removed; and
- hence, the weight of trade of the dollar zone increases in world trade;
- adding new countries which are traditionally more open to the dollar zone, strengthens this exposure.

But this effect is of a second order, as it only amounts to an increase by 0.6 percentage points in the indicator, relative to a level of 11.7, that is to say an increase of 5 per cent.

At a sector level, the effects are rather mixed. Two sectors lessen their exposure to the dollar zone: plastics by –0.2 percentage points and above all other transport equipment by –1.8 percentage points, that is by more than 6 per cent. This sector chiefly spans the aeronautics industry, an up-market segment of high technology in the American manufacturing sector. It is the main sector to benefit from the enlargement to the three potential applicants. Half of this effect stems from the magnitude of these sectors in the United Kingdom and in Sweden – by the means of a kind of 'consolidation' in the zone – and the other half comes from the decrease of competition in third markets.

Electrical machinery and computers are the main sectors that experience a sizeable increase in their exposure. In nearly all cases, the increase is first of all due to a deeper penetration of the European internal market. The entry of new countries that are very open to exports from the dollar zone increases the exposure of European industry. But this cannot necessarily be considered a negative effect, as the link with the dollar might provide low-cost imports of electronics goods to other European industries. But as far as the dollar effect is concerned, it is correct to underline that these sectors are more exposed than others.

This analysis shows that EU enlargement to other European countries might not necessarily reduce exposure to the dollar zone.

In summary, the indicator computed for EU-15 and EU-11 against the dollar zone is above average for the manufacturing sector for about the same list of industries with the exception of textiles (see Table 7.4). The chemicals industry is not included in the list as it has just about the same level of exposure as average in EU-11.

Table 7.3   *Indicators of exposure of EU-15 and EU-11 to competition from the dollar zone, 1996 (%)*

	Market of EU-15/EMU-11		Market share of the $ zone		Market share of third zone		Total		
	EU-15	EU-11	EU-15	EU-11	EU-15	EU-11	EU-15	EU-11	Diff.
Manufacturing	**5.0**	**4.3**	**7.1**	**6.7**	**0.3**	**0.7**	**12.4**	**11.7**	**0.6**
Publishing and editing	0.8	0.5	1.3	1.0	0.0	0.0	2.2	1.5	0.7
Tobacco	1.1	1.4	1.5	0.8	0.1	0.1	2.6	2.3	0.3
Refined petroleum and coal	1.5	1.7	1.6	1.4	0.0	0.0	3.2	3.1	0.1
Wood products except furniture	2.6	2.2	1.4	1.6	0.0	0.1	4.0	3.9	0.1
Food	2.4	2.4	1.7	1.6	0.1	0.1	4.2	4.2	0.0
Glass and other non-metallic min. prod.	0.9	0.8	4.0	4.0	0.0	0.1	4.9	4.8	0.1
Furniture	2.2	1.9	3.8	3.8	0.1	0.5	6.1	6.2	0.0
Iron and steel	1.2	1.1	6.0	6.1	0.1	0.1	7.3	7.3	0.0
Paper	3.5	3.1	4.4	4.2	0.1	0.4	7.9	7.7	0.2
Beverages	2.0	1.9	5.9	5.6	0.1	0.2	8.0	7.6	0.4
Metallic products	2.8	2.4	5.9	5.8	0.1	0.3	8.8	8.5	0.3
Automobiles	2.0	1.7	6.3	5.6	0.3	0.6	8.6	7.8	0.7
Ceramics	2.0	1.6	6.8	5.9	0.2	0.6	8.9	8.1	0.9
Rubber products	4.1	3.3	5.2	5.1	0.2	0.6	9.4	9.0	0.4
Pharmaceuticals	2.9	2.8	7.0	6.3	0.2	0.3	10.0	9.4	0.6
Plastics	3.9	3.4	5.1	5.2	0.3	0.7	9.3	9.3	−0.2
Non-ferrous metals	5.5	4.5	5.4	4.9	0.2	0.7	11.2	10.1	1.1
Chemicals except pharmaceuticals	4.1	3.7	7.8	7.5	0.3	0.6	12.2	11.8	0.4
Textiles	6.6	5.4	5.7	5.7	0.5	1.3	12.8	12.4	0.3
Machinery and equipment	3.7	3.0	13.5	13.1	0.5	0.9	17.7	17.0	0.7
Electrical machinery	9.3	7.1	12.0	10.4	0.6	2.1	21.9	19.7	1.2
Wearing apparel	13.0	10.4	6.3	6.7	2.4	4.1	21.7	21.2	0.4
Transport equipment except cars	12.4	12.3	14.8	15.9	0.7	1.4	27.9	29.6	−1.8
Professional goods	10.6	9.2	13.3	12.7	1.4	2.7	25.3	24.6	0.5
Manufacturing n.e.s.	14.8	12.0	9.6	8.7	1.4	4.2	25.8	24.9	0.7
Office machinery and computers	21.3	16.5	10.6	8.3	2.1	7.7	33.9	32.5	1.4
Leather and shoes	15.7	13.0	14.5	14.8	2.4	4.6	32.5	32.5	0.0

Sources: Authors' calculations from CEPII CHELEM database for trade; UNIDO and national sources for production.

Table 7.4   Comparison of exposure of EU-15 and EU-11

EU-15	EU-11
Computers	Computers
Leather	Leather
Transport except cars	Transport except cars
Manufactured products n.e.s.	Manufactured products n.e.s.
Professional goods	Professional goods
Electrical machinery	Electrical machinery
Wearing apparel	Wearing apparel
Machinery and equipment	Machinery and equipment
	Textiles

7.3   SECTORS' TRADE ELASTICITY TO EXCHANGE RATE FLUCTUATIONS

Data Issues

To estimate sectors' elasticity to exchange rate fluctuations a typical regression relates trade volumes to exchange rate variables, cost variables and other control variables. In this chapter, we are also interested in identifying the impact of market structure on sectors' elasticity. Hence, four data sets were collected: trade, production, exchange rate and market structure data.

The analysis of sectors' exposure to competition from the dollar zone used a 3-digit sector classification. Ideally, one should use a similar classification for the econometric analysis. However, to conduct such an analysis, two sets of variables (trade and costs) should be collected on a time series, bilateral (including non-European partners), and sectoral basis. Given the available data sets, it is not possible to fulfil these requirements at the finest level of disaggregation. For instance, it is possible to collect trade flows at the 3-digit level but it is not possible to collect the corresponding costs series especially for non-European partners. Hence, a trade-off among the various dimensions of the data was made and we ended up with the following sample. (Note however, that when the results of Sections 7.2 and 7.3 are combined in Section 7.4, a coherent framework will be used.)

The analysis focuses on imports and exports of 11 declaring countries: Belgium-Luxembourg, France, Denmark, Germany, Greece, Ireland, Italy, the Netherlands, Portugal, Spain and the United Kingdom. Bilateral trade flows between these countries and 17 partners are analysed. The partners are the 11 declaring countries plus Austria, Finland, Sweden, the United

States, Canada and Japan. The sector disaggregation is defined according to the NACE revision 1 classification (see Table 7.5). The dependent variables, that is, bilateral export and import volumes, are drawn from Eurostat's trend database. Exports from country I to country J in sector S will be termed X_{IJS}, whereas imports in country I from country J in sector S will be termed M_{IJS}.

Table 7.5   Estimation results of equations (7.4) and (7.5)

	Imports	Exports
Prices of the declaring country	−0.10	−0.73
	(−0.20)	(−3.33)
Prices of the partner country	−0.43	−0.17
	(−2.04)	(−0.49)
Production of the partner country	0.63	0.25
	(5.10)	(1.75)
Production of the declaring country	0.01	0.66
	(0.04)	(6.56)
Volatility	−0.06	0.01
	(−2.99)	(0.50)
Exchange rate coefficient per sector		
Food products, beverages and tobacco	−1.01	0.24
	(−4.24)	(1.26)
Textiles and textile products	−0.46	−0.29
	(−0.97)	(−0.73)
Leather and leather products	−0.08	−0.50
	(−0.25)	(−1.65)
Wood and wood products	−0.42	0.00
	(−1.25)	(−0.01)
Pulp, paper and paper products, publishing and printing	−1.05	0.40
	(−2.74)	(1.21)
Energy products	−4.37	3.86
	(−4.87)	(4.20)
Chemicals, chemical products and man–made fibres	−0.79	0.55
	(−2.88)	(2.29)
Rubber and plastic products	−0.85	0.47
	(−3.42)	(2.14)
Other non–metallic mineral products	−0.85	0.77
	(−3.72)	(3.96)
Basic metals and fabricated metal products	−0.55	0.35
	(−0.83)	(0.62)

Table 7.5   continued

	Imports	Exports
Machinery and equipment n.e.c.	−1.21	1.07
	(−4.25)	(4.55)
Electrical and optical equipment	−1.03	0.34
	(−1.69)	(0.66)
Transport equipment	−0.68	2.45
	(−1.14)	(4.37)
N	568	565
R^2	0.21	0.30
F-stat	2.1874	2.361
H-stat	12.4130	14.7780

Source: Authors' calculations.

Note: Figures in brackets denote the *t*-statistics; R^2 is the adjusted *R*-square; N is the number of observations; *F*-stat is the Fisher statistics for the non-existence of fixed effects; *H*-stat is the Hausman statistics for the existence of fixed effects versus random effects. *F*-stat is distributed as a $F_{(12.527)}$ in the case of imports and as a $F_{(12.519)}$ in the case of exports. *H*-stat is distributed as a $\chi^2(12)$ for imports and as a $\chi^2(14)$ in the case of exports.

Nominal exchange rate series are drawn from the IMF's *International Financial Statistics* (CD-ROM). The US exchange rates are used to obtain other bilateral rates. They are collected on an annual and on a monthly basis. The latter is used to compute exchange rate volatility as the standard deviation, over twelve months, of exchange rate changes. Expectations of future exchange rate changes are measured using the interest differential between the exporter and the importer. The 12-month euro interest rates are drawn from the IMF CD-ROMs. The bilateral exchange rate between country *I* and country *J* will be termed E_{IJ} and is defined as the number of currency units of the declaring country *I* for one currency unit of the partner country *J*. Therefore, an increase in E_{IJ} means a depreciation of country *I*'s currency with respect to country *J*'s currency. By analogy, volatility and the expectations of exchange rate changes are denoted respectively V_{IJ} and R_{IJ}. A positive R_{IJ} implies an expected depreciation of the declaring country *I* currency with respect to the partner country *J*.

As a proxy for costs, producer price indexes in ECU for each country and each sector are used. Sector production, measured in constant ECU of 1995, for each country and each sector is also used to take account of possible demand or supply effects. The respective total production of the declaring country and of the partner country in sector *S* are noted VD_s and VP_s. In the same way, $PPID_S$ and $PPIP_S$ will respectively denote producer prices of the declaring country and of the partner country in sector S. These two sets of data were drawn from Eurostat's European Business Trends database.

Finally, four market structure indicators are considered: concentration, segmentation, differentiation and the degree of scale economies. Concentration is measured as the 5-firm concentration ratio, and the data are drawn from Davies and Lyons (1996). Segmentation and differentiation data are taken from Martin et al. (1996). These are dummy variables taking value 1 for segmented (differentiated) sector and zero otherwise. A sector characterized by the existence of large establishments, covering a large proportion of output and employment is termed segmented while differentiation is approximated by R&D intensity. In order to measure the degree of scale economies, we use the minimum efficient scale, that is, the theoretical scale of the plant at which all economies of scale are exhausted. These data are provided by the European Commission. Note that this indicator is closely related, although richer, to the segmentation indicator.

Difference in Elasticity across Sectors

To investigate whether exchange rate fluctuations have differentiated impacts on trade volumes across sectors, the following equations were estimated:

$$X_{IJS} = \beta_0 + \sum_S \beta_{1S} \left(E_{IJ} \times SEC_S \right) + \beta_2 V_{IJ} + \beta_3 VD_S + \beta_4 VP_S + \beta_5 PPIP_S + \beta_6 PPID_S + \varepsilon_{X_{IJS}}$$

$$(7.4)$$

$$M_{IJS} = \gamma_0 + \sum_S \gamma_{1S} \left(E_{IJ} \times SEC_S \right) + \gamma_2 V_{IJ} + \gamma_3 VD_S + \gamma_4 VP_S + \gamma_5 PPIP_S + \gamma_6 PPID_S + \varepsilon_{M_{IJS}}$$

$$(7.5)$$

Where:

X_{IJS} = Exports from country I to country J in sector S
M_{IJS} = Imports into country I from country J in sector S
E_{IJ} = Bilateral exchange rate between country I and country J. An increase in E_{IJ} means a depreciation of country I's currency
V_{IJ} = Volatility of exchange rate changes
VD_S, VP_S = Total production of the declaring country and of the partner country in sector S

$PPID_S$, $PPIP_S$ = Producer prices of the declaring country and of the partner country in sector S.

SEC_S = Dummy variable that takes the value 1 for sector S and 0 otherwise.

Equations (7.4) and (7.5) can be derived from a structural model of exporter's behaviour (see for instance Sekkat, 1998). They were first estimated using yearly growth rates. The results failed to show a consistent and robust impact of market structure indicators on exchange rate coefficients. Such a result is considered to be due to two factors. On the one hand, the market structure indicators are available only for one point in time. Compared to the rest of the sample they do not display enough variance and hence a correlation may not show up. On the other hand, the impact of market structure is mainly a long-term phenomenon and may not appear using a short-term approach, that is, regression on yearly growth rates. It was therefore decided to abstract from short-term effects by estimating equations (7.4) and (7.5) using the average annual growth rates over the period 1989–97. Volatility is the logarithm of the average volatility over the same period.

When the sample combines various dimensions of the data (for instance time-sector-countries), a typical issue concerns the dimension according to which coefficients are allowed to vary. The focus of the econometric analysis is on the elasticity of each sector to exchange rate changes. Such an elasticity depends mainly on the sector's characteristics, that is, technology, product differentiation, scale economies and so on. While the importance of a given sector may differ across European countries (which may be accounted for by using fixed effects) there is no reason why its response to exchange rate changes would differ across countries of a similar level of development and hence using similar technologies. Hence, while the exchange rate coefficients are allowed to vary across sectors they are assumed to be similar (for a given sector) across countries.

The most natural way to conduct the investigation is to run a panel regression. We introduced fixed effects for sectors and countries. The fixed effects of importing countries proved to be significant. Hence, in addition to sector fixed effects, dummies for partners are included in the exports equation and reporters dummies are included in the imports equation. To save on space, fixed effects coefficients are however not reported. Estimation results are presented in Table 7.5 below

From Table 7.5, it appears that the F-test for common intercepts rejects the null hypothesis both for imports and exports and that the Hausman test statistics for random versus fixed effects is not significant. These two observations justify the focus upon fixed effects models. The adjusted R^2 in

Table 7.5 are of medium level. This is not surprising for regressions using growth rates.

A first interesting result shown in Table 7.5 concerns the effect of prices. In general, increases in the declaring country's producer prices should increase its imports from the partner countries and significantly decrease its exports towards them. The effects of price in Table 7.5 are significant only for the exporter. Coefficients for producer prices have the correct sign and are significant for *PPIP* in the case of imports and for *PPID* in the case of exports. When the domestic country's producer prices increase by 1 per cent, its exports fall by about 0.75 per cent. In the same way, an increase in the partner country's producer prices significantly decreases its exports towards the reporting country. When the partner country's producer prices increase by 1 per cent, its exports towards the reporting country decrease by about 0.5 per cent.

Coefficients of total production variables are significant in three cases out of four. Both an increase in total production in the partner country or the declaring country raise imports from the partner country to the declaring country. The impact of total production is of comparable magnitude to the impact of producer prices: a 1 per cent increase in total production for the partner country or the declaring country induces an increase of about 0.5 per cent of imports from the partner country to the declaring country.

Regarding exchange rate variables, one must separate exports and imports. For exports, a depreciation of the declaring country's currency should increase exports towards its partners. This is the case for six sectors. The leather sector, however, has a significant and unanticipated sign. For imports, a depreciation should decrease imports. The results show that the exchange rate coefficients are significantly different from zero, and negative in eight imports cases. Overall, exchange rate coefficients prove generally higher or comparable to the costs coefficients. The energy sector displays high coefficients for both imports and exports reflecting a high elasticity of demand in the long run.

An increase in exchange rate volatility has a consistently negative impact upon imports, which is understandable if producers are risk-averse. Increases in exchange rate uncertainty reduce international trade.

In Table 7.5, one can easily notice that the coefficients of exchange rate are different across sectors for both imports and exports. We have computed the *t*-statistics for the test of equality of coefficients for every pair of sectors. There are many cases where the *t*-statistic is significant, that is, sectors respond differently to exchange rate changes. For instance, exports of machinery and equipment and energy (coke, refined petroleum products and nuclear fuel) display a significantly different response to exchange rate fluctuations than food products, beverages and tobacco. Exchange rate depreciation, that is, an increase in E_{IJ}, boosts machinery and energy exports by a significantly larger amount than in the case of food and drink. The same depreciation reduces energy imports significantly more than food imports.

The Role of Market Structure

In this section, we examine whether the heterogeneous responses of trade volumes to exchange rate fluctuations can be accounted for by sector-specific characteristics. We consider three sector characteristics related to the competitiveness in the various sectors: scale economies in sector S (MES_S), segmentation in sector S (SEG_S) and concentration in sector S (CON_S).

The following interaction variables were then constructed:

$$ESEG_{IJS} = E_{IJ} \times SEG_S \tag{7.6}$$
$$ECON_{IJS} = E_{IJ} \times CON_S \tag{7.7}$$
$$EMES_{IJS} = E_{IJ} \times MES_S \tag{7.8}$$

Clearly, the regression coefficient associated with, for instance, $ESEG_{IJS}$ represents the role played by segmentation in generating the response of trade volume to exchange rate fluctuations. The same holds for the other interaction variables.

Following the analysis by Sapir and Sekkat (1995) we should take account of dynamics. For sectors where dynamics are important, expectations of exchange rate changes play a significant role. The issue here is to determine sectors for which dynamic considerations are important, although there is no available classification identifying such sectors. Hence, one should rely on conceptual analysis. Looking at the literature, it appears that dynamics is in general associated with consumer loyalty, that is, a consumer is likely to buy a given brand if he or she bought it in the past. Consumer loyalty was documented for various products such as software, computers or cars. These are in general goods involving product differentiation. Indeed, there is almost no consumer loyalty for homogeneous unmarked products such as bread, oil or paper. Hence, to avoid arbitrary choice, we rely on the differentiation indicator to identify those sectors for which dynamics may play a role.

We first compute expected exchange rate movements. This is done by postulating uncovered interest parity and, hence, the expected exchange rate change between countries I and J is given by:

$$R_{IJ} = R_I - R_J \tag{7.9}$$

This is the (one-year) interest rate differential between country I and country J. The next step defines an interaction variable, ERW_{IJ}, between the expected exchange rate change and sectors where dynamics is assumed to be important:

$$ERW_{IJ} = R_{IJ} \times DIFFs \qquad (7.10)$$

The equations to be estimated are the following:

$$X_{IJS} = \beta_0 + \beta_1 E_{IJ} + \beta_2 V_{IJ} + \beta_3 VD_S + \beta_4 VP_S + \beta_5 PPIP_S + \beta_6 PPID_S$$
$$+ \beta_7 Eij^* CHAR_S + \beta_8 ERW_{IJ} + \beta_{XIJS} \qquad (7.11)$$

$$M_{IJS} = \gamma_0 + \gamma_1 E_{IJ} + \gamma_2 V_{IJ} + \gamma_3 VD_S + \gamma_4 VP_S + \gamma_5 PPIP_S + \gamma PPID_S$$
$$+ \gamma_7 Eij^* CHAR_S + \gamma_8 ERW_{IJ} + \gamma_{MIJS} \qquad (7.12)$$

Where $CHAR_S$ denotes the characteristics of sector S. Thus, for a given sector S, the elasticity to actual exchange rate changes is given, respectively for exports and imports, by:

$$\beta_1 + \beta_7 CHARs \qquad (7.13)$$

and

$$\gamma_1 + \gamma_7 CHARs \qquad (7.14)$$

As imperfect competition reduces the elasticity to exchange rate, the expected signs are $\beta_7 < 0$ and $\gamma_7 > 0$. With respect to β_8 and γ_8 we expect the same sign as for β_1 and γ_1 because when dynamics is important, future exchange rate evolutions has the same impact as the actual evolution.

We will consider separately each of the characteristics and also perform a regression with all the characteristics. These equations are estimated in a similar way as before.

For each regression, we only present the fixed-effects results. The Hausman test for fixed versus random effects indeed systematically pleads in favour of a fixed-effects specification. Moreover, the F-test systematically rejects the null hypothesis of common intercepts.

The results are displayed in Table 7.6. In all specifications, the coefficients associated with the exporter price variables, $PPIDS$ (for exports) and $PPIPS$ (for imports), have the expected sign and are highly significant. They have the same order of magnitude as in Table 7.5. The 'price effect' already detected is confirmed as an important feature of the data. As in Table 7.5, the coefficients for VD_S and VP_S are significant in three instances, and are positive. Their magnitude, again, is comparable to the coefficients for producer price variables: a 1 per cent increase in VP_S boosts imports into the country by about 0.5 per cent.

The exchange rate coefficients E_{IJ} have the expected sign and are significant both for imports and for exports. Point estimates suggest that a 1 per cent depreciation of the domestic currency increases exports by 0.38 per cent and decreases imports by 0.86 per cent. The elasticity is not homogeneous across sectors. Concentration, indeed, proves significant for imports. The more concentrated the sector, the less depreciation will decrease imports. Accrued exchange rate variability significantly decreases trade volumes. Estimates suggest that this effect is significant only for imports: a 1 per cent increase in volatility decreases the growth rate of imports by about 0.06 per cent. The expected exchange rate variable also proves significant, for both imports and exports. In that case, for sectors where dynamics matter, a 1 per cent expected depreciation induces a 0.03 per cent drop in imports.

Segmentation has a significant sign in the export equation only. The sign is, however, positive. Exports seem to increase more in response to depreciation in the more segmented sectors. This is not in accordance with theory. The segmentation indicator may capture other effects than only imperfect competition.

The scale economy variable is significant in the export equation only. When economies of scale are important, depreciations have a higher impact on exports. A similar problem to the segmentation indicator appears. This is not surprising since the two indicators are closely related.

A final round of regressions was performed using all the sector characteristics (except *SEG* which is related to *MES*) in the same regression. Scale economies are not significant for imports and have an unexpected sign for exports. Compared to the regression with only the concentration ratio, the results now also reveal an effect of concentration on exports. Note that the samples are different due to data availability on scale economies. The sample underlying the results includes two additional sectors (leather, wood). The interaction variable with the expected exchange rate is significant and has the right sign in both equations. For these sectors where dynamics matters, point estimates suggest that the impact of an expected depreciation is very close in magnitude for both imports and exports.

To sum up, the estimation results show that cost considerations and the exchange rate are important determinants of trade. Hence competitiveness, as measured by the real exchange rate, is one of the most important determinants of European trade. Exchange rate volatility has an adverse effect on imports. Such a conclusion seems robust to various specifications

Table 7.6   Estimation results of equations (7.11) and (7.12)

Explanatory variables	Estimation using							
	Concentration		Segmentation		Scale economies		Concentration and scale economies	
	Imports	Exports	Imports	Exports	Imports	Exports	Imports	Exports
Prices of the declaring country	-0.50	-0.79	-0.33	-0.86	0.02	-0.72	-0.46	-0.61
	(-1.14)	(-3.80)	(-0.76)	(-4.21)	-0.05	(-3.51)	(-1.01)	(-2.90)
Prices of the partner country	-0.49	-0.27	-0.40	0.00	-0.51	-0.01	-0.49	-0.24
	(-2.51)	(-0.78)	(-1.95)	0.00	(-2.51)	(-0.04)	(-2.41)	(-0.70)
Production of the partner country	0.54	0.30	0.54	0.39	0.73	0.29	0.69	0.33
	(4.50)	(2.05)	(4.37)	(2.81)	(5.69)	(1.91)	(5.31)	(2.12)
Production of the declaring country	0.25	0.60	0.10	0.61	0.15	0.75	0.21	0.72
	(1.64)	(5.87)	(0.67)	(6.02)	(0.92)	(7.23)	(1.27)	(6.83)
Bilateral exchange rate	-0.86	0.38	-0.72	0.12	-0.88	0.41	-1.05	0.57
	(-5.08)	(2.44)	(-3.69)	(0.72)	(-5.39)	(2.76)	(-5.82)	(3.45)
Dynamics	-0.04	0.04	-0.02	0.03	-0.02	0.02	-0.03	0.03
	(-3.43)	(3.90)	(-2.44)	(4.00)	(-2.11)	(3.03)	(-2.99)	(3.75)
Volatility	-0.06	0.01	-0.06	0.02	-0.05	0.01	-0.05	0.01
	(-3.38)	(0.73)	(-3.21)	(0.93)	(-2.59)	(0.42)	(-2.57)	(0.27)
Concentration	0.03	-0.01					0.03	-0.03
	(1.98)	(-0.59)					(2.18)	(-2.21)
Segmentation			-0.08	0.45				
			(-0.38)	(2.42)				
Scale economies					0.01	0.03	0.00	0.04
					(0.77)	(2.68)	(-0.03)	(3.26)
N	562	560	568	565	499	496	499	496
R^2	0.21	0.26	0.19	0.26	0.23	0.31	0.24	0.32
F-stat	2.43	2.20	2.09	2.87	3.35	2.86	2.98	2.98
H-stat	13.03	11.06	12.60	18.14	11.00	9.80	11.32	9.84

Note: Figures in brackets denote the *t*-statistics; R^2 is the adjusted *R*-square; N is the number of observations; *F*-stat is the Fisher statistics for the non-existence of fixed effects; *H*-stat is the Hausman statistics for the existence of fixed effects versus random effects; *F*-stat is distributed as a $F(11.532)$ in the case of imports and as a $F(11.525)$ in the case of exports. *H*-stat is distributed as a $\chi^2(11)$ for imports and as a $\chi^2(12)$ in the case of exports.

Source: Authors' calculations.

of imports equations though the literature has never reached a consensus in this respect. The impact of exchange rate changes on trade varies across sectors. Concentration and dynamics explain the variations. The more concentrated a sector is, the less exchange rate changes will affect its trade. For goods subject to hysteresis either on the supply or the demand side, the more temporary exchange rate changes are, the less trade will be affected.

7.4   EURO/DOLLAR EXCHANGE RATE AND EUROPEAN TRADE

The objective of this chapter is to identify sectors which are the most likely to be affected by euro/dollar fluctuations. Such an impact depends on the exposure of a given sector to competition from the dollar zone and on its trade elasticity to exchange rate variations. For this purpose, the econometric results and the exposure index are combined. Note that the industrial classification used in Section 7.2 is more detailed than the one used in Section 7.3. For reasons of consistency, the exposure index was recalculated using the classification adopted in Section 7.3. Finally, to shed further light on the impact on Europe as a whole, the importance and the characteristics of the various sectors will be examined.

Trade Elasticity and Exposure to the Dollar Zone Competition

To identify the sectors most sensitive to exchange rate fluctuations, we focus only on those coefficients which are significant. The energy sector has the highest coefficient both for imports and exports. Because of its specific characteristics, this sector will be left aside in what follows. With respect to imports, one can distinguish two subsets of sectors. One with relatively high coefficients (equal to or above 1) including food, paper products, machinery and electrical products; the other with coefficients below 1, including chemicals, rubber and non-metals. Turning to exports, two subsets of sectors can also be distinguished: machinery and transport equipment have coefficients higher than 1; while leather, chemicals, rubber and non-metals have coefficients lower than 1. Note that the 'low elasticity' sectors are broadly similar for imports and exports.

Matching the exposure index with the sector classification used for the econometric analysis (Table 7.5) implies that textile products, leather products, machinery and equipment, electrical optical equipment and transport equipment and, to a lesser extent, chemicals are the sectors facing the most important competition from the dollar zone. Competition affects both European and foreign markets except for the machinery and equipment and the chemical sectors where competition is greater in foreign markets. The estimated coefficient for textile products is not different from zero in the imports or in the exports equations. The estimated coefficients for leather and chemicals were found to be lower (significantly in the case of exports) than those (when significant) of machinery, electrical and transport equipment. Combining the exposure index and the elasticity estimates, the classification in Table 7.7 emerges where machinery and equipment, electrical and optical products and transport equipment are sectors having the highest elasticity and the highest exposure.

Table 7.7   Four sectoral types

Trade elasticity to exchange rate	Exposure to competition from the dollar zone	
	High	Low
High	Machinery and equipment n.e.s.	Energy products
	Electrical and optical equipment	Food products, beverages and tobacco
	Transport equipment	Pulp, paper and paper products, publishing and printing
Low	Textiles and textile products	Wood and wood products
	Leather and leather products	Rubber and plastic products
	Chemicals, chemical products and manmade fibres	Other non-metallic mineral products
		Basic metals and fabricated metal products

With respect to the importance in the economy, Table 7.9 shows that in general the most important sectors are the same irrespective of the ratio considered (production or employment). These sectors are food, paper products, chemicals, metals, machinery, and electrical products and transport equipment. The three sectors which are highly sensitive to the exchange rate are important and represent together about one-third of European manufactured output. Except for basic metals, the low elasticity–low exposed sectors are of low importance in Europe. Among the remaining sectors, chemicals (low elasticity–high exposure) food and paper (high elasticity–low exposure for both) are important to the European economy.

A detailed assessment of the effect of dollar depreciation on sectoral trade may be conducted using the estimated coefficients. The effects on exports and imports can be separated. The coefficients Eij in Table 7.5 are the elasticity of trade volume to exchange rate changes and have a straightforward interpretation. For instance, a depreciation of 1 per cent of the dollar should decrease the export of machines to the dollar zone by 1.07 per cent. It is possible to go beyond such a direct assessment in order to determine the effects on market shares. Combining the estimated coefficients with the market shares computed in Section 7.2 does this. Abstracting from income effects, the coefficients multiplied by the market share and the assumed dollar depreciation give the change in market shares. This is of course a crude measure but sufficient as an indicator of the effect of dollar changes on sector trade.

Table 7.8 presents the effects of a 10 per cent dollar depreciation on the market share of each sector. The last two columns give respectively the

Table 7.8 Changes in market shares following a 10 per cent depreciation of the dollar

| Sector | E_{IJ} coefficients | | Market shares | | Changes | |
	Imports	Exports	The dollar zone in the euro zone	The euro zone in the dollar zone	The dollar zone in the euro zone	The euro zone in the dollar zone
Food products, beverages and tobacco	-1.01	0.24	2.4	1.1	0.24	-0.03
Textiles and textile products	-0.46	-0.29	10.5	2.2	0.48	0.06
Leather and leather products	-0.08	-0.50	21.8	10.7	0.18	0.54
Wood and wood products	-0.42	0.00	2.3	0.7	0.10	-0.00
Pulp, paper and paper products, publishing and printing	-1.05	0.40	1.9	1.2	0.20	-0.05
Energy products	-4.37	3.86	1.7	0.8	0.74	-0.31
Chemicals, chemical products and manmade fibres	-0.79	0.55	4.3	4.1	0.34	-0.23
Rubber and plastic products	-0.85	0.47	5	2.8	0.42	-0.13
Other non-metallic mineral products	-0.85	0.77	1.2	2.4	0.10	-0.18
Basic metals and fabricated metal products	-0.55	0.35	2.8	3.2	0.16	-0.11
Machinery and equipment n.e.s.	-1.21	1.07	4.3	9.1	0.52	-0.97
Electrical and optical equipment	-1.03	0.34	14.1	4.4	1.45	-0.15
Transport equipment	-0.68	2.45	4.8	4.1	0.33	-1.01

Source: Authors' calculations and the CEPII.

change of the dollar zone's market share on the euro zone market and the change of the euro zone market share on the dollar zone market. For instance the 10 per cent depreciation will decrease the European market share in the dollar zone by one percentage point in the transport equipment sector, that is, the market share becomes 3.1 per cent instead of 4.1 per cent.

On the import side the most affected sectors are energy and electrical products. The dollar zone market shares in the European market increase by 0.74 and 1.45 percentage points respectively. While the energy products sector may be left aside because of its specificity, the electrical products sector deserves more attention. It is one of the most important sectors in the economy with an already high penetration by the dollar zone and a high elasticity to exchange rate fluctuations. European producers will suffer greatly from such a depreciation.

Looking at exports the larger impacts concern machinery and transport equipment. Both are among the most important sectors in Europe. Depreciation will decrease European market share in the dollar zone by 1 percentage point, that is, from 9.10 to 8.10 per cent and from 4.1 to 3.1 per cent respectively.

Overall the results suggest that the effect of dollar depreciation will affect the European economy both through a reduction in its market shares in the dollar zone and through a higher penetration of this zone in the European market. On the import side, energy and electrical and optical equipment will be the most affected while on the export side, machinery and transport equipment will be the most affected.

A Detailed Analysis of Sector Characteristics

The impact on sectors of euro/dollar fluctuations was examined on the basis of the exposure indicator and the exchange rate coefficients. The theoretical review in Section 7.1 has shown that the two determinants in turn depend on the barriers to trade and market structure. Moreover the impact on the European economy as a whole depends on the size of the various sectors in Europe. Hence, to shed further light on the impact of euro/dollar fluctuations on the European economy, this section examines the importance of such characteristics in Europe.

Barriers to trade
Different sectors are more or less protected against international competition. Different forms of protection exist, of which tariff protection is the only form compatible with the principles of the GATT and its successor the WTO. Although most tariffs have been reduced in the past decades, non-tariff protection has become more common in the form of voluntary export

restraints, import quotas, anti-dumping measures or technical and sanitary regulations. The effects of the different types of protection are difficult to analyse. Messerlin (2000) has proposed a method to estimate tariff equivalents of non-tariff barriers by measuring the increase of consumer prices resulting from protection. Although he used controversial methods, we adapt Messerlin's estimates to our classification (presented in Table 7.9) as a pedagogic exercise without giving any approval to its estimates. The most protected sectors are, by decreasing order, food, for which protection adds 30 per cent to the price, clothing, iron and steel and car manufacturing.

Market structure
The role of prices in competition also depends on the degree of product differentiation. As differentiation can be based on various characteristics, it is difficult to find criteria to classify products. Nevertheless, two types of differentiation can be identified (see Martins, et al. 1996). The sale of different product varieties at the same price is referred to as horizontal differentiation. Products are vertically differentiated when they are sold at different prices which customers associate with brands with different qualities. The vertical positioning of a firm on a range of products requires heavy investments in R&D and/or marketing to achieve a brand image. In this chapter, only horizontal and vertical product differentiation are distinguished.

Homogeneous products are characterised by great elasticity of demand to price changes. On the basis of a variety of studies, Cortes and Jean (1996) estimated average Armington elasticities at the 2-digit level. Except for refined petroleum, coal and rubber products, they found that low-differentiated products have demand elasticities above 3. The high demand elasticity for clothing originates from the heavy competition from emerging countries, which sell at low prices thanks to their cheap labour costs.

In concentrated sectors, the number of firms remains constant with increasing production volumes. High levels of concentration are found in sectors with high entry costs (for example, with high fixed costs and therefore large-scale economies). In sectors with low levels of concentration, the number of firms increases with production volumes. Entry costs to these sectors are low and concentration ratios fall with an increase of market size. The degree of concentration determines the role of prices in competition. Concentration is measured here by the share of the five largest firms in European production, as given in Davies and Lyons (1996).

The cross-section of the two dimensions of concentration and the two of differentiation gives four market types (see Table 7.10). Firms included in the first and the fourth panels compete mostly through prices. Yet in the latter case product variety also plays a role. European firms

Table 7.9 Industry and market structures in the EU-15, 1996

ISIC code		Employment structure	Value added structure	Total rate of protection (% of retail price)	Degree of product differentiation	Demand elasticity[b]	Exposure to competition (relative to the mean)	Exports as a share of production			Imports as a share of final demand		
								Total	INTRA Europe	EXTRA Europe	Total	INTRA Europe	EXTRA Europe
1	311	Food products	11.6	9.5	30.4	High	1.5	-8.0	22.6	16.3	6.3	22.2	16.4	5.8
2	313	Beverages	1.4	2.6	22.5	High	1.5	-4.0	29.8	16.9	12.9	22.7	18.6	4.1
3	314	Tobacco	0.3	1.6	66.6	High	1.5	-10.0	14.5	10.1	4.4	12.1	10.4	1.6
4	321	Textiles	5.8	3.2	20.3	Low	8.0	1.0	61.3	38.1	23.2	58.3	41.1	17.3
5	322	Clothing	4.5	1.9	31.4	Low	8.0	10.0	78.4	52.5	25.8	84.2	38.5	45.7
6	323/324	Leather products and shoes	2.2	0.9	11.4	Low	8.0	20.0	94.9	50.3	44.6	94.8	51.2	43.6
7	331	Wood products except furniture	3.1	1.7	6.2	Low	4.0	-8.0	17.1	11.5	5.5	17.8	11.4	6.4
8	332	Furniture	3.8	2.0	5.7	Low	1.5	-6.0	38.6	24.3	14.3	35.2	25.6	9.6
9	341	Paper and paper products	3.0	3.0	7.6	Low	4.0	-4.0	49.7	31.9	17.8	43.7	35.6	8.1
10	342	Printing and publishing	5.6	4.7	7.5	High	4.0	-10.0	9.5	5.4	4.1	7.1	5.5	1.5
11	351	Chemical products	5.4	7.9	8.9	High	1.5	0.0	50.3	29.8	20.5	45.2	32.8	12.4
12	3522	Pharmaceuticals	1.9	2.5	n.a.	High	1.5	-2.0	42.1	21.5	20.6	34.5	24.4	10.1
13	353/354	Refined petroleum and coal	0.5	4.3	6.7	Low	1.5	-9.0	17.4	10.4	7.0	16.6	10.5	6.1
14	355	Rubber products	1.4	1.2	7.8	Low	1.5	-2.0	59.3	42.7	16.5	57.4	44.7	12.7
15	356	Plastic products	3.8	3.3	7.7	Low	8.0	-2.0	72.9	51.7	21.3	69.8	57.5	12.3
16	361	Ceramics	1.1	0.6	8.4	Low	3.0	-3.0	46.9	26.8	20.1	38.5	31.1	7.4
17	362/369	Glass, other non-metalic prod.	4.3	4.0	5.8	Low	3.0	-7.0	25.2	15.1	10.0	20.2	16.1	4.0
18	371	Iron and steel	3.7	3.5	17.7	Low	3.0	-5.0	43.7	27.8	16.0	37.8	30.7	7.0
19	372	Non-ferrous metals	1.4	1.5	6.8	Low	3.0	-1.0	50.5	34.5	16.0	54.9	31.5	23.4
20	381	Metallic products	10.5	7.8	10.6	High	1.5	-4.0	41.6	24.9	16.7	36.0	27.3	8.7
21	382-3825	Machinery and equipment	10.9	8.3	4.2	High	1.5	5.0	64.2	28.9	35.3	52.7	38.1	14.6
22	3825	Computer and office equipment	1.1	1.1	9.6	High	1.5	22.0	93.0	63.7	29.3	94.0	54.1	40.0
23	383	Electrical machinery	11.6	9.6	7.4	High	1.5	9.0	70.6	37.8	32.8	67.5	41.8	25.7
24	384-3843	Transport equip. except cars	3.5	2.7	7.5	High	1.5	16.0	46.6	13.9	32.7	39.1	15.9	23.3
25	3843	Cars	8.2	7.7	14.6	High	1.5	-3.0	67.6	46.8	20.9	62.9	53.7	9.2
26	385	Professional equipment	2.3	1.8	5.9	High	1.5	16.0	84.5	42.1	42.4	83.3	45.2	38.1
27	390	Other manufacturing	1.8	1.1	7.2	Low	8.0	16.0	92.2	57.2	35.0	94.6	69.1	25.6
	300	Total	100.0	100.0	11.0			0.0	48.6	28.9	19.7	44.6	31.1	13.5

Table 7.10 *Four market types*

Product differentiation	Degree of concentration	
	Small	Large
Small	**1**	**2**
	356 Plastic products	355 Rubber products
	331 Wood products except furniture	371 Iron and steel
	322 Clothing	372 Non-ferrous metals
	323/324 Leather products and shoes	353/354 Refined petroleum and coal products
	332 Furniture	
	342 Printing and publishing	
	321 Textiles	
	361 Ceramics	
	341 Paper and paper products	
	390 Other manufacturing	
	362/369 Glass and non-metallic products	
Large	**4**	**3**
	381 Metallic products	3825 Computers and office equipment
	382-3825 Machinery and equipment	314 Tobacco
	311,2 Food products	3843 Cars
	3522 Pharmaceuticals	351 Chemical products
		384-3843 Transport equipment except cars
		383 Electrical machinery
		385 Professional equipment
		313 Beverages

Notes:
Sectors are little concentrated if the share of the five largest firms in production is below 25 per cent.
The sectors in the first and fourth panels are arranged by decreasing order of concentration, whereas sectors in the second and third panels are classified by increasing concentration ratios.

229

belonging to the first panel compete mostly with emerging countries. In the second and third panels, prices are of lesser importance in competition. Firms in the second panel achieve economies of scale in the production of homogeneous goods, and compete mostly on the basis of production volumes. Enterprises in the third panel produce mostly high value-added goods, which require large investments; their competition is based on the brands offered. Often they have substantial market power.

Sectoral Importance in Europe

The effect of devaluation for European manufacturing depends above all on the size of the sectors, which are subject to international competition. Size is estimated by their shares in value-added and employment of total manufacturing. Metal products and machinery are the largest industries in European manufacturing, and are also the sectors in which Europe is specialised.

Among the sectors subject to competition from countries of the dollar zone, the most important ones in terms of employment are electrical and machinery and equipment, and to a lesser degree textiles and clothing. The impact of a monetary shock on total employment in manufacturing depends therefore on the consequences for those particular industries. Other sectors under competitive pressure, such as professional equipment, computers and office machinery and equipment, are relatively intensive in qualified personnel and represent only a small share of industrial employment in Europe.

Clothing, leather products, shoes and toys are sectors whose share in total value-added is far smaller than their share in employment. Therefore labour productivity is smaller than the average of manufacturing. In clothing, European firms compete with firms of the dollar zone (for a large part located in Asia), whose advantage is mainly based on relatively low unit labour costs. The same is true for other sectors, which are relatively less important in terms of employment and even more so in value-added terms, such as leather products, shoes and toys. Heavy price competition mainly results from little product differentiation, high demand elasticities, and low sector concentration levels. Despite the protection of European producers of clothing and leather products, firms from the dollar zone manage to compete with them.

Other European sectors which compete heavily with countries of the dollar zone (professional goods, transport equipment, computers and other office machinery) have quite different characteristics: labour productivity is close to or above the average of manufacturing, little protection against competition outside Europe, the products sold are highly differentiated with low demand elasticities, concentration ratios are high as well as the degree of openness. Instead of prices, product differentiation is the key factor in competition with the dollar zone.

The most important sectors in terms of employment among those least exposed to competition from the dollar zone, are food manufacturing, printing and publishing, and glass and other non-metallic products and to a lesser extent wood, furniture and tobacco. In terms of the share in value added, refined petrol is important. Labour productivity in petrol refining and tobacco is largely superior to average manufacturing productivity.[2] The limited competition from the dollar zone in petrol refining originates mostly from the small price differences of crude oil between continents. A possible price advantage elsewhere is therefore counterbalanced by transport costs. The globalisation of this sector is mostly through foreign direct investment. High concentration rates in tobacco manufacturing, which enable firms to influence prices, are an important entry barrier for firms of the dollar zone. Moreover, as demand elasticities for tobacco and petrol are low in the short run, prices matter little in competition.

The absence of competition in food manufacturing results from the relatively high rates of protection, as well as high concentration ratios and substantial transport costs relative to the unit values of products.

7.5 CONCLUSION

This chapter examined the likely impact of euro/dollar fluctuations on European Union manufacturing. It classified European sectors according to their sensitivity to dollar exchange rate fluctuations. Such a sensitivity is assumed to depend on the exposure to competition from the dollar zone and on the elasticity of sectors' trade to exchange rate fluctuations

Exposure is measured by an indicator which takes into account the fact that the dollar zone is larger than just the United States and concerns competition not only on the export markets but also on the domestic market as well as on third country markets. For imports of manufactured products, the share of goods coming from the dollar zone is equivalent to 5.8 per cent of final demand in Europe, with 86.7 per cent of goods provided by European producers. The exposure index of European producers to competition in the dollar zone is 5 per cent. To this should be added competition for exports to the dollar zone (7.1 per cent) and in third markets (0.3 per cent), calculated for each country. Overall, the average exposure index of European producers to competition from the dollar zone is 12.4 per cent. The analysis shows that textile products, leather products, machinery and equipment, electrical optical equipment and transport equipment and, to a lesser extent, chemicals are the sectors facing the highest degree of competition from the dollar zone. Competition concerns both the European and foreign markets except for the machinery and equipment and the chemical sectors where competition is more important in foreign markets.

The elasticity estimates show that cost considerations and the exchange rate are important determinants of trade. The impact of exchange rate changes on trade varies across sectors. The variations are explained by concentration and dynamics. The more concentrated a sector is, the less exchange rate changes will affect its trade. For goods subject to hysteresis either on the supply or the demand sides, the more temporary exchange rate changes are, the less trade will be affected. The sectors having the highest elasticity of trade to exchange rate fluctuations are energy, food, paper products, machinery, electrical products for imports and energy, machinery and transport equipment for exports.

Combining the exposure indicator and the elasticity estimates, a sectoral classification emerges where the three sectors having the highest elasticity and being the most exposed are machinery and equipment, electrical and optical products and transport equipment. These sectors are important and represent together about one-third of European output. Textiles and leather (low elasticity–high exposure) are of little importance in the economy. Except for basic metals, the low elasticity–low exposed sectors (wood and wood products, rubber and plastic products, other non-metallic mineral products and basic metals and fabricated metal products) do not account for much total value-added in Europe. On the other hand, among the remaining sectors, energy, food and paper (high elasticity–low exposure) are important to the European economy.

APPENDIX 7.A   THREE ZONES

European Union (15 countries)	Dollar zone (25 countries)	Others (14 countries)
Austria	Algeria	Czech Republic
Belgium-Luxembourg	Argentina	Hungary
Denmark	Australia	Japan
Finland	Brazil	Morocco
France	Canada	New Zealand
Germany	Chile	Norway
Greece	China	Poland
Ireland	Colombia	Romania
Italy	Ecuador	Russia
Netherlands	Egypt	South Africa
Portugal	Hong Kong	Switzerland
Spain	India	Tunisia
Sweden	Indonesia	Turkey
United Kingdom	Israel	Venezuela
	Korea	
	Malaysia	
	Mexico	
	Pakistan	
	Peru	
	Philippines	
	Saudi-Arabia	
	Singapore	
	Taiwan	
	Thailand	
	United States	

APPENDIX 7.B   SECTORAL BREAKDOWN: PRODUCTION (ISIC, NACE) AND TRADE (CHELEM)

	ISIC, Rev 3	NACE	CHELEM
Total manufacturing	300	D	
1. Food products	311	15	KA...KG
2. Textiles	321	17	DA+DD
3. Clothing	322	18	DB+DC

4. Leather products and shoes	323+324	19	DE
5. Wood products except furniture	331	20	EA
6. Furniture	332	36	EB
7. Printing and publishing	342	22	ED
8. Plastic products	356	25	GH
9. Metallic products	381	28	FA+FB
10. Machinery and equipment	382–3825	29	FC. FH
11. Professional goods	385	33	FI. FK
12. Other manufacturing	390	36+37	EE
13. Chemicals except pharmaceuticals	351+352–3522	24	GA..GE, GG
14. Beverages	313	15	KH
15. Tobacco	314	16	KI
16. Paper and paper products	341	21	EC
17. Refined petroleum and coal	353+354	23	IG+IH
18. Rubber products	355	25	GI
19. Ceramics	361	26	BB
20. Glass and other non-metallic products	362+369	26	BA..BC
21. Iron and steel	371	27	CA+CB
22. Non-ferrous metals	372	27	CC
23. Electrical machinery	383	31+32	FL..FN, FP..FR
24. Pharmaceuticals	3522	24	GF
25. Computers and other office equipment	3825	30	FO
26. Transport equipment except cars	384–3843	35	FV+FW
27. Cars	3843	34	FS..FU

APPENDIX 7.C   DATABASES

Production

Sources

UNIDO, *Industrial Statistics Data Base 1999*, CD-ROM

Other sources

UNIDO, 'Industrial Development Global Report 1997' and UNIDO website: Saudi Arabia, Pakistan, Peru, Thailand

OECD, STAN Database: Australia, Mexico, New Zealand

OECD, Economic Studies: Romania
European Commission, DEBA Database: Germany, France, Italy
National Sources: Czech Republic, Hong Kong, Egypt.

Bilateral Trade

Sources
CEPII, CHELEM Database, CD-ROM 1999

Other sources
IMF, *Direction of Trade Statistics*, for Saudi Arabia, Czech Republic, Russia.

NOTES

* This chapter is based on Fouquin, M., Sekkat, K., Nayman, L., Malek Mansour, J. and Mulder, N. (2002), 'Sector sensitivity to exchange rate fluctuations', in *European Integration and the Functioning of Product Markets*, European Economy: Special Report, no. 2.
1. Or ten, if we consider that in practice the Belgian franc and the Luxembourg franc were de facto a single currency.
2. These findings are partly explained by the high taxes on these goods. As value-added is estimated on market prices, they include these taxes.

REFERENCES

Athukorala, P. and Menon, J. (1995), 'Exchange rates and strategic pricing: the case of Swedish machinery exports', *Oxford Bulletin of Economics and Statistics*, **57**(4), 533–45.

Baldwin, R. and Krugman, P. (1989), 'Persistent trade effects of large exchange rate shocks', *Quarterly Journal of Economics*, **CIV** (4), November, 635–55.

Bénassy-Quéré, A. (1996), 'Potentialities and opportunities of the euro as an international currency', *Document de travail*, 96–09, CEPII.

Campa, J. and Goldberg, L. (1997), 'The evolving external orientation of manufacturing: a profile of four countries', *Economic Policy Review*, July, Federal Reserve Board of New York.

CEPII (1998), *Compétitivité des Nations*, Paris: Economica.

Coppel, J. and Durand, M. (1999), 'Trends in market openness', OECD, Economic Department, Working Papers, no. 221.

Cortes, O. and Jean, S. (1996), 'Pays émergents, emploi déficient?', Working Paper, no. 96–05, CEPII, Paris.

Davies, S. and Lyons, B. (1996), *Industrial Organization in the European Union*, Oxford: Oxford University Press.

Dixit, A. (1989), 'Entry and exit decisions under uncertainty', *Journal of Political Economy*, **97**(3), 620–38.

Dornbush, R. (1987), 'Exchange rates and prices', *American Economic Review*, **77**(1), March, 93–106.

Feenstra, R. (1989), 'Symmetric pass-through of tariffs and exchange rates under imperfect competition: an empirical test', *Journal of International Economics*, **27**, August, 25–45.

Feinberg, R. (1986), 'The interaction of foreign exchange and market power effects on German domestic prices', *Journal of Industrial Economics*, September, 61–70.

Feinberg, R. (1989), 'The effects of foreign exchange movements on U.S. domestic prices', *Review of Economics and Statistics*, **71**(3), August, 505–11.

Feinberg, R. (1991), 'The choice of exchange rate index and domestic price passthrough', *Journal of Industrial Economics*, **39**(4), June, 409–20.

Froot, K. and Klemperer, P. (1989), 'Exchange rate pass-through when market share matters', *American Economic Review*, **79**(4), September, 636–54.

Mann, C. (1989), 'Prices, profit margins, and exchange rates', *Federal Reserve Bulletin*, 72, 366–79.

Martins, J., Scarpetta, S. and Pilat, D. (1996), 'Mark-up ratios in manufacturing industries: estimates for 14 OECD countries ', OECD, Economics Department Working Papers, no. 162.

Martson, R. (1990), 'Pricing to market in Japanese manufacturing', *Journal of International Economics*, 29, 217–36.

Messerlin, P.A. (2000), *Measuring the Cost of Protection in Europe*, Washington, DC: Institute for International Economics.

Ohno, K. (1989), 'Export pricing behaviour of manufacturing: a US-Japan comparison', *International Monetary Fund Staff Papers*, 36, September, 550–79.

Sapir, A. and Sekkat, Kh. (1995), 'Exchange rate regime and trade prices: does the EMS matter?', *Journal of International Economics*, 38, 75–94.

Sekkat, Kh. (1998), 'Exchange rate variability and EU trade', European Commission Economic Papers, no. 127, February.

UNIDO (1997), 'Industrial Development Global', Report, Vienna.

8. Product market integration and EU exposure to euro/dollar fluctuations

Adriaan Dierx, Fabienne Ilzkovitz and Khalid Sekkat[*]

INTRODUCTION

The process of European integration in the past decade has been closely associated with the Single Market Programme (now evolved into the Internal Market Strategy) and Economic and Monetary Union. This process has been pushed forward by highly publicised deadlines and target dates (1992 for the SMP, 1999 and 2002 for EMU) giving a first impression of abrupt change in the economic environment. In practice, however, businesses and consumers tend to anticipate such change and modify their behaviour even before the formal change is made. On the other hand, often the full impact of the economic reforms is felt only years after their introduction. This implies that European integration is a continuous process, one in which the speed of progress may be affected by policy initiatives such as the SMP and EMU and which takes place in conjunction with other events influencing the behaviour of economic agents and the performances of the economy, such as globalisation or the ICT revolution.

Moreover, while at a superficial level the timing of these key policy initiatives may appear to coincide between EU Member States, in practice it can be quite different. Some Member States for instance have received temporary derogations on key elements of the Single Market Programme. Others have experienced serious delays in implementing all its provisions. Also, the SMP does not concern all sectors equally or simultaneously. To the extent that a Member State is specialised in SMP-sensitive sectors,[1] it will be more immediately affected by the SMP. Finally, not all Member States participate in the first wave of EMU. All of this implies that the impact of the European integration process is likely to differ between Member States. To that one should add the different starting points of the current EU Member States in the early 1990s (with some countries not yet being EU members).

The major effects of the SMP and EMU can be summarised as follows (see Chapter 1 for a more detailed presentation of these effects). In the first instance, the SMP and EMU modify the framework conditions under which firms compete by facilitating market entry and making it more difficult to geographically segment national markets. The lower barriers to market entry and the increased price transparency are both seen as factors that raise the level of competition in product markets, leading to a reduction of profit margins. In response firms change their strategic behaviour, affecting the range and characteristics of products that they sell, the geographical spread of their sales territory and the location of their production facilities. The gains in productive efficiency due to such changes in company strategy should be reflected in cost reductions and thus contribute to the restoration of profit margins to sustainable levels. At the industry level, these changes in strategies should be reflected in the degree of concentration of production, the spatial distribution of economic activity and, associated with that, the degree of industrial specialisation of the EU Member States.

The focus of this chapter is on how, by changing the conditions of competition and the structure of European industry, this ongoing but uneven integration process affects the exposure of EU Member States to euro/dollar fluctuations. The focus on euro/dollar fluctuations is important for two reasons. First, the use of a single currency by all members highlights the dependence of their trade on the euro fluctuations with respect to the dollar and the yen.[2] Second, the dollar occupies the most important position among non-European currencies for international trade invoices[3] and it is a currency that is often subject to substantial fluctuations.[4]

The rest of this chapter is organised as follows. Section 8.1 briefly presents the framework for analysing the exposure of EU Member States to euro/dollar fluctuations. Two main questions are addressed. First, do euro/dollar fluctuations represent an asymmetric shock? Second, if so, does the European integration process – through its impact on competition and industrial specialisation – affect the exposure of EU Member States to such a shock? Section 8.2 discusses the first question while sections 8.3 and 8.4 provide empirical evidence on the impact of integration on competition and industrial specialisation to answer the second question. Finally, Section 8.5 concludes on the likely impact of European integration on the exposure to euro/dollar fluctuations.

8.1   A FRAMEWORK FOR THE ANALYSIS

An important feature of the EMU is the transfer of monetary policy to the European Central Bank (ECB). This feature raises questions about macroeconomic stabilisation because the centralisation of monetary policy at ECB level deprives the national authority of an economic policy instrument. Mainstream macroeconomic theory implies that the main determinant of the cost for a country of losing this policy instrument is the degree of asymmetries of shocks affecting the economy. In the European context if a country is affected differently by a shock it can only rely on fiscal and structural policy instruments to react to its specific situation. Furthermore the scope for individual countries to use fiscal policy is constrained by the provisions of the Growth and Stability Pact. Hence both academics and policy makers remain concerned with the loss of exchange rate as a policy instrument and the diminished ability of countries to react to national specific shocks (see Sapir and Buti, 2001, for a broad discussion).

Shocks affecting the economy can be symmetric or asymmetric. A shock that is affecting all countries in the same way is called symmetric, while a shock that is affecting countries differently is called asymmetric. With a symmetric shock, there is no need for using national policy instruments to deal with the situation. A centralised economic policy (for example, ECB policy) is able to cope with the problem. In contrast, with an asymmetric shock, it is necessary to have adjustment mechanisms or to keep some policy instruments under national control in order to allow nationally targeted response.

Asymmetric shocks being the more problematic, the question is to identify the conditions of their occurrence. They may occur either because they are specific to the country or because the country reacts differently to a non-specific shock. The most common examples of country-specific shocks are domestic shocks such as a domestic wage increase or a politically induced shock. Empirical evidence has shown that country-specific shocks are relatively unimportant in the European context. Therefore, it is shocks of the second type that we will investigate in more detail in this chapter.

An example of a country non-specific shock is a decrease in the demand of a specific product, for example, cars or chemical products. In this case all countries producing such products face the same shocks. However, the effect of such a shock on countries depends on their response to it. Country non-specific shocks may have different effects across countries if countries' responses to a common shock differ. The main reason for this is the difference in the structure of the economies, such as industrial specialisation. For instance if countries are specialised in different industries and one industry is affected by a shock, countries will be affected differently.

In the context of EMU, exchange rate change is a typical example of a shock which is not country specific but might have asymmetric effects across countries. Indeed the euro is now the unique currency in twelve Member States. Hence, all of them face the same fluctuations of the euro.

However, the impact of such fluctuations may differ across countries if the two following conditions are met: (1) there is a variation between sectors in terms of their sensitivity to exchange rate fluctuations, implying that some sectors can be identified as 'sensitive to exchange rate fluctuations'; and (2) there is a difference between countries in the economic weight of these so-called 'sensitive' sectors.

Section 8.2 examines whether these two conditions are met. If this is the case, the euro/dollar fluctuations can be considered as an asymmetric shock. The follow-up question is whether and how product market integration affects the exposure of EU Member States to asymmetric shocks originating in exchange rate fluctuations. To answer this question, the two following issues need to be considered.

First, product market integration may affect the exposure to exchange rate fluctuations by affecting the conditions of competition. A number of papers have indeed shown that the impact of exchange rate fluctuations on trade varies across sectors according to market structure. In a seminal paper, Dornbush (1987) used industrial organisation models to examine the impact of market structure on sectors' elasticity to exchange rate changes. He showed that this elasticity depends on the type of competition (prices vs. quantity), the degree of product differentiation and the number of home and foreign firms. Extending the analysis in a dynamic perspective, Baldwin and Krugman (1989) and Sapir and Sekkat (1995) showed that the sensitivity to exchange rate fluctuations also depends on market dynamics. The predictions of these models received empirical support (Feinberg, 1986; Martson, 1990; Feenstra, 1989; Menon, 1995, and others). For instance, Feinberg (1986), the only one who has explicitly tested for the impact of market structure, found that increased market concentration reduced pass-through on the relative price of traded to non-traded goods in Germany. The conclusions from these papers are that the differences between sectors in the trade elasticity to exchange rate fluctuations is explained by the conditions of competition and that sectors less exposed to competitive pressures should also be less affected by exchange rate fluctuations.

Second, European integration may increase the risk of asymmetric shocks if it increases differences in industrial specialisation between countries. The literature holds two opposing views on the impact of integration on industrial specialisation. The first is associated with Krugman and the new economic geography approach. Krugman (1993) asserted that the removal of barriers to trade associated with European integration would allow firms to reallocate their activities and, due to economies of scale and a reduction in transport costs, lead to an increased inter-industry specialisation of the EU Member States, making them vulnerable to asymmetric shocks. The second view was expressed by Frankel and Rose (1996), who argued that

European integration would, on the contrary, strengthen intra-industry trade linkages between participating countries and make their economic structures more similar. The choice between these two views is not easily made as both arguments have found some empirical support.

8.2   DO EURO/DOLLAR FLUCTUATIONS REPRESENT AN ASYMMETRIC SHOCK?

In order to answer this question, we have first to examine whether there is a variation between sectors in terms of their sensitivity to exchange rate fluctuations and second whether there is a difference between countries in the economic weight of the so-called sensitive sectors.

Sectoral Sensitivity to Exchange Rate Fluctuations

Fouquin et al. (2002); and Fouquin and Sekkat (Chapter 7, this volume) analysed the likely impact of euro/dollar fluctuations on European Union manufacturing. Leaning on previous theoretical and empirical research, the Special Report of the European Commission (2002), tries to classify European sectors according to their sensitivity to exchange rate fluctuations which is determined first by their exposure to competition from the dollar zone and second, by the elasticity of trade to exchange rate fluctuations. The study in Chapter 7 of this book also investigates the extent to which market structure influences such sensitivity. Combining the results of the two classifications, sectors that may be highly affected by euro/dollar fluctuations are identified.

The exposure indicator takes account of both competition by imports from the dollar zone[5] into the European market and competition to European exports in the dollar zone and in third markets. The analysis shows that textile products, leather products, machinery and equipment, electrical optical equipment and transport equipment and, to a lesser extent, chemicals are the sectors facing the most competition from the dollar zone. Competition concerns both the European and foreign markets except for the machinery and equipment and the chemical sectors where competition is more important in foreign markets.

Countries are not equally exposed to competition from the dollar zone. Fouquin et al. (2002) has recomputed the exposure index for three large European economies: Germany, the United Kingdom and France. The results show that in four cases France experiences an exposure to the dollar zone well above that of its partners: in the glass industry, in steel, beverages and in other transport equipment (mainly aeronautics). This concerns competition in both home and export markets. The UK exhibits more contrasted features. The most-exposed industries in the export markets are tobacco, refined petroleum and automobiles, ceramics, non-ferrous metals, computers and professional goods. In the British market, the most exposed sectors are publishing and editing, paper and metal products. Finally in Germany four industries stand out with respect to exports, that is plastics, fibres and other manufacturing products and professional goods.

The econometric analysis assessed the difference across sectors with respect to the elasticity of their trade to exchange rate fluctuations and the extent to which market structure and goods' characteristics determine such a difference. The regression related trade volumes in the different sectors[6] to exchange rate variables, cost variables and market structure variables. The analysis focused on bilateral imports and exports of eleven European countries from or to seventeen partner countries (including the United States, Canada and Japan). Exchange rate variables include volatility, exchange rate changes and expectations of future exchange rate changes. Finally, four market structure indicators are considered: concentration, segmentation, differentiation and scale economies. The estimation results[7] show that the impact of exchange rate changes on trade varies across sectors and that the variation in the trade elasticity to exchange rate fluctuations is explained by market structure. The more concentrated is a sector, the less exchange rate changes will affect its trade. The sectors with the highest elasticity to exchange rate fluctuations are energy, food, paper products, machinery, and electrical products for imports and energy, machinery and transport equipment for exports.

Weights of the Sectors Sensitive to Exchange Rate Fluctuations

Combining the results of both analyses, machinery and equipment, electrical and optical products and transport equipment are the most exposed sectors to competition and have the highest elasticity of trade to the dollar fluctuations. Together these three sectors account for about one-third of manufacturing output in the EU. The textiles and leather (low elasticity–high exposure) sectors, on the other hand, represent a relatively small share of total manufacturing output. Except for basic metals, the low elasticity–low exposed sectors (wood and wood products, rubber and plastic products, other non-metallic mineral products and basic metals and fabricated metal products) do not account for a high share of manufacturing output either. However, the remaining sectors, energy, food and paper (high elasticity–low exposure) are relatively important to the European economy.

While the exposure indicator shows that countries are not equally exposed to competition from the dollar zone, combining exposure with the elasticity of trade suggests that the three most sensitive sectors at the European level are the same at the country level. There are, however, differences in the economic weight of the most sensitive sectors across countries. Figure 8.1 shows that it may vary by up to a factor of four between Member States. These sectors are the most important in Germany and the least important in Greece. Differences also show up amongst countries of similar size and level of development. The importance of the sectors is about 10 percentage points higher in Germany than in France and about 15 points higher than in Italy. These figures suggest that the impact of exchange fluctuations can differs markedly across European countries.

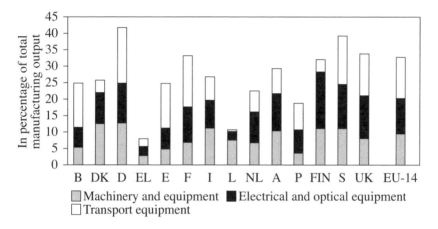

*Figure 8.1   Production share of US dollar sensitive sectors (average
1995–99)*

This analysis shows that there is a difference between sectors in terms of their sensitivity to euro/dollar fluctuations and that the economic weight of the so-called sensitive sectors varies between countries. One can thus conclude that the euro/dollar fluctuations represent an asymmetric shock. The next question is whether the changes in the conditions of competition and in industrial specialisation lead to an increase in the exposure of EU Member States to such a shock.

8.3   INTEGRATION AND COMPETITION

This section provides a review of the effects of product market integration on the conditions of competition in the EU. First, the expected effects of integration on competition are summarised. Thereafter, a short survey of recent empirical work analysing the pro-competitive effects of the SMP and EMU is given. Finally, the consequences of the changing competitive environment on the strategies of European companies are described. Two main conclusions that are relevant for the assessment of the impact of product market integration on the exposure of the EU to euro/dollar fluctuations can be drawn from this section. First, despite strategic action by European companies to regain market power, product market integration should increase the degree of competition in the EU. This means that one may expect an increase in sector sensitivity to euro/dollar fluctuations. Second, the pro-competitive effect should be more pronounced in industries which were more concentrated and which were previously more protected from competitive pressures by non-tariff barriers and, therefore, one should observe some decline in the differences of competition between sectors. As a result, one should expect a decline in the differences between sectors in their sensitivity to exchange rate fluctuations.

Expected Effects of Integration on Competition

With the increased integration of European product markets the ability of consumers to compare prices across borders and to purchase products from foreign producers has gradually risen. This wider choice for consumers is reflected in an increase in the elasticity of demand for any specific product. Under imperfect competition, an increase in demand elasticity implies a greater incentive for suppliers to lower prices and raise production levels. In other words, market integration forces companies to compete harder on price and market share and this should put downward pressure on mark-ups.[8] At the same time, the removal of barriers to trade and investment has facilitated market entry by foreign firms. Firms are no longer operating in different national markets, but increasingly take a European or even world market perspective. As a result, enterprise behaviour is no longer based only on national considerations, but rather it reflects the increased multinational character of the firm.

The welfare implications of such a scenario would be positive. On the one hand, product market integration would improve allocative efficiency by increasing the number of competing firms, thus reducing the degree of concentration, and by widening the choice of consumers, thus increasing the elasticity of demand. As a result, price levels would move closer to marginal costs.[9] On the other hand, product market integration would raise productive efficiency, leading to a reduction in average costs. Increased competitive pressures would induce firms to diminish their misuse of technical, financial and human resources and managerial slack and would reduce the number of firms on the market by forcing the exit of the least efficient firms. As the number of firms goes down, production per firm has to rise substantially to satisfy not only the demand of the former clients of the exiting marginal firms but also the increase in demand due to the decline in prices. As production levels increase, surviving firms should benefit from economies of scale, which should be reflected in a greater productive efficiency.[10] The conclusion is that in the absence of a strategic reaction by enterprises market integration has positive effects on both the allocative and productive efficiency of the European economy.[11] The following section presents an overview of empirical results supporting this conclusion.

Pro-competitive Effects of the SMP and EMU

Several empirical studies have been made to assess the pro-competitive effects of the SMP. Smith and Venables (1988) have made the pioneer work, defining a theoretical model allowing measurement of the welfare effects of the reinforcement of competition within the Single Market. Their results suggest that the more positive effects are likely in industries in which national market concentration is high and pre-integration behaviour less competitive. Building on this work, Allen et al. (1998) show that on average, price–cost margins have fallen by 3.9 per cent in the sectors more sensitive to the SMP. Using a computer generated equilibrium (CGE) model they have compared the competition effects across manufacturing industry. They conclude that the pro-competitive effects of the Single Market are stronger in the more concentrated sectors and in the sectors previously protected from international competition by non-tariff barriers.

This conclusion is confirmed by empirical work made by Botasso and Sembenelli (2001) on Italian firms, by Griffith (2001) on UK firms and by Notaro (2002) on eight European countries. Botasso and Sembenelli compared the pre-reform (1982–87) with the post-reform (1988–93) performances of Italian manufacturing industries in order to estimate the impact of the SMP on market power and productivity. They find in 1993 that in the most sensitive sectors, Italian firms decreased their market power by 50 per cent during the implementation of the SMP, while no similar pattern emerged in the other sectors; and that in these sensitive sectors, productivity growth increased during 1985–87, indicating that sensitive firms anticipated an increase in competitive pressures by reducing inefficiencies. Using panel data on UK establishments over the period 1980–96, Griffith finds that the mark-up fell by 1 per cent more in the sensitive industries than in the non-sensitive ones. Notaro analyses the impact of the SMP on productivity and concludes that productivity in the sensitive industries increased by approximately 2 per cent in 1992–93.

Finally, an interesting approach is proposed by Sauner-Leroy (2003) to analyse the effects of the SMP on price–cost margins. Using the BACH database on the harmonised accounts of European companies, he analyses the respective contributions of price and cost developments in the variation of price–cost margin over the period 1987–99. High price–cost margins can indeed be interpreted as a consequence of low competitive pressures (leading to higher prices) but they can also result from efficient behaviour of firms (leading to lower costs). The conclusion of this analysis is that two phases can be distinguished in the evolution of price-cost margins in European manufacturing industry. Over the period 1989–92, the fall in price–cost margins was mainly due to a decrease in prices greater than that in costs while subsequently, price–cost margins recovered mainly thanks to efficiency gains. These results are consistent with the analytical framework provided in Chapter 1. They indicate that European companies have anticipated the consequences of the full implementation of the SMP and this has led to a strong increase in competition, leading to a price fall while firms have not yet fully adapted their strategies. Subsequently, some firms have succeeded in reducing their costs while others have been forced to exit the market.

Contrary to studies on the SMP, empirical work analysing the pro-competitive effects of EMU is relatively rare. Gasiorek et al. in Chapter 2 have explored the effects of increased price transparency in EMU. They assume that the greater impact of this higher transparency of prices will be felt on consumers because before the arrival of the euro, the large European producers already had good information on prices across markets. The increased awareness by consumers of price differences between Member States encourages price arbitrage and makes it more difficult to segment the EU market. If the greater impact is to come from improved consumer transparency, simulations made with a CGE model show that EMU should lead to increased output and lower mark-ups in a large majority of manufacturing sectors. This chapter also shows that the pro-competitive impact of greater consumer price transparency should be higher in less competitive industries, that is, more differentiated and concentrated industries.

Finally, the chapter by Gasiorek et al. confirms the conclusions of Smith and Venables (1988) and Allen et al. (1998): if the Single Market and EMU not only increase the intensity of competition (by encouraging entry and arbitrage) but also lead to the elimination of market segmentation (that is, producers treat the EU market as a single market and adopt a unified pricing strategy), the pro-competitive effects should be much greater.

Strategic Responses by Enterprises

In the new competitive environment where the least efficient firms are forced to exit from the market, every firm would have an interest in taking action to ensure that it would be amongst the group of survivors. Such action could take various shapes. However, a distinction can be made between two main types of action. First, a firm could focus its efforts on reducing the production costs. Second, a firm could attempt to increase its market power, permitting it to charge higher prices. In reality, firms will of course apply a combination of these two strategies.[12] Nevertheless, here the two strategies and their consequences for the economy as a whole are considered in turn.

Cost reduction strategies
There are several ways in which a firm can bring down its average production costs. Over the period of increased product market integration, European companies have chosen the two following strategies: they have increased the multinational character of their production by expanding operations across Member States and they have refocused their activities on core business. On the one hand, increasing geographical diversification allows expansion of the scale of production and consequent benefit from increasing returns to scale (associated, for example, with fixed overhead and marketing costs). On the other hand, reducing industrial diversification aims at concentrating production in areas where the company has particular expertise or other cost advantages.

Rondi et al. (see Chapter 3 and European Commission, 2002) provide empirical evidence suggesting that EU firms have reduced their industrial diversification and increased their geographical diversification over the period 1987–97. For example, they show that whereas in 1987, EU firms in their sample were on average active in three countries, this number increased to an average of 4.5 countries in 1997.[13] Other evidence indicating that firms have expanded the geographic scope of their activities is provided by data on trade, FDI, cross-border mergers and acquisitions (see European Commission, 1996, 2000a and 2000b). It also seems that firms surviving the pressures of competition displayed at the origin a relatively high degree of industrial diversification and that they have chosen to scale back their operations in marginal industries. Finally, this analysis confirms that the SMP has an asymmetric impact across industries: firms in high-tech industries characterised by a high percentage of public procurement which are more sensitive to the increased competitive pressures coming from the SMP have strongly reduced their industrial diversification, while at the same time strongly increasing their geographical diversification.

Strategies aimed at increasing market power
Amongst the strategies used by enterprises to increase their hold on the market, a distinction can be made between supply-side and demand-side

strategies. Supply-side strategies aim to limit the number of companies effectively competing in the market, while demand-side strategies aim to reduce the elasticity of demand, giving firms more leeway in setting their prices at relatively high levels.

There are several ways to limit the number of players in the market. The strategy of a 'return to core business' would imply – if implemented by a broad set of large enterprises – a division of the market place between spheres of dominance. Every segment of the market would be dominated by one or two enterprises having designated that section as their core business. The national champions of the pre-integration period would be replaced by the European sectoral champions of the post-integration period. There are of course more crude ways to create and maintain monopoly power. The construction of barriers to entry, collusive behaviour in terms of price setting or of dividing up the market, and the creation of a monopoly through expansion or well-targeted takeovers are all possible (but possibly illegal) means towards limiting effective competition, raising price levels and restoring profitability. The increased price transparency for producers under EMU could facilitate collusive practices but Gasiorek et al. in Chapter 2 argue that the risk of increased collusion under EMU is relatively limited because in most industries producers were already well aware of existing differences in price levels between EU Member States before EMU.

Product differentiation strategies can contribute to reducing the elasticity of demand. These strategies can take two forms. On the one hand, a firm may attempt to set its products clearly apart from that of its main competitors. This implies increased investments in advertising and/or R&D. Product differentiation may go hand in hand with a reduction in the diversification of a firm's activities across different sectors in order to avoid spreading the available investment resources too thinly. This outcome is consistent with the observation in Rondi et al. (Chapter 3) that firms operating in industries where either advertising or R&D expenditures are important strategic instruments have reduced their diversification quite remarkably. On the other hand, the firm has an interest in more clearly differentiating its own products sold in different EU Member States. But in EMU the greater comparability of prices should limit the possibilities for the firm to engage in price discrimination. In response to such a development, firms have considered two alternative strategies. First, to forgo the potential profits associated with discriminatory behaviour and to adopt a pan-European pricing and marketing policy instead (and, associated with that, reductions in the unit cost of advertising). Second, to attempt to re-segment the now integrated European market by selling differentiated products in the different national markets, thus impeding cross-border arbitrage. While from such a perspective this second option is contrary to the spirit of the process of

European market integration, it can also be seen as a way of satisfying local or national tastes that are culturally determined and not easily changed.

Impact of Such Strategies on Industrial Concentration

As we can see, the new competitive environment resulting from product market integration leads firms to adapt their strategies both to improve their efficiency and to increase their market power. Therefore, it is difficult to draw conclusions about the net impact of these strategies on the conditions of competition.

One interesting indication can be given by the observed change in market structure. In that respect, Veugelers (in Chapter 4) shows that in 2000, the top five firms in a typical EU industry account for 25 per cent of EU production. The average five-firm concentration ratio (C5) did not change very much over the period 1987–2000 but has increased in the period 1997–2000. However, this average hides a rich diversity across industries and highly concentrated sectors in particular have witnesses a decline in concentration. There has also been considerable turbulence in market leadership in EU manufacturing industries: over the period 1987–2000, the leading top five companies have lost more than half of their market share position. This instability of market shares indicates that there was a lot of rivalry between European companies and that competitive pressures have had an impact on the position of main players. To sum up, this empirical evidence supports the thesis that the SMP and EMU have had a pro-competitive effect and that this effect is stronger in sectors which were highly concentrated and previously more protected.

8.4 THE EVOLUTION OF INDUSTRIAL SPECIALISATION WITHIN THE EUROPEAN UNION

Through the creation of more integrated and competitive markets in Europe, the Single Market Programme has encouraged European companies to reorganise their production processes and to redeploy their activities across European territory. Economic and Monetary Union should reinforce some of the benefits associated with the SMP. In particular, by making prices and costs more transparent and facilitating cross-border transactions, the introduction of the euro should lead to increased trade and foreign direct investment flows within the euro area (see Emerson, 1999; Ilzkovitz and Dierx, 1999; and Dierx et al., 2000).

Monitoring the speed and direction of changes in industrial specialisation across Europe is crucial not only to see whether European companies exploit the opportunities created and adapt to the new economic conditions but also to detect whether the risks associated with such a process of specialisation do materialise. Among such risks, the vulnerability of EMU to asymmetric shocks is the focus of this chapter.

Empirical Evidence

This section first reviews various studies that aim at evaluating changes in the inter-industry specialisation of the EU Member States. In these studies, inter-industry specialisation is defined as the distribution of a given country's activities[14] across different manufacturing sectors. This short review of the literature on inter-industry specialisation is followed by an assessment of recent trends in intra-industry trade, which appear to support the Frankel and Rose (1996) hypothesis.

Amiti (1999) constructed Gini coefficients of specialisation using production and employment data of 10 European countries (the EU-12 minus Luxembourg and Ireland) over the period 1968–90. The results showed an increase in specialisation in all the EU countries between 1980 and 1990.

Aiginger et al. (1999) chose to work with value-added and trade data for 22 manufacturing sectors and 95 manufacturing industries. At this level of aggregation, data were available for the period 1988–98 only, which is a relatively short period when looking at changes in specialisation patterns. This may be a reason why the data show only modest changes in production and trade specialisation in a majority of EU Member States (see Figure 8.2). Figure 8.2 also illustrates that the largest changes in specialisation tend to occur in some of the smaller EU Member States. The study by Midelfart et al. (2000) used production and export data for the period 1970–97. By going back further in time, the study made a useful reminder that in the 1970s the industrial structures of the European economies were still converging. Since the early 1980s, however, production specialisation has increased gradually (see Table 8.1). This change in trend was particularly striking for countries that had just entered into the European Union. Export specialisation, however, has not changed significantly, which may be indicative of an increased importance of intra-industry trade.

The rise of the Grubel–Lloyd index in all Member States confirms the increased importance in the European Union of intra-industry trade (see Table 8.2), which appears to support the argument that the industrial structures of the EU economies are converging. The catching up of lagging EU Member States may be associated with a convergence of factor endowments and technology (see Table 8.3). A study carried out by Centre d'Etudes Prospectives et d'Informations (CEPII) for the European

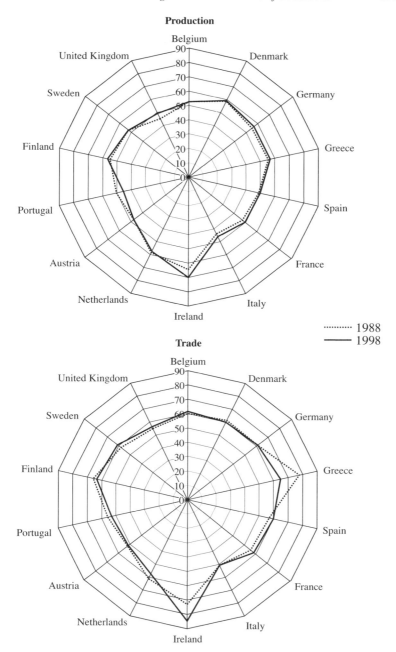

Source: WIFO (1999).

Figure 8.2   Changes in production and trade specialisation (1988–98)

Commission (1997) shows that most intra-industry trade involves the exchange of vertically differentiated products. This implies that countries may not be specialised in specific industries but rather in quality ranges within the same industry. The northern Member States are more specialised in the medium and high-quality products, while the southern Member States (Greece, Italy, Portugal and Spain) are more specialised in the low-quality range. However, even in these countries the share of high-quality products in intra-EU trade is increasing.

Table 8.1   Evolution of the production and trade specialisation of the EU Member States (1970–97)

Krugman specialisation index	70/73	80/83	88/91	94/97
Production	0.43	0.40	0.44	0.47
Exports	0.67	0.62	0.63	0.63

Source: Midelfart et al. (2000).

Table 8.2   Evolution of intra-industry trade inside the EU (1980–2001)

	1980	1985	1990	1995	2001
Austria	0.34	0.36	0.41	0.42	0.46
Belgium-Luxembourg	0.45	0.44	0.51	0.55	0.57[a]
Germany	0.51	0.51	0.58	0.60	0.59
Denmark	0.35	0.36	0.42	0.42	0.46
Spain	0.28	0.32	0.43	0.50	0.57
Greece	0.08	0.09	0.11	0.14	0.11
France	0.58	0.56	0.62	0.64	0.68
Finland	0.20	0.22	0.26	0.25	0.25
Italy	0.38	0.40	0.44	0.44	0.45
Ireland	0.33	0.32	0.32	0.28	0.37
Netherlands	0.45	0.44	0.56	0.57	0.48
Portugal	0.09	0.13	0.23	0.26	0.32
Sweden	0.33	0.34	0.41	0.43	0.43
UK	0.48	0.45	0.54	0.55	0.52

Notes:
The closer the indicator is to 1, the more a Member State's trade with its EU partners is intra-industry in nature, and so the more comparable are their industrial structures.
[a] Data for Belgium.

Fontagné and Freudenberg (1999) estimated the impact of exchange rate variability on trade patterns (inter versus intra) and demonstrated that intra-industry trade had been weakened by exchange variability over the period 1980–94.[15] EMU, on the contrary, eliminates exchange rate variability within the euro area and thus should help to strengthen intra-industry trade.

While the CEPII study focused on intra-industry specialisation at the Member State level, the study by the CEPR had a closer look at changes in the production specialisation of the different countries. Ten out of fourteen Member States became less specialised between 1970/73 and 1980/83, while between 1980/83 and 1994/97 all countries except the Netherlands experienced an increase in production specialisation.

Table 8.3 Convergence of factor endowments between EU Member States (%)

Share of the top three Member States	1980	1995	Change
R&D capital stock[a]	80.1	75.9	–4.2
Physical capital stock[b]	62.4	61.5	–0.9
Active population[c]	54.4	56.5	2.1

Notes:
[a] Out of DK, D, E, F, I, Irl, NL, Fin, S and the UK.
[b] Out of B, DK, D, EL, E, F, I, NL, A, P, Fin, S and the UK.
[c] Out of B, DK, D, EL, E, F, I, Irl, NL, A, P, Fin, S and the UK.

Source: Aiginger et al. (1999).

To see in what type of industries the different countries were specialised, Midelfart et al. (2000) identified fourteen key industry characteristics (economies of scale, technology level, R&D intensity, capital intensity, share of labour, skill intensity, higher skills intensity, agricultural input intensity, intermediate goods intensity, intra-industry linkages, inter-industry linkages, sales to domestic consumers and exports, sales to industry and industrial growth) and compared the prevalence of each of these characteristics between countries. The results showed that the industrial structures of France, Germany and Great Britain were characterised by high returns to scale, high technology, and a relatively highly-educated workforce. In contrast, Greece and Portugal were more specialised in industries with low returns to scale, low technology, a workforce with relatively little education, a high dependence on final demand and a low share of non-manual workers. It appears that the production specialisation of the EU Member States is heavily influenced by structural factors which are unlikely to change rapidly even during a period of important progress in European integration.

8.5 CONCLUSION

The loss of the exchange rate instrument in EMU has brought the issue of asymmetric shocks affecting the EU Member States to the forefront. Different authors point to the risk of shocks arising from fluctuations in the euro exchange rate against the dollar. Although all countries face the same shock, its effect may be different across countries. This may occur for two reasons. First, exchange rate fluctuations may have different impacts across sectors. Second, countries may have a different industrial specialisation.

The chapter confirms that these two conditions hold, implying that fluctuations in the euro/dollar exchange rate indeed constitute an asymmetric shock. On the one hand, the sensitivity of sectoral trade flows to exchange rate changes varies across sectors with differences in sensitivity being explained by the degree of competition in these sectors. The less intensive is competition in a given market, the weaker will be the exchange rate effect on trade in the corresponding sector. On the other hand, the empirical evidence shows that countries are indeed specialised in different industries and that the weight of exchange rate sensitive sectors can vary by a factor of four across Member States.

The follow-up question is whether and how European integration affects the exposure to asymmetric shocks originating in exchange rate fluctuations. To answer this question, one needs to examine the impact of European integration on the conditions of competition and on industrial specialisation.

The chapter concludes that the integration process has raised the level of competition on European product markets, resulting in efficiency gains. While these gains may have been affected by changes in the strategies of enterprises aimed at restoring their market power (for example, return to core business, collusive behaviour or product differentiation), empirical evidence shows that the efficiency gains of integration are unlikely to have been completely negated by such strategies. For example, there has been a lot of turbulence in market leadership in the EU, the leading top five companies having lost more than half of their market share position over the period 1987–2000.

Empirical analysis also shows that the pro-competitive effects of the SMP are stronger in the more concentrated sectors and in the sectors previously sheltered from international competition by non-tariff barriers. As the differences between sectors to their sensitivity to exchange rate fluctuations can be explained by the differences in the conditions of competition and as the process of European integration has raised the level of competition in the least competitive sectors in particular, one should expect a decline in the differences between sectors in terms of sensitivity to exchange rate fluctuations. As a result, country differences in exchange rate sensitivity should decline as well.

The exposure to asymmetric shocks due to exchange rate fluctuations in EMU is also affected by the impact of integration on industrial specialisation. In that respect, the Single Market Programme was an occasion for enterprises to review the location of their production facilities and to redeploy their activities in other Member States if found profitable. Such a redeployment could have significant effects on the industrial specialisation of the EU Member States. Recent trends show an increase in the production specialisation of the Member States and a rising importance of intra-industry trade. The industries and the quality ranges within industries in which Member States are specialised both appear to be shaped first and foremost by the factor endowments of those Member States. The convergence of factor endowments between Member States observed is particularly relevant in this respect. As we have witnessed since the early 1980s simultaneous increases in production specialisation and intra-industry trade – which work in opposite directions – no major net effect on the Member States' exposure to asymmetric shocks is expected.

Combining this result with the observation of increased competition, one can conclude that the fears that the European integration process would significantly increase the exposure of the EU Member States to asymmetric shocks associated with exchange rate fluctuations do not receive strong support.

NOTES

*. We are indebted to Jan Host Schmidt and Reinhilde Veugelers for helpful comments on an earlier version of this paper, to Karel Havik and Alberto Garralon Perez for statistical assistance and to Sarah Vitiello for secretariat support. The usual disclaimer applies.
1. See Buigues et al. (1990) for a definition of industrial sectors most likely to be affected by the Single Market.
2. The impact is far from negligible because extra-EU trade still represents about one-third of total EU trade.
3. In particular, most Asian emerging countries belong to the dollar zone, as do countries in Latin America. Hence, exchange rate variability, particularly euro/dollar variability, is an important determinant of European trade performance.
4. Gros and Thygesen (1992) pointed to the risk that the euro/dollar exchange rate might go beyond its equilibrium level and impact the external competitiveness of European producers. Moreover, Kenen (1995) and Benassy-Queré et al. (1997) argued that

the adoption of the euro might increase the volatility of its exchange rate vis-à-vis the dollar.

5. The definition of the dollar zone is based on an empirical indicator suggested by Bénassy-Quéré (1996). According to this definition a country is considered to belong to the dollar zone if its currency is less volatile with respect to the dollar than to other currencies.

6. Given that the estimation is conducted at a disaggregated industry level (that is, the NACE rev. 1 two-digit level), simultaneity between trade and exchange rate movements is not an issue.

7. The estimated elasticities reflect the final impact of exchange rate changes on trade. This includes not only the sector's reaction but also possible economic policies initiated by the government in order to deal with the shock.

8. A mark-up is defined as (price – average costs)/price.

9. The Lerner index (LI) which measures the degree of market power or the monopoly rent can be defined as (price – marginal costs)/price and is equal to s_i/η with s_i equal to the share of firm i in industry output and η defined as the industry price elasticity of demand. Maximum allocative efficiency is obtained when firms produce until their price equals marginal cost and in this case, the Lerner index is equal to zero.

10. See Griliches and Regev (1995), Nickell et al. (1997), and Bottasso and Sembenelli (2001) for an empirical assessment of the importance of such productivity effects.

11. By increasing competitive pressures, product market integration could also stimulate dynamic efficiency by inducing firms to improve their technology and to innovate. These effects are not taken into account here.

12. It is not always straightforward to classify specific actions taken. A 'return to core business' strategy, for example, could be seen as part of a strategy to reduce costs, or as a way to strengthen market power.

13. This analysis is based on firm-level data on the leading firms in European manufacturing industries; a firm qualifies as a 'leader' if it is one of the five largest EU producers in at least one manufacturing industry.

14. Measured in terms of production, value-added, employment or trade.

15. The underlying argument is that firms which are adverse to variability in terms of sales have an incentive to locate in the country where macroeconomic shocks to exports are correlated with the shocks these firms face.

REFERENCES

Aiginger, K., Böheim, M., Gugler, K., Pfaffermayr, M. and Wolfmayr-Schnitzer, Y. (1999), 'Specialisation and (geographic) concentration of European manufacturing', WIFO Background Report, DG Enterprise Working Paper, July.

Allen, C., Gasiorek, M. and Smith, A. (1998), 'The competition effects of the single market in Europe', *Economic Policy*, **13**(27), October.

Amiti, M. (1999), 'Specialization patterns in Europe', *Weltwirtschaftliches Archiv*, **135**, 1–21.

Baldwin, R.E. and Krugman, P.R. (1989), 'Persistent trade effects of large exchange rate shocks', *Quarterly Journal of Economics*, **104**(4), 635–54.

Bénassy-Quéré, A. (1996), 'Potentialities and opportunities of the euro as an international currency', *Economic Papers*, no. 115, European Commission, Directorate-General for Economic and Financial Affairs.

Bénassy-Quéré, A., Mojon, B. and Pisani-Ferry, J. (1997), 'The euro and exchange rate stability', CEPII Working Paper, 1997–12.

Blanchard, O. and Giavazzi, F (2001), 'Macroeconomic effects of regulation and deregulation in goods and labor markets', NBER Working Paper, no. 8120, February.

Bottasso, A. and Sembenelli, A. (2001), 'Market power, productivity and the EU Single Market Program: evidence from a panel of Italian firms', *European Economic Review*, **45**, 167–86.

Buigues, P., Ilzkovitz, F. and Lebrun, J.F. (1990), 'The impact of the internal market by industrial sector: the challenge for the Member States', *European Economy*, special edition.

Dierx, A., Ilzkovitz, F. and Schmidt, J.H. (2000), 'Economic and Monetary Union – reinforcing the Single Market', in M. Darmer and L. Kuyper (eds), *Industry and the European Union: Analysing Policies for Business*, Cheltenham, UK and Northampton, MA: Edward Elgar.

Dornbush, R. (1987), 'Exchange rates and prices', *American Economic Review*, **77**(1), March, 93–106.

Emerson, M. (1999), 'Euro strategies for business: going for AAA', Report of a Centre for European Policy Studies (CEPS) working party, Brussels.

European Commission (1996), 'Economic evaluation of the Internal Market', *European Economy*, no. 4.

European Commission (1997), 'Trade patterns inside the Single Market', *The Single Market Review*, subseries IV, vol. 2.

European Commission (2000a), 'Economic reform: report on the functioning of Community product and capital markets', abridged version of COM(2000)26, Brussels.

European Commission (2000b), 'Mergers and acquisitions', *European Economy*, supplement A, no. 5/6.

European Commission (2002), 'The impact of integration on the functioning of product markets', *European Economy*, Special Report, no. 2.

Feenstra, R. (1989), 'Symmetric pass-through of tariffs and exchange rates under imperfect competition: an empirical test', *Journal of International Economics*, **27**, August, 25–45.

Feinberg, R. (1986), 'The interaction of foreign exchange and market power effects on German domestic prices', *Journal of Industrial Economics*, September, 61–70.

Fontagné, L. and Freudenberg, M. (1999), 'Endogenous symmetry of shocks in a monetary union', *Open Economies Review*, **10**, 263–87.

Fouquin, M., Sekkat, K., Nayman, L., Malek Mansour, J. and Mulder, N. (2002), 'Sector sensitivity to exchange rate fluctuations', in 'The impact of integration on the functioning of product markets', *European Economy*, Special Report, no. 2.

Frankel, J. and Rose, A.K. (1996), 'The endogeneity of optimum currency area criteria', NBER Working Paper, no. 5700.

Griffith, R. (2001), 'Product market competition, efficiency and agency costs: an empirical analysis', Institute for Fiscal Studies, Working Paper, 01/12, June.

Gros, D. and Thygesen, N. (1992), *European Monetary Integration*, London: Longman.

Griliches, Z. and Regev, H. (1995), 'Firm productivity in Israeli industry 1979–1988', *Journal of Econometrics*, **65**, 175–203.

Ilzkovitz, F. and Dierx, A. (1999), 'Du marché unique à la monnaie unique. L'impact sectoriel de l'euro', *Economie Internationale*, 4th quarter.

Kenen, P. (1995), *Economic and Monetary Union in Europe: Moving beyond Maastricht*, Cambridge: Cambridge University Press.

Krugman, P.R. (1993), 'Lessons of Massachusetts for EMU', in F. Torres and F. Giavazzi (eds), *Adjustment and Growth in the European Monetary Union*, Cambridge: Cambridge University Press.

Martson, R. (1990), 'Pricing to market in Japanese manufacturing', *Journal of International Economics*, **29**, 217–36.

Menon, J. (1995), 'Exchange rate pass-through', *Journal of Economic Surveys*, **9**(2), 197–231.

Midelfart, K.H., Overman, H.G., Redding, S. and Venables, A.J. (2000), 'The location of European industry', *Economic Papers*, no. 142, Economic and Financial Affairs Directorate-General of the European Commission, April.

Nickell, S., Nicolitsas, D. and Dryden, N. (1997), 'What makes firms perform well?', *European Economic Review*, **41**, 783–96.

Notaro, G. (2002), 'European integration and productivity: exploring the gains of the Single Market', London Economics, working paper, May.

Sapir, A. and Buti, M (2001), 'EMU in the early years: differences and credibility', CEPR Working Paper, no. 2832, June.

Sapir, A. and Sekkat, Kh. (1995), 'Exchange rate regime and trade prices: does the EMS matter?', *Journal of International Economics*, **38**, 75–94.

Sauner-Leroy, J.-B. (2003), 'The impact of the implementation of the Single Market Programme on productive efficiency and on mark-ups in the European manufacturing industry', *Economic Papers*, no. 192, Economic and Financial Affairs Directorate-General of the European Commission, September.

Smith, A. and Venables, A.J. (1988), 'Completing the Internal Market in the European Community: some industry simulations', *European Economic Review*, **32**(7), 1501–25.

Index

accrued exchange rate variability, decreases trade volumes 221

ACNeilsen and current PLI data, less dispersion inside than outside the core 30

aggregate production, concentrated in regions closest to largest markets 4

Aiginger, K. 5, 250

alcohol and spirits 35–6

Allen, C. 245–6

Amiti, Mary 115, 250

analytical framework 2–5

arbitrage between countries, consumers, distributors and wholesalers 6

arbitrageurs, additional suppliers to consumers 21

Asian emerging countries 198, 207

asymmetric shock
  affects countries differently 239
  do euro/dollar fluctuations represent? 241–2
    sectoral sensitivity to exchange rate fluctuations 241–2
    weights of sectors sensitive to exchange rate fluctuations 242–3

asymmetries of shocks, losing policy instrument and 239

Austria 16, 25, 100, 122
  bilateral differences 1980/83 and 1994/97 123–4
  employment in service sector 152
  impact of transparency 53
  imports and exports 213
  industry characteristic bias 1994/97 132
    (economies of scale, technology) 129
    factor intensities 130

intermediate goods usage and functional destination of output 131
intra-industry trade (1980–2001) 252
Krugman specialisation index 119
  exports and imports 126
PLI data 33
regional structure of manufacturing 133

BACH database 246

Baldwin, R. 205, 240

barrier reduction, structural change which impacts on allocative and structural changes 17

Barro, R.J. 108–109

basic chemicals, fall in market concentration 90

Belgium 25
  bilateral differences 1980/83 and 1994/97 123–4
  employment in service sector 152
  industry characteristic 1994/97 132
    (economies of scale, technology) 129
    factor intensities 130
    intermediate goods usage and functional destination of output 131
  Krugman specialisation index 119
    exports and imports 126
  PLI data 33
  regional structure of manufacturing 133

Belgium-Luxembourg
  diversification, industrial and geographical (1987–93–97) 72
  impact of transparency 53
  imports and exports 213
  intra-industry trade (1980–2001) 252
  treated as single country 41